Peter Ross is a journalist based in Glasgow. He has worked on the staff of Scotland On Sunday, The Sunday Herald and The List, and is a six time winner at the Scottish Press Awards. He is married with two children and lives in the south of the city.

He is on Twitter as @peteralanross

DAUNDERLUST

Peter Ross

SANDSTONEPRESS
HIGHLAND | SCOTLAND

First published in Great Britain
and in the United States of America in 2014
Sandstone Press Ltd
PO Box 5725
One High Street
Dingwall
Ross-shire
IV15 9WJ
Scotland.

www.sandstonepress.com

Editor: Robert Davidson
All but 'Glasgow Central' © Scotsman Publications
Glasgow Central © Peter Ross

The publisher acknowledges subsidy from Creative Scotland
towards publication of this volume.

ISBN: 978-1-908737-76-2
ISBNe: 978-1-908737-77-9

Cover design by Mark Ecob
Typeset by Iolaire Typesetting, Newtonmore.
Printed and bound by Totem, Poland

For Jo, James and Jack – with all my love.

Acknowledgements

I'd like to thank the editor and publishers of Scotland On Sunday for allowing the publication of these stories in this book. They were written under the guidance of Kenny Farquharson and Fiona Leith, and I am indebted to them for advice, encouragement and support. Thanks, too, to my colleagues on the paper – writers, photographers and editors – for their inspiring comradeship. I am also grateful to Robert Davidson of Sandstone Press for his belief in this book. Finally, a word of thanks to the many wonderful people who appear in these pages, without whom Scotland, and my writing, would be much poorer.

daunder *v&n* – saunter or stroll in a leisurely way: "Shall we take a wee daunder up Sauchiehall Street?"

lust *n&v* – desire, ardour, compulsive need; a sensation experienced often on said street, *esp* on a Friday night.

Contents

Introduction

THERE are more things in Irvine and Perth than are dreamt of in our philosophy. That, anyway, has long been my philosophy when writing about this country for the newspapers. Scotland and its people are endlessly surprising, funny, moving, maddening, wise, weird, industrious and daft. When you go out on a story you never know quite what you are going to see and hear. The one certainty is that it will be worth paying attention. For me, that means carrying a pen and notebook.

In five years of writing for Scotland On Sunday, I have carried these everywhere: to villages and cities, islands and forests; on to canal barges and into karaoke bars, monasteries and morgues; I have written down the words of drag queens and drug addicts, sheep farmers and street preachers, monks, drunks and dudes smoking skunk. In doing so, I have developed what can best be described as an addiction to Scotland, or more specifically an addiction to making journeys within it – a need, an urge; a daunderlust.

These articles represent the spoils of that urge. We live in a culture completely in thrall to the idea of celebrity. For me, though, the great characters of these pages – Tommy Farmfoods, Jesus George, Val Morrison and Woijech the Fly to name just four – are far more enthralling than most famous people; some, indeed, are superstars within their own milieu. To call them ordinary people would be plain wrong, but it is true that their lives are largely unsung, even Luigi Corvi, the 25 stone chip shop owner who performs operatic arias while serving fish suppers at Glasgow Cross. This has been one of the great delights of my work – to seek out these extraordinary folk and bring them to the attention of the reading public.

I am struck, too, reading back over these articles by how many are elegiac in tone. Everywhere there is a sense of loss and passing. Literally so in the case of the Renfrew Ferry, to take one example, but in a wider sense, too. These stories yearn for a more colourful, characterful age and seek to document what traces of it remain. It is possible that the tone has also been influenced by the period during which these stories were written – the years of increasing austerity from late 2008 to 2013, a period during which the Blair years strut was hobbled and humbled. The background to these articles, the mood muzak, is one of growing anxiety about the economy and the environment. To put it simply: everyone was skint and it never bloody stopped raining.

There is sadness, then, but I hope there is more often humour. So many of the people in these stories are very funny, usually deliberately so. Humour, in this country, comes black. For proof, see Raymond Morris, the Laird of Balgonie Castle, near Markinch, Fife, who – each January 1st – paints on the lid of his home-made coffin a new year of death. Or ask Davy, a forklift driver from Balornock, whom – on the last Friday night before Christmas 2009 – I witnessed suffering a cardiac arrest in the back of a Glasgow ambulance. The quick work of a paramedic saved his life, but it was a near thing. Recovering consciousness and pulling away the oxygen mask from his face, Davy's first words to his trembling wife were a joke: 'There,' he said, 'goes ma Sunday shift.'

As that little quote suggests, I have reported much of the direct speech in these articles using the Scots language, and individual regional dialects, in which it was uttered. I am grateful to my editors at Scotland On Sunday for allowing me to do this, as the usual newspaper way is to present everything in Standard English. If I had been writing for the news pages, I would have followed this convention as it allows for the clarity and sense of objectivity necessary for the reporting of news. However, in these articles I have tried to depict events with intense realism, describing in detail the experiences of my own senses – what background noise I could hear, what I could smell, the whole texture of the day. It seems to me important, therefore, to report how people actually talk; the rhythms of their speech and the words they use. To do otherwise is to fall short of the truth.

It has been sometimes suggested to me that quoting in Scots risks appearing as patronising or sneery, as those being quoted are often members of – to use an old-fashioned term which I still rather like – the working class. I can see that argument, and it is a worry. But what concerns me is the perception of readers rather than any uncertainty about my own motives. I do not regard Scots as worthy of mockery or in any way a lesser form of Standard English. In fact, it is exactly because it is so expressive, because the words and their use display so much verve and emotional punch that I am keen to get them in my articles. I am jealous, in fact, of those with quick, creative Scots tongues, and I am grateful to them, too – they make my work better.

I am delighted that these articles are being collected together as a book. I have always thought of them as one piece of work. They add up, I hope, to a portrait of a nation. An unfinished portrait, of course, of what some might consider an unfinished nation – one on the cusp of deciding whether it should continue to sup at the same table as the rest of the United Kingdom or fetch its own tea instead. This book offers no view or answer. What it does submit is a snapshot of a people during a period of change, and reveals the independence of character which they already have without having to vote for it. The Scots in this book, like a huge number of those out of it, are doughty, big-hearted individuals, each with his or her own quirks, passions and eccentricities.

Character, more than oil, more than wind and wave, is Scotland's greatest natural resource. These folk are worth knowing. I am very glad to have made their acquaintance, and I hope you will enjoy meeting them, too.

Peter Ross
Glasgow
2014

Murmuration

GORDON rubs his chin, stumped for an answer, and places his pint back on the bar of the Gretna Inn.

'Davey!' he shouts to a white-haired old man sitting, nursing an ale, in a dim corner. 'Davey, how many years has the starlings been coming?'

'Aw, yonks,' says Davey. 'They've been here since I was a boy, and that's a long time.'

In the pubs of Gretna, in the schools and shops and pews, they talk about the starlings which, between November and February, at dusk, darken the skies in great swirling clouds, tens of thousands strong, known as murmurations. 'They're always out at about four o'clock,' says Lauren, a young woman who works behind the counter in WH Smith at Gretna motorway services. 'I was walking up the High Street yesterday and it was like zombies. Everyone was stood still just looking up at them.'

To those of us who see photographs of this phenomenon, the starlings seem wondrous enough. To the people of Gretna, it is a little bit of everyday magic and an important seasonal marker; the shrill call of the birds' sounds, to them, like the squeaking hinge of the changing year. I was keen to witness the murmuration for myself, so set off south from Glasgow on a dry day between two downpours.

Glasgow, by the way, once had its starling display, an estimated two and a half million of them swooping through the gloaming above the City Chambers and Central Station. But the council, in its wisdom, saw them off during the 1960s and 1970s, frightening them with loudspeakers, flashing lights and, memorably, a piper playing on Jamaica

1

Bridge. Edwin Morgan, in 1968, wrote a poem about these efforts, in which he described the birds' 'sweet frenzied whistling' and asked: 'I wonder if we really deserve starlings?' Edinburgh, too, was known at one time for the birds. The cables of the Forth Road Bridge were black with starlings, and there was a great roost at Leith from the 1950s through to the 1970s; commuters heading home after a day's work would see thousands high above the city's crooked skyline, great flocks making for the docks.

A starling weighs little on its own, but in sufficient numbers they can cause significant damage to trees and buildings. The most famous incident occurred on 12 August, 1949, when listeners to the nine o'clock news were surprised not to hear the chimes of Big Ben. Starlings roosting on the minute hand had caused the clock to run four minutes slow. There is something delicious about this idea, starlings being so punctual in their habits.

If we now see far fewer starlings in our cities then this is because there are fewer everywhere. There are thought to be about four million starlings in the UK, a decrease of 80 per cent in 40 years. They are now on the critical list of birds most at risk. The causes of this steep decline are not understood fully, though it is believed to be related to intensive farming methods and changes in architecture; most buildings constructed these days lack the nooks starlings love.

In the early afternoon, when I arrive in Gretna, the Solway starlings are nowhere to be seen. They will still be outwith the town, in the fields and moors and on the coastal strand. Starlings travel up to 20 miles from their feeding grounds to their evening roosts. There are, however, plenty of clues for those who seek their flight path. Down a quiet cul-de-sac, not far from the Gateway shopping centre, Raymond Park, 74, is up a stepladder wiping white streaks from his windows. 'Starlings?' he says. 'Hellish. They come over here as it's getting dark, thousands of

2

them, going to that bit of wood over there. Do I like them? No. They may be a nice enough sight, but there's an awfa lot of shite to clean.'

This is a familiar lament. The starlings of Gretna are loved best by those who do not own property directly beneath where they fly. That said, the Reverend Bryan Haston, minister of Gretna Old Parish Church, is a model of Christian forgiveness: even though roosting starlings killed three large conifers in the manse garden, he still likes them. 'It's quite amazing,' he says, 'to look up late in the day and see the lovely patterns they make in the sky.'

On Croft Road, 25-year-old Steph Nixon laughs when I ask about the starlings and points to the spattered Vauxhall Vectra in her drive. 'Oh, it's a nightmare,' she says. 'I've given up cleaning my windows, and I can't put a washing out at all. We have to time our run into the house from the car, and when they are overhead it comes down so hard it sounds like it's raining above the conservatory.'

At approximately 2.30 pm, I spot my first starling – a gallus chap atop the church tower, perhaps one of those vandals that did for the minister's conifers. Starlings are underrated. They appear drab at first, a plainly dressed beauty unnoticed at a busy dance. But when they catch the light, one sees the iridescent purples and greens, like oil in water, and the pearly feather tips. In the golden winter sunlight they are especially beautiful, clicking and chittering in the sycamores above the bus shelter and from Gretna's red-brick chimneys.

Isobel Tranter, head of the community council and owner of a B&B, likes to watch them flock from her lounge. They are, she says, mesmerising. Already, there is some evidence tourists are being drawn to Gretna by the spectacle. Isobel's husband Philip, a driving instructor, is a great admirer of the birds, though he is concerned by the numbers of people pulling over at the side of the roads to take photographs. 'I don't mean to sound like David

Attenborough,' he says, 'but what's going on here, with the starlings and the barnacle geese, it's almost as if nature is making a comeback.'

As 4.00 pm nears, anxiety rises. Will this be the day when, for whatever reason, the birds choose not to perform? Then, suddenly, it happens. The starlings are in the air. One hundred, two hundred, five hundred, a thousand, ten thousand, 50, 60, 70 thousand. The murmuration grows all the time as new flocks join from every direction. And that gorgeously apt word, murmuration, is part of the appeal. Its earliest known usage is in The Book of St Albans, published in 1485, where – as 'a murmuracion of stares' – it is one of several collective nouns set out in a treatise on hunting.

Murmuration, certainly, expresses rather well the sound made by so many starlings as they pass overhead. What you hear, more than their song, is the shush of their wings – like a whole town's whispered secrets.

The way they move is astonishing. Twisting, massing, diffusing, seeming to act as one creature, never ever colliding. The starling cloud is hundreds of feet wide and about a hundred feet deep. The mind reaches for metaphors – a shoal of fish, a spreading stain, television static; observed through the binoculars they resemble bacteria under a microscope. Describing a murmuration has given pause to several poets and novelists. John Clare, who knew them as starnels, wrote in the 1830s that they 'darken like a clod the evening sky'. Coleridge, on 27 November, 1799, looked out from a coach heading for London as vast flights formed arcs and orbs, 'glimmering and shivering, dim and shadowy, now thickening, deepening, blackening'. George Orwell, on 5 November, 1939, while hard at work in his Hertfordshire garden, watched tens of thousands of starlings fly overhead with a noise of heavy rain.

No-one knows for sure why the starlings do this; the consensus among ornithologists is that it is to somehow

4

deter birds of prey. However, watching the murmuration it is difficult to escape the perhaps wrongheaded conclusion that the starlings take great pleasure and some pride in their display. Joy is the word that springs to mind. Certainly, the sight increases the joy of Scott and Claire Staszek, a young couple from Dunfermline, who married in Gretna earlier that day and break off from their wedding meal, in the Solway Lodge Hotel, to step outside and admire the starlings as they swirl, like dark confetti, above their heads. 'Millions of them, eh?' says the father of the bride. 'I've never seen so many thegither.'

Scotland is home to a summer population of 170,000-300,000 breeding pairs of starlings. But in the winter the population grows to between two and three million, as birds seeking a milder climate arrive from Russia, Scandinavia and the Baltic states. Similarly, birders will make significant journeys in order to see the starlings. At the side of the B7076, on the outskirts of Gretna, I meet Barry Jackson, 40, who has travelled here from Essex. He is a connoisseur of murmurations, having observed those at Brighton Pier and Minsmere. 'But this is the best I've ever seen,' he says. 'Absolutely spectacular.'

Sandy Gill, 62, taking photos from the side of the road, nods his agreement. 'It's a true wonder of nature.' He has made the short trip from Langholm twice this week and says he will be back again.

By half past four, it's all over. As suddenly as they appeared, the starlings are gone, dropping from the sky as if in response to some telepathic signal, funnelling downwards into a small wood at the side of the Gretna Gateway. Inside, in the dying light, the noise is extraordinary, a ceaseless trebly pulse, almost electronic in character, and the birds are just visible in silhouette on the trees, strange fruit on laden branches.

Soon it will be dark and only the noise – and the memory – will remain.

The Fetish Club

'CAN I ask,' says Charlotte, 'what you're wearing tonight, sir?'

The balding man in the leather blouson and blue jeans sweeps a drunken hand down the length of his body to indicate that this, and nothing else, is his intended outfit.

'I'm sorry, sir, that is not appropriate dress. Rubber, leather, lingerie, uniform, cross-dressing; we're looking for people who have made a real effort. Hence, you're not dressed. This is my party and you can't come in.'

Charlotte Hellicar, manager of Torture Garden, often described as the world's leading fetish club, turns to the next person in the long queue waiting on Edinburgh's shadowy Niddry Street. 'And what are you wearing tonight, sir?'

'It's PVC,' says a tall thin pale fellow in a long black coat.

'Can I have a quick flash?'

The man holds open his Jenners bag. Charlotte nods at the contents. They pass muster. The man has his hand stamped and walks inside, looking for a nook in which to get changed. It is freezing tonight in Edinburgh, too cold to walk the streets in latex catsuits. But even if it were not, the usual thing at Torture Garden is to show up in your civvies, either carrying your fetish gear in a bag or wearing it beneath your warmest clothes. One club-goer unzips his thermal anorak to reveal a clerical collar; his partner opens her vintage mink wrap to show Charlotte she is wearing a lacy purple thong. In contrast to the usual cliché about Edinburgh, here it often seems to be a case of fur coat *and* knickers.

There are around 500 people cramming into The Caves, an atmospheric warren of stone vaults, used in the 18th century to store whisky. Scotland has its own domestic fetish, bondage and S&M scene, based around clubs such as Violate and DV8 in Glasgow and Edinburgh, but Torture Garden – which runs monthly in London – always whips up a lot of excitement as its visits north are infrequent. This is just the sixth time it has been held in Scotland in ten years.

What's striking is the wide age spread. Revellers range from their twenties to their sixties, with most, I'd estimate, being in their thirties and forties. One woman, in fishnets and leather corset, shows up on a mobility scooter. There is a tremendous atmosphere of tolerance and bonhomie; no sense of threatened violence. As Charlotte puts it, 'You can't have a fight in rubber pants and take yourself seriously.'

Inside, it's not just the bosoms which are heaving. The place is packed with folk on the lash. Everyone has changed into their finery: pirates, pervs and punks; regency dandies drunk on brandy; middle-aged gents dressed as middle-aged ladies and vice-versa; a vampire in a codpiece; a zombie in a tux. 'This is an escape, it's fantasy land, an indulgence,' says one chap wearing a Napoleon shirt and Mexican wrestler mask. 'I'm middle-aged and middle-class. I've got the usual boring commitments. This is how I want life to be. To hell with lawn bowls.'

Another man, this one wearing a silver skull mask, is employed by a pensions company and says he has come along tonight because he couldn't face attending a work night out. As he says: 'I could hardly wear this to the pub.'

Issy, a slender usherette, is here with her boyfriend Stephen, a musician. Both are in their twenties. She is wearing gold latex hotpants with matching nipple pasties, and has patches of gold leaf stuck to her face and body; Stephen has on a matching outfit, albeit sans pasties. 'I can't go almost naked anywhere else, and I don't know anyone here so it's okay,' Issy laughs. 'And even if I do bump into someone I know, I can be confident they're never going to tell a soul.'

A buxom young Londoner introduces herself as Ophelia Blitz and explains that she is in Edinburgh to scout locations for vintage porn films she plans to screen during the Fringe. She is wearing fishnets and a leopard-print slip and is leading her boyfriend, Paul, by a leather strap fastened round his neck. Paul is bare-chested beneath a tuxedo waistcoat. 'The waistcoat is borrowed from a showgirl friend of mine,' Ms Blitz explains. 'There are three show-girls and a showboy and we all live on a World War Two torpedo boat. It's pretty awesome. If you're ever in Chelsea, please do pop in.'

The music at Torture Garden is loud and it is great: Bad Romance; The Model; I Love Rock'n'Roll; and, perhaps inevitably, Louis Prima hollering about being king of the swingers. That last seems to be something of an anthem. Although many people who attend Torture Garden are simply into the flamboyance of it all, there are also significant numbers for whom fetish is a lifestyle and an important part of their sexuality.

In the dark cobbled lane outside, taking a fag break, are John and Pet. John is a big man, burly and bald in a black T-shirt that shows off considerable biceps. He's Pet's brother-in-law. The husband is somewhere back inside, I think. Pet is 31 years old, quite plump, wearing a leather hood with batlike ears, a present for her 10th wedding anniversary. She is sipping from a can of Red Bull. John is holding a chain which leads to a pink leather collar round Pet's neck – 'I'm just taking her out for a bit walk for my bro,' he explains.

Pet is beaming and chatty. 'I've been with my master since I was 19,' she says. She usually wears a wedding ring but has taken it off tonight as shackles make her fingers swell up. Three months after her marriage she was given the collar which meant, formally, that she was a submissive in a deep and committed relationship with her husband. This ritual is known as collaring and – being just between the two of them – it meant more to Pet than the marriage ceremony itself.

'I like knowing I'm always going to be under the same master; it's like knowing you're married for life,' she says in a strong Edinburgh accent. 'It's the old-fashioned way.'

What, though, does her family think of it all? Is this the sort of thing she has to keep secret? 'Oh, my family know all about it. My mother was a dominant when she was younger.'

Two rooms, known as dungeons, are set aside at Torture Garden for S&M. In the upstairs dungeon, a woman dressed in the manner of Marie Antoinette is striking with a riding crop the exposed buttocks of a man stretched out on a black leather bench of the sort you may remember vaulting over during gym lessons. Other equipment includes medieval-style stocks and a wooden St Andrew's cross.

Even here, perhaps especially here, there is a prevailing health and safety culture. A sign on the wall outlines some house rules: 'No wax, no blood.' In fact, drawing blood is an extreme rarity, I'm told. The real problem is with spilt Baileys, which is a bugger to scrub off one's bondage bench.

Roy, the dungeon master, explains how it all works. He is a silver-haired paunchy fellow wearing sensible glasses, perspex stilettos, sheer stockings and a hoop-skirt made from the inner tyres of several bicycles. He also has hairy chest and a rubber tail. 'I am basically a referee,' he says. Roy is there to ensure the house rules are obeyed, and that when anyone says the safe word – in this case, 'red' – play must stop. 'The most important thing is that it's safe, it's sane and it's consensual. People here gently bring others up through pain to pleasure and to get the endorphin rush.'

Back downstairs, the party is peaking. Over by the bar,

a group of friends in elaborate latex costumes drink cock-tails and people-watch. One, a gentleman known as Miss Britné, is forced to sip through a straw as most of his mouth is covered by a mask, part of a rubber milk-maid outfit, leaving just one small hole. Drinking straws are essential part of Torture Garden kit, and a number of people carry them in small vanity cases alongside their floggers.

Herbie, a Glaswegian woman of middle years in a tight latex dress, explains the appeal of that particular material. 'It's the visualness, it's the way the light bounces off it. It emphasises the contours of your body, showing the good bits and hiding the bad. Anybody can wear latex and look fabulous regardless of size, age and shape.'

Daz, a graphic designer wearing a black rubber suit and clinging green mask, says, 'In my normal life I'm a pretty shy guy. But this is your classic superhero scenario. Once you've got the mask on, you feel you can take over the world.'

This is the crucial point, I think – the fetish scene, it seems to me, is all about transformation, about sloughing off the everyday, the deadlines and worries, and becoming someone else entirely. The last record of the evening is Iggy Pop's Lust for Life, and to see so many people up dancing, make-up smudged, leathered in leather, backs striped with lash marks, is to witness a tremendous moment of abandon and a weird kind of innocent joy.

Too soon it is all over, and the clubbers spill out into the cold night in search of what, at 3.00 am, are the greatest fetish objects of all – shiny black taxis. As one man says, quite sensibly: 'I really don't fancy risking the night bus in this gimp mask.'

The Anatomy Rooms

DEEP in the heart of Edinburgh's New Town, in a fashionable flat down a cobbled mews, Tim Maguire is contemplating his own death over a pot of Earl Grey tea. 'It doesn't frighten me,' he says. 'I just hope I will be some use.'

Maguire, who is 55, has arranged to bequeath his body to Edinburgh University Medical School. He is a humanist celebrant, and thus has no belief in the afterlife. However, it is fairly certain what will happen to him when he dies, in a physical sense at least. His body will be taken by a firm of undertakers to the grand 19th-century building on Teviot Place. It will be stripped, embalmed and dissected – the muscles, blood vessels and organs exposed – and used to instruct medical students in the wonders of human anatomy. Within three years of arriving at the university, his body will be cremated and his ashes scattered in the grounds of the crematorium.

He is quite blithe about all this. He has signed up for it. He is one of around 160 Scots each year who arrange to donate their bodies to medical science. Five university medical schools in Scotland accept bodies – Aberdeen, Dundee, Edinburgh, Glasgow and St Andrews. The act of giving away your body feels quite dramatic, but the process is mundane, a simple filling in of forms. The university sends out a Declaration of Bequest in which you fill your details and tick boxes giving or refusing consent for, to give one example, the extended retention of parts of your body. Most people tick everything. Their attitude to their corpse is intensely pragmatic – once you're dead, you're dead.

For Maguire, the decision was prompted by learning that there was a shortage of bequests. 'I was surprised to find that in the city of Burke and Hare, Edinburgh's Medical School weren't getting the bodies brought to them that they need,' he says. 'It's a way of being altruistic at a point when it costs you nothing. It's a way of being generous with yourself.'

It didn't take long, did it, for Burke and Hare to be mentioned? That Edinburgh is strongly associated with the study of anatomy is largely due to the murderous reign of the infamous 'resurrectionists' who killed 17 people between 1827 and 1828 and supplied their bodies to Dr Robert Knox, who ran a popular anatomy school. They were caught and Burke was executed. Afterwards, his body was dissected publicly by Alexander Monro, the third Professor of Anatomy of that name to hold the post at Edinburgh University.

Burke's remains are displayed high up in the Medical School on Teviot Place. 'Irish (Male),' reads the sign. 'The skeleton of William Burke, the notorious murderer hanged at Edinburgh, 28th January, 1829. Dissected by Monro, Tertius.' The terror of the West Port reduced to just another labelled specimen behind dusty glass.

One far-reaching consequence of the Burke and Hare murders was the passing of the 1832 Anatomy Act which allowed licensed anatomists legal access to unclaimed corpses, a group which often included those who died in prison or the workhouse or the fetid backstreets, as well as individuals who arranged to donate themselves to medical science. Previously, executed criminals had been the only group legally available for dissection.

Since 2006, the Human Tissue Act has allowed bequeathed bodies to be used for the practice of surgical techniques as well as for the study of anatomy. Edinburgh University requires in excess of 40 bodies each year for postgraduate surgical training. The other fundamental change brought about by the Human Tissue Act is that individuals who want to bequeath their bodies must now state that in writing and have it witnessed. In the mid-Eighties, Edinburgh University required around sixty bodies each year in order to teach anatomy; they now get by with about twelve for undergraduate teaching. This is the result of a UK-wide change in emphasis on how medicine is taught which has meant that few students now dissect bodies themselves. Instead, they observe and handle bodies which have already been dissected by departmental staff and post-graduates. This is known as prosection.

But what exactly happens when you donate your body to medical science? To find out, we must enter those quarters that are usually closed to all except the dead and those who deal with the dead – the anatomy rooms.

*　*　*

The Medical School on Teviot Place is a brooding Victorian building entered through grand wooden doors above which is engraved: SURGERY. ANATOMY. PRACTICE OF PHYSIC. The sense of history is tangible. Britain's first ever Professor of Anatomy, Robert Elliot, taught in Edinburgh from 1705.

In a modest office sits a man who, though he would likely deny it, is the descendent of that eminent teacher. Dr Gordon Findlater, 59, is the senior lecturer in anatomy and head of the department. Bald on top, with a white beard and blue eyes, he is originally from Nairn. He speaks with passionate eloquence about anatomy. What he says is candid and often unexpected.

'When you are producing a dissection, I do honestly think it's like a work of art,' he explains in a soft Highland accent. 'There's a challenge to present this in the best way possible, to make it – what's the word? – attractive. It's not a case of just doing it. It's got to be aesthetically pleasing. I can show you an atlas and you'll see what I mean.'

He gets up from his desk and pulls a book from the hundreds of volumes on his shelves, flicking through until he finds the page he wants. 'Have a look at that. Now you might not find this particularly attractive. This is the back of your forearm. Just look at the intricacy.' The picture shows the tendons as a series of lines converging towards the palm; there's a balance to it, an elegance of proportion, and a level of abstraction that is undeniably aesthetic.

'You have to understand how difficult it is to produce something like that. Just like a sculptor removes bits of stone, we remove fat and skin, fascia, to reveal the underlying tissues and structures. So what you end up with is something that is not just useful from a teaching point of view, but which is pleasing to the eye. I think you owe it to the family to not just chop up a body.'

Findlater's experience of dissection is fascinating. 'You can lose yourself in it. You can get completely engrossed. It's a challenge, and very body-dependent. Some bodies are easy to dissect. Some are difficult. It's therapeutic. It's relaxing. When I'm teaching students the skills, I'll say, 'Look, I'll show you how to do that,' and 20 minutes later I'm still doing it. I get carried away because I enjoy it.'

Is it reasonable to derive pleasure from this, given it's based on someone else's misfortune? 'I think so,' Findlater replies. 'Somebody left the body to you, so you owe it to the dead person to do them justice. It's a wonderful gift to leave your body to students to look at, and we have so much respect for a dead body. My colleagues and I try to get across to students that this isn't just a body. This is actually somebody's mum, somebody's dad, somebody's brother, somebody's sister. They are to remember that when they are handling the body. We also expect them to dress accordingly. We don't want to see flip-flops or hats. We ask them to present themselves in a decent way.'

Each May, the Medical School hosts a service at Greyfriars Kirk for family and friends of those whose bodies have been received. First-year medical students are expected to attend. It's a way of expressing gratitude. Findlater is fond of quoting Winston Churchill's famous line about Battle of Britain pilots. 'Never have so many owed so much to so few. The so few being the twelve bodies we receive in one year. That will educate 250 medics. And how many thousands will they go on and treat?'

Students working on a body are not told the name. Although they are expected to remember that this was a person, there are protocols that make the situation bearable emotionally. When a body comes in, the hair is removed, as hair is considered one of the signifiers of individual personality. Similarly, the faces of bodies are kept covered at first, for the sake of new medical students who may be as young as seventeen with no personal experience of death; grief, for them, is as abstract as that dissected forearm.

Bodies that come into the Medical School are given a unique four-digit code. Gender stereotyping continues even after death; signifying male and female, the labels on the bodybags are either blue or pink. It would be easy, in these circumstances, for the person's living identity to be entirely forgotten. Findlater, however, always makes a point of knowing whose body has come into his department.

'I want to personalise it,' he says. 'I want to know their name and where they came from. I see dead bodies every day, but it doesn't make death any easier when somebody in your own family dies. My brother was in a wheelchair and was hit by a drunk driver. I was starting my degree when he was killed. I wasn't aware then, and I'm still not aware of there being any link between his death and the body I was working on. They felt quite separate. This work doesn't make you immune to death. If it's family, it's just as traumatic.'

Two bodies have come into the department that day, and are to be embalmed. Downstairs, through a number of locked doors, is what is known as the receiving room. It is painted magnolia with pale blue wall tiles, and dominated by two silver tables. The atmosphere is cheery and professional. This is a workplace, not so different from any other.

Drawers are labelled for the implements inside – hemostatic forceps, scissors, knives, bone-cutting forceps. A blackboard, divided into a grid, tells staff in chalked code which bodies are on which shelf of which room. The embalmed bodies are kept separate from those which are frozen. The former are used to teach anatomy, the latter for surgical training. Freezing flesh allows it to keep the 'life-like' consistency necessary for attempting techniques that will later be used on living patients.

A body is wheeled into the room and lifted on to one of the tables. The white sheet is removed to reveal an elderly man. He died the day before and is still in his pyjamas. Those pyjamas are the hardest thing to look at. Dead bodies often appear fake somehow, waxen and too small, but to see someone in his clothes makes him real and begins to tell a story about who he was and what he might have meant to others.

Most of the bodies received by the Medical School are elderly. The youngest person to bequeath his body to Edinburgh was a 39-year-old who died of a brain tumour. Recently, paperwork was sent out to a 103-year-old.

The pyjamas are removed and a technician makes an incision in the inner left thigh in order to access the femoral artery. A tube is inserted and embalming fluid is pumped into the body from a machine. The technicians wear face masks during this part. Every anatomy department has its own embalming solution, but all use the same basic mix; here, it is known as the 'Edinburgh formula' – a blend of formaldehyde, phenol, alcohol and water. Around fifteen litres, depending on size, will 'fix' a body so it does not decompose.

Findlater moves his hands through the air above the body and intones the names of those parts through which the embalming fluid will move: 'Femoral artery, external iliac, common iliac, abdominal aorta, thoracic aorta, arch of aorta, ascending aorta, left ventricle, left atrium, pulmonary veins, lungs.' The movement of his hands and the Latin terms are striking. It feels as though a sacrament is being given. Findlater is an elder in the Church of Scotland. You might think a job like his would be a challenge to faith. In fact, it appears to strengthen his belief. He can see, in these mortal remains, that something – 'for want of a better word, the spirit' – is absent.

Later, we go upstairs to the teaching room. It's a large white space flooded with light from the roof and from arched windows looking out over an internal courtyard. Anatomy has been taught here since the late 19th century, yet – were it not for the insistent smell of formaldehyde, and the gentle outlines of bodies under sheets – you might think yourself in the loft studio of a successful artist or couturier. The anatomical paintings on the walls are a century old.

Findlater folds back the sheet on the embalmed body of a woman. He uses scalpel and forceps to remove part of the skin on the left foot. He points out tendons and nerves on the leg, explaining how easily these can be injured, and the great saphenous vein which is used in coronary bypass surgery.

He lifts off the front of the ribcage to reveal the organs beneath. The colours are autumnal. The branching aorta looks like a tree root. 'This is the abdominal cavity,' says Findlater. 'We're looking at the blood supply to the bowel, the small intestine in particular. This is what we call an arterial arcade. I think it's beautiful.' The organ is roughly fan-shaped. The deep brown bowel is the rim. Dissection has revealed the blood vessels running to it. They have a delicate skeletal quality, like antique lace, or fallen leaves.

'You could look at that in a textbook, but it would be nothing like as meaningful as seeing it for yourself,' says

Findlater. 'There's a lot of argument about why do we need bodies? Why not just use plastic models or computers? Because you wouldn't have the experience. The difference is that it's real. True understanding comes from handling the body.' He presses the aorta. 'Hear it cracking? That's atherosclerosis, hardening of the arteries. You can't get that from a book.' He puts the ribcage back and covers the woman with the sheet. 'We've got the perfect 3D model here. It's called a body.'

* * *

On a wet afternoon in Edinburgh, Iain Campbell, senior technician in the anatomy department, is busy preparing bodies for cremation. The law states that bodies can be kept for up to three years. Today, ten are leaving the building. They are placed in white cardboard coffins.

'We get special requests sometimes,' says Campbell. 'I had to dress one with American flags and put a photograph of his father in with him.'

Two undertakers in sober suits carry the coffins out to a silver Mercedes van with darkened windows. They drive to Mortonhall Crematorium, a striking modernist building, and unload through the side entrance. In the dim chapel, the pews are empty, the curtain still, and no one seeks comfort by gazing upon the wooden cross. There is no music, no mourners. The tears were shed when these men and women died.

This lack of ceremony may seem sad and a little lonely, but the true ritual and remembrance took place when the bodies were dissected and examined. The dead were honoured through use, and their memory will live on, not only in the hearts of their families and friends, but also in the skills of the doctors who held their stilled hearts and learned, through them, how to heal.

In Edinburgh, in Scotland, and no doubt throughout the

world, there will be people unaware that they owe their lives to the generous few who, years ago, chose to sign their names on some simple forms. Though their flesh is now ash, they could not hope for a more enduring and impressive memorial.

Luigi Corvi

THERE'S a guy works down the chip shop you'd swear was Pavarotti. His name, in fact, is Luigi Corvi. He is 53 years old, weighs 25 stone, and runs Val D'Oro, an old-fashioned chippy at Glasgow Cross.

A red neon sign in the window proclaims Val D'Oro 'Home of the Great Glasgow Fish Tea', but it has, arguably, a greater claim to fame. Corvi is an accomplished tenor and loves to sing. Regular customers have grown used to their black pudding suppers being served to the strains of Nessun Dorma.

'A lot of people come in and ask for a song,' says Corvi. 'And they get a song. There are some very rowdy Celtic fans from Ireland. When they are over for games, they come in here and I sing them Meeting of the Waters.'

By reputation, Val D'Oro is Glasgow's oldest chippy, located since 1875 on the vague boundary where town centre blurs into east end. Sited between a pub and a hairdresser's, saloon and salon, its gold and red frontage locates it aesthetically in the mid-20th century.

On the exterior wall above the entrance is a large work by the artist David Adam, Corvi's brother-in-law, depicting Christ being crucified. It was put there in honour of the Pope's visit. Corvi is in the picture, holding a fish supper, and so is his most regular customer, Mary Paterson, who is in her nineties and has been eating at Val D'Oro for at least seventy years. It is very much a Glaswegian crucifixion. Christ, leaning out from the cross, is being offered a restorative swig of Irn-Bru.

Inside, the wood and Formica tables and booths date back to 1950. The mirrored tiles on the pillars are a little chipped. The floor, which was apparently laid by Mario Lanza's cousin, 'old Mr Cocozza', has seen better days. 'You don't think it got like this by accident, do you?' says Corvi. 'Fifty, sixty, seventy, eighty years of neglect. We had to work hard to get it looking like this.'

In fact, he is proud of Val D'Oro's authenticity, and so he should be. This is a real Glaswegian place. He is considering having the paint removed from the walls to expose, at the back of the seating area, the initials and love hearts carved into the wood by generations of 'winchin' couples'. It would be a sort of Glasgow Lascaux.

The Corvi family have owned Val D'Oro since 1938, before which it was called The Swiss Restaurant and belonged to the Beltramis, a name that still rings out in the city thanks to Joe Beltrami's career as a criminal defence lawyer. Corvi is proud of the long association with Val D'Oro, and points his kin out among the many photographs on the walls. 'That's my Uncle Guido on the day he came back from the war. That's my father's cousin Pierino who met his girl here in the shop. And that's Frank Sinatra, a member of everyone's family.'

Corvi, known to familiars as Gee-gee, is wearing a yellow polo shirt and white apron. So neatly does he slot into the space between counter and shelves that Kath, a friendly middle-aged woman who is helping out this Friday lunchtime, struggles to squeeze by on her way to the serve customers. His gold bracelet rattles on the silver countertop as he talks, especially when he slaps down his palm to emphasise points. He is vehement and verbose.

My first question is about his forthcoming debut single, a spoof of the Go Compare adverts. His reply lasts 28 minutes, and takes in topics including Catholicism, prejudice against fat people, Robert Burns, Scottish independence, Islamic terrorism, Roman theology, Victorian architecture

('How can you not think of God when you look at the Forth Bridge?') and – inevitably – the price of fish.

He also gives me a song, the first of a few I'll hear over the next hours. Corvi performs part of Gaetana Donizetti's 1832 opera L'elisir d'amore. As he sings, he closes his eyes, a thumb and finger pinched together, his left hand moving gently through air heavy with hot oil. All the while, the business of the shop continues, the sounds of customers ordering and being served mingling with that of the love song. The total effect is that of a bathetic duet.

'Adina, credimi, te ne scongiuro,' sings Corvi.

'Small fish supper, please,' a customer says to Kath.

'Non puoi sposarlo ... te ne assicuro.'

'Would you like salt and vinegar?'

'Aspetta ancora ... un giorno appena ...'

'There's your fish. Your haggis is just coming.'

' ... un breve giorno ... io so perch.'

'And ten Mayfair please, hen.'

Corvi, who is unmarried, is passionate about opera. His mother, Anna-Maria, played it constantly in the house when her three children were growing up. She is still glamorous at 78, going by the photographs Corvi has on his phone, and seems to have always been an extrovert. She was a Communist in Italy but moved from Salerno to Scotland after the war. In Glasgow, she and Corvi's late father, Peter, were introduced by a matchmaker called Mr Valenti.

Young Luigi would play in the shop as a child. By the time he was twelve he was working here every weekend without expectation of pay. It seems to have been a close, strict family upbringing; he didn't spend a single night away from his parents until he was 21. Work was the priority, but it wasn't a narrow life. The family home in King's Park was full of books. As a child, Corvi read Dante's Divine Comedy and Gibbon's Decline And Fall Of The Roman Empire. The Broons annual seems not to have been on the agenda.

It was a cultured life, but pragmatic, too. It's surely impossible to run a chippy in that particular part of Glasgow without being conversant with the realities of existence. Corvi's grandfather, after whom he is named, responded to a gangster demanding protection money with a threat of his own – a brandished axe-handle. Peter Corvi used a vinegar bottle to see off a hoodlum who considered himself entitled to a free fish supper. Luigi Corvi, too, is no pushover. He once sat upon two neds who were threatening his staff, holding them immobile till the police arrived. That incident might be worthy of an opera itself – perhaps La Chaviata.

At one point while I'm there, a young man with short brown hair and a blue hooded tracksuit comes into Val D'Oro. He seems to be on edge, keeps looking out the window, and makes no attempt to order food.

'Awright, big man?' he says to Corvi in that weirdly camp nasal voice peculiar to Glasgow's fighting classes. He's ducked in here, he admits, to elude his pursuers. 'Just wee boys. Fourteen, fifteen year auld. But when there's three o' them and they've goat blades, whit can ye dae?'

Corvi grants him sanctuary. After five minutes he goes on his way. Corvi returns to telling me about the time he saw La Bohème in Torre del Lago.

He trained as a singer for a time at the RSAMD and later studied opera in Italy under the tutelage of the Italian tenor Carlo Bergonzi. Returning to Glasgow, he was shocked to find his father had lost a great deal of weight. It was cancer. Peter Corvi died in 1992. His portrait takes pride of place in Val D'Oro. Beneath it is the epitaph – 'A life's work'.

Luigi had prospects back then. He'd been invited to audition for Covent Garden, but couldn't attend as his father was dying. After the death, he felt a responsibility to keep the family business going, to swap craft for graft. It wasn't a chore, it was a duty. It was the way things were. So he more or less gave up all thoughts of a professional career as a singer. Arias behind the fryer – that was going to be as far as it went.

Then, quite recently, one of his impromptu performances was heard by the songwriting and production duo, Iain and David Sim. The plan now is to make an album and try to get a record deal. Corvi's profile is rising. He has been giving concerts, and appears as himself in the Scottish film, Donkeys. He does not seem especially ambitious, but would love to sing with Susan Boyle, whose voice he considers 'primeval'.

His own voice is quite something. The jars of beetroot and pickled onions fairly rattle when he gives Lohengrin laldy. More moving, though, is when he translates Stefano Donaudy's Vaghissima Sembianza into English, keen I appreciate the words. Suddenly, he begins to cry.

'Sorry,' he says, wiping the tears with his apron. 'You must think I'm some sort of nut. These songs are so beautiful that talking about them is more difficult than actually singing them.'

It's rare in life that you meet someone as openly emotional as Luigi Corvi. He sits there behind the counter, a half-pizza visible through the glass glowing like the setting sun, and it's clear that for him song is solace. There's joy in his face when he performs that just isn't there at other times. I want to ask him a hundred things. Is he lonely? What does it feel like inside when he sings? But first there's a customer with an important question of her own. 'Huv ye no' goat nae fish, naw?'

Later, at home, I can smell Val D'Oro on my clothes. But what truly lingers is the sound of the chip shop owner's voice and the glimpse he gave of his soul.

The Forth Bridge

IT is Saturday night, almost Sunday morning, and 150 feet above the chill, black water of the Forth, in a sheet-metal bothy the colour of blood, the men of the bridge are waiting to begin work. 'Sweetie?' Someone offers a barley sugar. 'That's what gets you through these shifts. Better than a hip flask.'

The bothy has been part of the Forth Rail Bridge since the 1930s. It is slightly below the level of the railway tracks and has the look of an air-raid shelter. Inside, it is small and plain – white walls, water-stained ceilings, stickers of Old Firm stars and pin-up girls and the Bash Street Kids stuck around the darkened windows. There are around fifteen or so men in here, bleary-eyed and midnight-stubbly, dressed in bright orange overalls and dirty jackets. They drink coffee from plastic cups, scan the tabloids and wind each other up about the day's football. The chat is a mix of technical jargon and swear-strewn banter. 'Right,' says the gaffer, 'we need to be off the track at ten to seven. Wheels-free at ten to seven.'

A man walks in – slight and gaunt, middle-aged, switching off the light on his helmet. He looks like a miner straight from the pit, and is greeted with a warmth that must be welcome, given the freezing temperatures outside. 'Pistol Pete! Y'awright? Is it rainin' oot there?'

'Batterin' doon.'

'Coulda had another coupla oors in bed, man.'

There is a low rumble nearby that you can feel in your guts. One of the workers cocks an ear. 'Is that a train? Cannae hear fuck all over that wind.'

The wee small hours of Sunday morning is the only time in the course of the week that trains do not run over the Forth Bridge. Usually, they pass back and forward, between Edinburgh and Fife, at a rate of eight an hour. So this shift is an opportunity for the workers of Balfour Beatty, the company charged with repainting and restoring the bridge these last ten years, to bring on and take off all the materials necessary for their work. The bridge is owned and operated by Network Rail; this weekly handover of the tracks is known as 'taking possession'. But it isn't an exact science, and sometimes there is a lot of waiting around for the phone call, hence these men crowded into the bothy, bored and restless, passing the time with coffee and craic. 'This is torture, eh?' says George Lowe, the general foreman, wryly. 'All these men eager to work and they cannae go. Look at him, lying like a burst couch over there.'

The worker on the receiving end of this pleasant simile, Gordon McAulay, is a short, stocky Glaswegian of middle years. He's reclining with his head on the radiator and his boots up on the back of a chair. If he hears the foreman's remark, he chooses to ignore it, preferring instead to explain what it's like to graft away high on the bridge while most Scots are enjoying either a warm bed or last orders. 'We've been doing it so long we're used to it,' he shrugs. 'But there's some folk can't handle it because it's dark and they can't see the water. See when we first started this job? The fire brigade came out to do some safety checks and the chief fire officer, as soon as he got out over the water, just froze. Had to be carried off.'

There's laughter at this, a laughter containing pride, and cutting through it a mobile ring tone – Mozart's Symphony No 40, written less than a century before construction began on the Forth Bridge. It is 1.15 am and this is the call they have been waiting for. 'Right guys,' says the gaffer, 'let's roll.'

A downing of coffee, a grabbing of helmets, and we're

out the door. Straight away, the whole world is wind. Like an angry ghost, it howls in your ears and tries to shove past. It's dark on the bridge at night, the narrow walkways lit by a string of bulbs, protected by cages, rocking back and forth in the wind. Look down and it's just black. The water is invisible; the grey back and outstretched wings of a herring gull float, spectral, through the inky void. You can hear the phantom shriek of seabirds nesting on Inchgarvie but the island itself can't be seen. The flaring gas of Mossmorran refinery causes the horizon to flicker and glow, giving the hills of Fife the look of active volcanoes. Above, through the struts and braces and booms, you can see the stars.

The whole scene is quite astonishingly atmospheric, and the workers, despite having been here for years, are not inured to its charms. Standing in the dim buttery light of a walkway bulb, Aaron Paddon, a 22-year-old labourer from Bo'ness, takes a moment to contemplate what the bridge has come to mean to him. 'I'll be sad to finish,' he says. 'Working here is something I'll always remember.'

* * *

Endings. Beginnings and endings. Construction work began on the Forth Bridge in the summer of 1883, and the last of 6.5 million rivets was driven home on 4 March 1890. The bridge was built but needed constant care as it was lashed and scoured by wind, water and haar. The years passed and 'painting the Forth Bridge' came to mean a never-ending task. Start at one end, carry on to the end, taking so long about it that you must then start again – that was the way, each painter a Scottish Sisyphus. But all that is ending now.

In 2002, Network Rail gave Balfour Beatty the greenlight to begin the job, at a cost of over £130 million, of painting the Forth Bridge using a new technique and exceptionally durable paint, so that it would not need painted again for more than 20 years. The job is not purely aesthetic. 'The bridge was quietly decaying,' says Ian Heigh, sometimes known as the bridgemaster, who has overall responsibility for the bridge for Network Rail. 'It was rusting away. We had to arrest the corrosion before it got to a critical stage.' He regards himself and the team as custodians of the bridge's future. 'This,' he says, 'is the best bridge in the world.'

The work is due to finish on 9 December, 2011. By then, some 240,000 litres of paint will have been used. The paint, manufactured by Leighs of Bolton, is known officially as Transgard TG168, but everyone calls it Forth Bridge Red and it is used only here, nowhere else. It would cost you £6 per square metre if you wanted to apply the paint to your kitchen wall; putting it on the bridge, due to the difficulties of access, costs around £370 per square metre.

At the peak of the restoration work, there were up to 350 men working on the bridge. All men. You hear, from time to time, about a female abseiler who was employed for a brief period, but she is talked about as a remarkable sighting, akin to the pod of orcas spotted in the Forth a few years back.

Now, as the work reaches its end, there are still around 120 workers, and the bridge continues to have the feel of a community in the air, something like an old-fashioned pit village lying out there on the water. It is rough and tough, yes, but there is also a feeling of men looking out for one another, and not just in terms of their physical safety. Over the decade, many of them have experienced life's cyclical storms – bereavement, divorce, the challenges of new fatherhood – and have been consoled and steered by workmates.

A bridge is all about support, and the Forth Bridge is supportive in more ways than one. 'It's about the bridge,' says John Andrew, business development director at Balfour

Beatty. 'It's not about individuals. Everyone's working together to restore this wonderful icon.' And while that may be true, mostly, there is also a sense in which the work is meaningful precisely because it is about individuals; about the men who embody the same traditional Scottish values as the bridge on which they work – strength, ingenuity, comradeship, endurance, effort and a certain kind of masculine grace. Look at the old photographs of the men who built the bridge, those Victorian briggers with their blurred and shadowy faces – what a pity we do not know their names. However, that can be put right, now, as we meet their 21st-century descendants.

*   *   *

On a bright day in early September, Colin Hardie, the construction manager, walks up the steps outside the South Queensferry office compound and leads the way out on to the bridge. The plan is to walk right across to Fife, a distance of a mile and a half. Hardie is 48 and comes from Grangemouth, a big man with a surprisingly gentle and considered manner. You probably wouldn't want to cross him, but as a guide to the bridge he is expert and enthusiastic. He has worked on it for almost a decade and feels proud that, through his graft, he has written himself into the story of this place. 'I wish we had another ten years,' he says. 'The bridge gets in your blood.'

It is a fairly mild day, the sky blue, the water glittering through the girders. The weather is not always this kind. They've worked in minus fourteen before now. But it's not so much the cold that's the problem as the wind. Hardie explains that when it gets up to between 40-45mph they have to evacuate the workers as it becomes unsafe. Over the course of the decade, an entire year's work has been lost to the punishing Scottish climate.

High on the bridge, with a long view to all points of the

compass, you can see the weather coming from far away, eerie hail storms that drift in like solid walls of white. The workers are supplied with special thermal clothing, but it is not unknown for them to supplement these official garments with pairs of women's tights.

The weather gets to you. Matt Costello, an actor who for the last few years has worked as an electrician's mate, once stood on the top of the Fife cantilever, heartsick of the cold, and shouted lines from Macbeth into the wind and rain. 'Tomorrow and tomorrow and tomorrow/Creeps in this petty pace from day today/To the last syllable of recorded time.'

Keeping warm can be a state of mind, and so the bridge rings out, day and night, with the sound of yelling, whistling and kid-on slagging matches; all this on top of the clanging of work and sirens warning of approaching trains. Walking through, it's hard to tell where the noise is coming from, above or below. The scaffolding platforms are known as dancefloors, and this can on occasion be a literal description. 'Up on the catwalk, up on the catwalk,' bellows one young scaffolder near the top of the Fife cantilever, channelling Right Said Fred and shaking his touche some 300-odd feet above the Forth. He is, of course, secured to the bridge by his safety harness – as are all employees working at the so-called leading edge.

'Look!' he breaks off and points.'The peregrine!' And sure enough, there it is – one of a pair which nest on the bridge, stooping at a pigeon. The peregrines are cherished by the workers, who value such sightings and consider the birds as being under their protection. If the workers of the Forth Bridge had a heraldic emblem, it would be a peregrine perched on a girder and holding a paintbrush in its beak.

Not that the workers actually use brushes much. The rivets are all done by hand, but every other part of the bridge has paint sprayed on. First, the old lead paint and rust is removed by blasters dressed in protective clothing that gives them the look of astronauts; they are armed with high-pressure hoses firing grit and compressed air. The interior of the encapsulated areas – visible from outside as white 'bandages' wrapped around the bridge – fills quickly with dust and lead, making it difficult to see. The hoses are powerful enough to cut through flesh and bone, and the blasters know to work in a clockwise direction to avoid contact with workmates. The job requires trust and true grit. Primer, epoxy glass flake and finally an acrylic ure-thane finish is then applied; the bridge gets a further fourth coat at the level low enough to be splashed by waves. The paint is of a type used on oil rigs and has been compared in its toughness to the platelets of an armadillo.

From the top of the middle cantilever – known to the workers as Garvie – the vista is as extraordinary as you would expect, and then some. You can see the Pentlands, Fife, out to the Bass Rock, but what is unexpected is the view west – as far as Ben Lomond. Hanging off the under-side of the platform are dozens of 21ft-long 'droppers' – steel poles that end in a short T-bar, just wide enough for a man to stand on. Incredibly, the scaffolders climb down these in order to work, nothing below them but more than 300 feet of air and then the hungry water. These droppers represent a rite of passage – a man looking for work on the bridge will be invited to climb down. If he cannot bring himself to do it, he will not be hired. Of the 300 or so men employed on the bridge, another 700, roughly, did not have the required head for heights.

For those with the right stuff, working on the Forth Bridge is the equivalent of a campaign medal earned in a particularly hard-fought combat zone. 'If you can scaffold here,' says Andy Wright, the general foreman, 'you can scaffold anywhere in the world.'

Of course, for some with a particular temperament, the idea of working at great heights, above the Forth or speeding trains, is terrifically attractive. One abseiler spotted walking through the bridge has 'Living the dream' written across his helmet and describes the bridge as 'the biggest climbing frame in the world'.

Thrill-seeking is not encouraged, however. Safety is stressed constantly by the contractors, because this is very risky work. During construction of the bridge, at least 71 men died, and there have been deaths since. The most recent came during the current restoration work, in January last year, when Robert MacDonald, a 52-year-old painter working the nightshift, fell 150 feet and landed on scaffolding near the railway tracks. 'Every man on this bridge was affected,' Hardie recalls. 'Morale was down. Our programme probably fell behind at that point by as much as three or four months. We closed the site for ten days as a mark of respect. It's very hard to describe the feelings. I was devastated. That guy left for work, just like me, and didn't manage to get home in the morning. I'm quite a big man, I think I'm a man's man, but there's times even now when I look back and it does bring a lump to the throat. You are actually numb. You're numb. We are a working family, and we lost one of our own.'

Two workmates who were with MacDonald at the time of his fall testified at a fatal accident inquiry that he fell through a gap in a walkway while the crew were taking an unauthorised shortcut. His daughter Clare has spoken about her father's love for the bridge. He was proud to be part of the painting crew, she said, and considered the bridge as being his own. What makes this especially moving is that it is precisely what you hear from many of the bridge workers; it belongs to those who toil upon it, and though their devotion is sometimes sorely tested, it seems to endure like steel.

Just ask Fraser Marshall. He is 65, acts as a point of contact between the workers and the railway to make sure no one is injured by the trains, and will retire when the current work ends. He grew up in South Queensferry, in a house overlooking the bridge, and has seen it almost every day of his life. He remembers the steam trains passing in the days when passengers would throw pennies out of the windows and into the water for luck.

He loves the bridge, despite the fact that he has every reason to hate it. 'I was 15 when I lost my eldest brother, and then I was 26 when I lost my father,' he recalls. 'Both accidents out on the bridge there. My brother out on the north approach span, my father on Fife south.' Both were called John. His brother was a painter who fell from the bridge. His father, a rigger, was killed on Christmas Eve, 1972, when the platform on which he was working collapsed into the Forth; his body was never recovered.

The bridge has taken much from Marshall, but to hear him tell it he has gained a great deal too. He started here almost 30 years ago, working on the railway track, and considered that he had the best job in the world. 'You feel you're doing your bit for Scotland,' he says, 'keeping the bridge there and in use.'

*　*　*

Thole is a good Scottish word. It means to endure or bear. You might thole the death of a father or brother. The Forth Bridge was built to thole. Its 53,000 tonnes of steel are strong but are also intended to have the appearance of strength, thereby convincing its first nervous rail passengers that it would not collapse, as the Tay Bridge had done. What's striking, therefore, is that John Fowler and Benjamin Baker's design does not look brutish. It has, instead, a shiplike elegance that has led a number of the workers to refer to the bridge as she.

Walking within 'her' is an experience like no other. It feels, at times, like being inside an Escher print, especially when going up in one of the lifts, or hoists, and seeing the

Fife countryside tilting at a crazy angle, or when walking down the cloistered slope of an internal catwalk at the top of Garvie. Mostly, what you notice is the psychedelic geometry of the bridge – all those repeating X and W shapes, all those hypnotic vanishing points.

Down on the water, from the perspective of The Forth Linesman, a works barge, there is an incredible moment while rounding Inchgarvie, when the cross on what appears to be a small chapel at the eastern end of the island lines up precisely with the huge cross-shaped brace of the cantilever. Little wonder that Gary Hutchison, the 42-year-old skipper, is moved to write poetry about the bridge, describing it as 'a giant wrapped in steel' breaking through the waves.

That giant, come Christmas, will stand alone in the water. The work will be done, the workers departed to other bridges, other buildings or to the dole. There's a sadness in that, of course, but this is a new beginning too.

Standing on the promenade at South Queensferry early one Sunday morning, watching the sun rise behind the bridge, its awesome frame reddening in the dawn's rays, what strikes most forcefully is that this structure represents much of what is great about Scotland, what we value in ourselves, and so it is right that we should treat it with such passionate care.

It is 7.10 am, the overnighters are just finishing their shift, and one of them is visible on the level of the racks. A tiny figure, unidentifiable, he could be any brigger from any era, part of the crew who built this icon and who have acted as its guardians since. He is silhouetted against the pale morning sky, framed by the diamond struts of the walkway, and is soon lost to history amid the beautiful complexity of the Forth Bridge.

A Glasgow Ambulance

LYING at the foot of a flight of stairs in a Glasgow pub, a halo of blood round your head, the jukebox playing Blame It On The Boogie, half-cut punters peering round the door to see your crooked body – if you could choose a way to die, it probably wouldn't be like this.

The man is 53, but none of the three paramedics attending to him knows that yet. 'What's your best estimate of time?' Ray Hannah, asks. His female colleagues were first on the scene. 'Fifteen minutes we've been here' says one. 'Nobody knows who he is or where he's from.'

Hannah is a stocky 50-year-old with glasses and greying hair. He lies on the floor and uses a silver tool called a laryngoscope to try to open the man's windpipe for air. The man has a massive head injury, a crevice running back from above his right eye. A barmaid wanders over, chalk-faced and anxious. 'How is he?' she asks me. 'He wasn't really drunk. He was drinking Southern Comfort and they were teasing him because it was a girly drink. He nipped outside for a fag and must have had a funny turn.'

The paramedics, helped by a fourth colleague, 52-year-old Ricky Doyle, strap the man to a board and heave him up the stairs and out into the ambulance. Blood darkens their green overalls.

Doyle drives to the Royal Infirmary, siren and blue light going, while in the back Hannah and another paramedic give the man oxygen and CPR, injecting him with adrenaline in an attempt to increase the flow of blood to his heart. At the hospital, the doctors and nurses go to work immediately, but to no avail. He's dead. 'Big lad, wasn't he?' says Doyle, slipping effortlessly into the past tense.

It's around 5.00 pm on Friday, a week before Christmas. For Scotland's ambulance crews, this will be the busiest weekend of a busy year. 'See this job?' says Doyle. 'I would say that as much as 70 per cent of our work is alcohol-related. If it wasn't for drink, a lot of us wouldn't be in a job.'

Doyle is 52, solid and strong. He's been doing this for almost 30 years, and has been partnered with Hannah for most of those. He hardly ever takes a drink himself. 'What I see in this job puts you off. People ending up in jail because they've stabbed somebody, and it's the drink that's caused it.'

Hannah and Doyle are based at Springburn, the busiest ambulance station in Scotland. The paramedics sit around in a large room, slurping tea and watching telly, waiting for the phone to ring. They never wait long. The Scottish Ambulance Service, as a whole, responds to 600,000 call-outs each year. The average time between the call coming in and the ambulance arriving on the scene is 7.2 minutes. Emergency calls surge by around 20 per cent over the festive period.

Paramedics complain bitterly that they waste a lot of time attending incidents that aren't real emergencies. For instance, if someone falls and skins a knee, but they have an existing heart condition, then an ambulance will be sent. It's also common for people with drink or psychological problems or both to dial 999 and pretend to be seriously ill.

Then there are 'regulars' who phone every day. One paramedic tells me about a man who lives in a flat full of dog dirt and empty beer cans. 'It's always chest pains he says he has, and see when you get there? It's 'Ah can't get ma telly oan.'

Since NHS 24 replaced doctors making out-of-hours calls, the pressure on ambulance crews has also increased, they say. 'We are enemies of NHS 24,' says a paramedic who estimates that half his call-outs are referrals from the service, many of them non-life threatening. 'You cannae work wi' these people. They are rippin' the shite right oot eh us.'

At 5.40 pm, Doyle and Hannah respond to their second call. An old man has fallen in the Gorbals, his nose flattened, syrupy blood pooling in the gutter. 'Charlie, keep yer heid still!' growls the young man in a hooded top who has been watching over him. Hannah eyes this man suspiciously. Sometimes, when people are lying hurt in the street, they have their wallets and purses stolen.

They get the man into the ambulance and start taking his blood pressure, checking for signs of a stroke. The police go through his pockets and tell him his money is still there. 'That's in case I meet a big blonde,' he says. Charlie is wearing a grey suit jacket and has blood all over his face. He's 77 and a bit upset, worried that he's putting everyone to trouble. Hannah asks how much he's had to drink. 'I might have had a couple of pints and a couple of halfs,' he muses. 'Leave it at that. I don't want to make out I've had a lost weekend. Little Ol' Wine Drinker Me. Was that Dean Martin? I don't want to start fuckin' singing like him.'

Charlie is a charmer. A poor soul. Not everyone who gets in the back of an ambulance is so pleasant. It's common for paramedics to be verbally abused, or even assaulted, by the people they are trying to help. Doyle remembers someone throwing a hi-fi at him from fifteen floors up. Hannah says that, a few weeks back, he got kicked on the thigh by a man with a head injury. The police arrested him, but Hannah found out the next day that the man's wound was the result of someone attempting to kill him. 'I think if somebody tries to murder you, you'd be a bit upset.' He's considering dropping the charges.

At 8.55 pm we drive to Possilpark. Doyle gets there fast. Knows all the back roads. No need for satnav.

There's a 42-year-old lying in the street with a large bump on his right temple, two police on the scene. The man stinks of urine and is drunk and aggressive. His eyes glare out through the mud and blood. It's a struggle to get him into the ambulance. Taking a blood sample is a nightmare. 'Are you daein' ma heid in?' he asks Hannah. 'Cos ah will come and kill you.'

It goes on like this for a while, the man threatening to shoot everyone, but eventually they get him strapped in and drive to hospital.

'He's mild, by the way,' says Doyle. 'I've had two or three cops in the back, holding people down.' He shakes his head at the amount of manpower wasted. The paramedics are compassionate, 'but he stretches your patience, a guy like that'.

At 10.00 pm, another call-out. A man in Balornock with chest pains. David Miller, a 46-year-old paramedic, is already on the scene. 'This guy's having a really bad heart attack,' he explains, out of earshot of Eileen, the man's wife. Eileen and her husband Davy live in an upstairs flat. The living room looks lovely for Christmas. The telly's on with the sound down. The two daughters, 14 and 10, are in their room. It feels strange – normal family life with his life-or-death situation right in the middle of it.

Davy is lying on the couch, a monitor strapped to his chest. The paramedics examine the reading and transmit it to the Golden Jubilee Hospital in Clydebank which specialises in heart problems. 'He's never ill,' says Eileen, shaking her head as her husband is given morphine for pain.

We get into the ambulance. Eileen sits by her man's head. He's ghastly pale, but talking a bit, asking where his girls are, when suddenly his heartbeat on the monitor starts making crazy sawtooth arcs. It's a cardiac arrest. 'Pull over!' Hannah yells to Doyle. 'Davy, no!' Eileen pleads, cradling his head as it lolls to the side.

Doyle gets in the back. Eileen and I stand outside on Queen Margaret Drive and watch as the ambulance rocks. Inside, Hannah is thumping Davy's chest and giving him an electric shock with the defibrillator. Outside, Eileen's thinking her husband is about to die. She scrabbles in her handbag for a cigarette and lights it with shaking hands. 'Christ,' she says, 'I'm too young to be a widow. I'm only 43.'

It feels like a long time before the ambulance doors open, but when they do, it's good news. He's alive. What's more, he pulls away the oxygen mask from his face and makes a joke: 'There goes ma Sunday shift.' If you ever wanted proof that they breed them tough in Glasgow, there it is.

We drive at speed to the Golden Jubilee and Davy is immediately taken up to theatre. In the ambulance, Hannah reflects on what just happened. 'You don't want to see somebody that age breathing his last, especially in front of his missus. It was a disaster when he went into cardiac arrest, but if you can pull him out of that, that's definitely the outcome you want.'

He saved that man's life. There's one less widow in Glasgow tonight, two kids that still have their dad. These paramedics have been doing this job for three decades; imagine how many they must have saved in that time. It's a thought that makes Hannah grimace. 'We get them to the hospital and the doctors and nurses do the rest,' he says, turning back to his paperwork. 'I just like to think we help people.'

The Monks of Pluscarden

THE Latin chant drifts through the dim church in a beautiful echoing murmur; tidal, it flows and ebbs, flows and ebbs, the white-cowled men bowing, now rising, now bowing once more, as if caught in the sublime surf of their song. This scene could be taking place at any time in any of the last eight centuries, but it happens to be half-past four in the morning on the fourteenth of June in the year of our lord 2012. The monks of Pluscarden Abbey are at their prayers.

Pluscarden Abbey, near Elgin, is the only medieval monastery in Britain inhabited by monks and used as a place of worship. It is home to twenty-two Benedictines. They range in age from their twenties to their eighties. Some have pale unlined faces, some are lined and lame. It is likely that most, probably all, will spend the rest of their lives here and be buried, eventually, in the Abbey cemetery, their graves marked by simple wooden crosses, which, as time passes, will grow so thick with lichen that at last their names will disappear. Intrigued visitors, tracing with a finger the furred letters, will make out only this carved epitaph: 'After life's fit fever he slept well.'

If life is a fever, Pluscarden is immune, its natural resistance built up over centuries of isolation. There is a rare stillness here. No silence; birdsong and bells make sure of that. But there is a deep quiet. The Abbey is in a fertile glen at the foot of steep fields with a palisade of firs at the top. The hill and forest feel like a looming wall, keeping the monks in, the world out.

The Benedictines spend five hours each day in church,

three-and-a-half hours engaged in 'spiritual reading', and four hours on chores and manual labour, which can be anything from sowing chives to tending hives. Pluscarden is well known for its honey, but the bees which provide it do not do so in a spirit of Christian charity. 'We get these docile Buckfast queens but before too long they've developed a peppery temper,' Brother Michael explains. 'They are notoriously fierce. Poor Father Dunstan has been taken to A&E at least twice.'

Pluscarden's day begins at 4.30 am with Vigils and Lauds, at ninety minutes by far the longest of the eight daily services. At this hour, even the Abbey cat, Baxter, named for the soup, is still asleep. Yet the monks are up, among them Father Giles, who has been at Pluscarden for forty of his sixty-three years and is still so ill-suited to early rises that one of his brethren must, each morning, batter on the door of his cell.

For much of the year, Vigils and Lauds will be performed while outside it is frozen darkness. Even now, the dawn is dim. Looking at the sky through the church windows, as the monks sing, it's rather moving to think that for centuries this place was a ruin, that rooks once flew through unglazed arches and ivy choked the nave.

Founded in 1230, the monastery was dissolved in 1587 and went through a long period of decay, some of its stone used to build the kirk in Elgin. In 1948, five monks began to rebuild. By the time Father Gilbert arrived at the monastery on a dreich day in 1971, cycling up from Edinburgh, the church was still missing much of its roof and rain was running down the walls. 'It's astonishing,' he says, 'what has been achieved.'

Taking holy orders and becoming a monk at Pluscarden is to enter a self-contained world of seclusion and repetition. The point is to focus attention on God. External stimuli are thus removed. There is no television or radio, phone calls are rare, and internet access is restricted to those senior monks whose positions require them to retain contact with society. In theory, the Abbey receives a daily newspaper, but it does not arrive daily, and in any case is regarded as 'a snare and delusion' – probably the first time the Telegraph has ever been described in quite that way. The monks also make their own entertainment, singing songs and performing comic sketches. 'They are usually adaptations of ones we remember from the distant past,' says Brother Michael. 'Do you remember when the Two Ronnies did Mastermind? That was quite good.'

There are small signs that the brothers are more worldly than one would expect. The three Polish brethren, for instance, seemed to be cheerfully aware that their football team had drawn with Russia in Euro 2012. Then there was the fact that the guestmaster who arranged for me to stay joked, by email, that I might actually be a drug smuggler and asked whether I would bring him some Cadbury's Fruit & Nut. Such treats loom large at Pluscarden, I think. 'We eat liturgically,' Father Dunstan explained when I arrived, 'which means at Christmas it's mega-food, but tonight it's just a simple meal of bread and cheese.'

Lunch and supper are taken in the refectory at long wooden tables. Grace is sung, but during the meals no-one speaks. Instead, a monk ascends to a pulpit and reads aloud from some dry volume. He also reads out a necrology – a list of Benedictines round the world who died on that particular date. When the meal ends, the brethren wipe their cutlery and bowls with a cloth and return them to a shelf beneath the table. Each monk brushes the crumbs from his place and then passes the dustpan to his neighbour. All this without a word. Chat is reserved for the twenty minutes put aside each day for recreation.

To an outsider, the monastic life can appear narrow and relentless. Certainly, it is testing. The usual thing for a young man who thinks he would like to become a monk is to first stay for a month. He can then spend six months as a postulant, wearing the grey habit, followed by two years as a novice. He would then become a junior, and, after a total of five-and-a-half years, could take vows and become a monk, pledging himself under threat of hellfire to a life of poverty, chastity and obedience.

'One is still tempted,' says Father Benedict, a 53-year-old former soldier who is the Prior, or second-in-command, at the Abbey. 'I still find ladies terribly attractive and sometimes the idea of having a wife can overwhelm one. That's an ongoing battle till one dies. It's the same with things. It'd be quite nice if I could have a motorbike, or even an extra pair of socks.

'But for me, the joys outweigh the sorrows so much that the sorrows become irrelevant. Every single day, from the moment you get up to the moment you fall asleep, everything you are doing is completely worthwhile. There are moments when one is aware of really complete deep happiness. To lose the love of a wife to get the love of God more fully and directly, to be stripped of earthly goods in order to have the Kingdom, well what we get compared to what we give is ridiculously out of proportion.'

There are two postulants at Pluscarden at the moment, one of whom has been at the Abbey for three months and is being visited by his brother. The family are concerned to find out how he is coping. During the first year following the postulancy, a novice is forbidden visits from his family. During the second year, he will be allowed to meet them just once. To live like this must be overwhelming at first. Most would-be monks give up during the first two months. 'I remember,' recalls Brother Finbar, 'I burst out crying when I was putting on the habit. I thought, 'Of all the stupid things you've ever done, this takes the cookie.''

He is fifty-five now and has lived here joyfully since his mid-twenties, his former life as a chargehand in a Glasgow pub an ever fading memory. I was especially keen to meet Brother Finbar. He had been recommended to me by his friend, the actress Tilda Swinton. She said he was a cinephile, which he is happy to confirm – 'God, I think Tilda would be so good in an Almodovar film. I'll put that on my prayer list.' The monks are allowed to watch, en masse, around three films each year, selected by the Abbot, but when a monk is celebrating a significant anniversary he is allowed to choose. Finbar, to mark 25 years at Pluscarden, opted for The Blues Brothers, a very popular choice among his brethren.

In his Rule, written in the sixth century, Saint Benedict condemns laughter. The Benedictines of Pluscarden, sticklers in so many ways, allow themselves some laxity here. They are fond of a funny story, and this is to their credit. But make no mistake, theirs is a serious life – profound, solemn and deeply felt. What will stay with me, then, is attending Mass – the smell of wax and old stone, the clink of glass against golden chalice, the glug of wine and blood. The brethren, as they sip, look serene, like they are exactly where they are meant to be, doing exactly what they are supposed to be do. The altar candles, when gently extinguished, send blue smoke twining upwards.

'Everything is fragile nowadays,' Father Benedict says afterwards. 'Will we still be here in 40 years? Please, God. We'll see what happens.'

The Ba'

'THE rules of the Ba' game are simple,' says Len Wyse. 'There's nae rules.'

An amiable man with a neat white moustache, Wyse is a past provost of Jedburgh, a current councillor for the Borders town, and the proud owner of two horses and a dog named Bud. Yet before and above all that, he was and is an Uppie, a title conferred on him by virtue of his birth, in 1951, in the cottage hospital up behind the Castle Jail. 'You get a pride in it,' he says.

Jedburgh folk are either Uppies or Doonies, depending on where in the town they were born, and this geographical status decides the team for which they play in the Jethart Hand Ba' – a sporting occasion which has taken place here, once each year, for centuries. A small leather ball is thrown up on the site of the old Mercat Cross, and it is the task of the Uppies and Doonies to carry this back to their respective goal, known as a 'hail'. A distance of around one mile separates the two, and it can take an hour or more to score. After each hail, a new ball comes into play.

There is no upper limit on the numbers in each team, and the game is rough. Anyone taking momentary possession can expect to be battered into the street with a scrum of 40 or more burly men on top of them. After, say, ten minutes of being pressed to the pavement, they will emerge with a tomato-red face, two cauliflower ears and steam rising from their head as if they were a freshly prepared stew.

It's 11.00 am on Thursday when I arrive at Len Wyse's house. He has eight of the balls lined up on a radiator, drying out before the game. First there will be six balls played by the boys, he explains, and then up to sixteen by the men. The number varies, depending on how many people want to sponsor a ball. Most pubs in town do so, offering a gallon of beer to whoever scores the hail. Other balls are donated to mark important personal occasions. One this year is the gift of a couple celebrating their golden wedding; another is from a man in memory of his murdered son. The Ba' is a key moment in the emotional life of the town.

The balls, each three inches in diameter, are made by a local saddler. They are dark leather, each stuffed with moss from a nearby burn and a page from The Scotsman, and decorated with long, colourful ribbons which are stitched on by Wyse. The players can sometimes keep a ball if they score a hail, and these are cherished objects. 'My great-grandfather got that one well over a hundred years ago,' says Wyse, holding up a black and brittle orb.

At noon by the clock tower bell, the first ball of the day is thrown up by Andrew Nagle, a Doonie. The head boy at the local school is always given this honour. Nagle's grandfather, David Rose, did it back in 1945. Seven years later he scored a try in Great Britain's victory over France in the 1954 rugby league world cup final. 'La Rose! La Rose!' they yelled in the Parc de Princes. 'Guid yin, Nagle!' they yell now, as the 17-year-old secures the first hail of the day, running down the High Street with the ball and rolling it over the course of the culverted Skiprunning Burn.

Nagle is a tall, good-looking lad, and many of the spectating teenage girls, all skinny jeans and big hair, seem particularly impressed by his triumph, to judge from the shrieking. There is definitely a slightly hysterical, peacockish, puppy-love aspect to the Ba' as played by the youngsters. When a boy gives a girl a ribbon from one of the balls, it's understood as a serious romantic gesture.

Though there is no rule preventing their participation,

the women of Jedburgh show no obvious desire to play. 'No,' says 15-year-old Jade Thomson. 'We just scream.' This is a happy thing for the 'auld heids' who hold tradition dear and fear an ugly and embarrassing public conflict of the sort experienced by nearby Hawick over its all-male Common Riding.

There are no signs of such insurrection here. The women seem happy to encourage their menfolk with tactical advice. 'Gaun, Tom, push on son!' yells one proud mum. 'Gie him a wedgie!'

In the Sue Ryder shop just off the Market Square, the manager Liz Robson peers out between the thick slats of wood which are supposed to protect her window from being smashed by the scrum. Every shop in town is covered up like this. 'It's horrible when the sun goes down, and the mob are outside, smacking against the glass,' she says.

Jedburgh is handsome, all rough old stone and crow-step gables. It is a place where the famous names of Scots history feel very present. Walking around, you pass the houses where Robert Burns, Bonnie Prince Charlie and Mary Queen of Scots spent time, the court where Sir Walter Scott practised law.

Hand Ba', so physically engaged with these ancient streets, seems part of this living tradition. You can look at old photographs of games past, and the only thing that changes is the fashions. Bowler hats in one picture. Teddy boys in the next. Right up to today when players wear their work gear: hi-vis tabards, boiler suits, and 1950s-style blue jackets with 'Tulloch Potatoes' written on the back where you might expect to see 'Jets' or 'Sharks'.

These days, of course, most people are born outside of town, in the hospital in Galashiels, and their Uppie or Doonie status is decided by the direction from which they arrive in Jedburgh. The natural route is by the A68 from the north, which would make them a Doonie, but if the father is a die-hard Uppie then he will certainly go the long way round in order to ensure his child remains within the true faith.

And it is a faith. 'The Ba's a religion to me,' says Billie Gillies, a 66-year-old bricklayer – and Uppie. 'Ah think aboot it every day. If you took the Ba' away frae me, ah'd have nuthin'.'

Gillies is the Obi-Wan Kenobi of the Jedburgh Hand Ba' – keen to pass on the mystical skills he has acquired in almost 60 years of play. At one point he is walking up the street with his arm round a young man. 'The funny thing is that if the ba' likes you, it'll seem to come to you,' he tells the lad. 'Dinnae struggle and attract attention. Keep quiet if you want to be a Ba' player.'

While the boy's game is fast, Hand Ba' played by the adult men often descends into large piles of writhing bodies and limbs. It's hot and sore and stinking. 'People are complaining about the fermers,' says Len Wyse at one point. 'They've no' changed efter work and it smells like sheep in there.'

The men's game relies heavily on 'smuggling' – hiding the ball inside your clothes, sauntering away from the scrum, perhaps feigning injury, and then going on to hail surreptitiously. It's even possible, though not in the spirit of the game, to smuggle the ball into a car boot or hand it to a passing motorbike. Everyone knows smuggling goes on though, so there are always lots of intimate body-searches going on round the fringes of the scrum. No crotch goes ungroped.

What's remarkable in these heavily regulated times is that the Hand Ba' continues without interference from the health and safety lobby. The police are nowhere to be seen and there are no paramedics standing by. It takes place on a date worked out by a complicated procedure involving Candlemas and the new moon, but is not advertised and there isn't an organising committee. No-one is in charge. The Ba' is a 'happening' rather than an official event.

Yet there is no doubt that this game can be dangerous. At one point an Uppie gets hold of the ball and makes a break for a patch of countryside. This involves crossing the A68. A lorry, travelling at some speed and sounding its horn, bears down upon a group of players. No-one is hurt, but it isn't long afterwards that an 18-year-old called Daniel Brown runs smack into the brick wall of an electricity substation, cutting his head open above his right eyebrow.

The game has violent roots, explained to me by Rod Sharp, an 81-year-old retired teacher. The story goes that in the mid-16th century, English forces occupying nearby Ferniehirst Castle were besieged by the Scots. 'The English captain decided to surrender,' says Sharp, 'but the leader of the Jedburgh men, recognising him as the person who had ravished his wife and daughters, cut off his head, picked it up by the long hairs, and flung it over the castle walls.' This is symbolised today by the ball and ribbon; the Uppies score a hail by throwing it over the walls of the Castle Jail at the top of the High Street.

This year's Hand Ba' ends in the freezing darkness, shortly before nine, with the Doonies the victors by eight hails to seven, and the players repair to the pubs to collect their liquid winnings. Ronnie Notman, 51, a garage worker and proud but weary Uppie, rubs his hands together against the cold. 'It's in the blood this, eh?'

Barlinnie

BARLINNIE at dawn on a freezing February morning presents to the world a forbidding aspect, the brutal silhouette of its vast Victorian halls suggestive of a factory from the Industrial Revolution, albeit one in which the raw material and finished product are the same: men.

Bad men, some would say, and no doubt there are people in Scotland's largest prison – the defilers of children, the tracksuited cleavers of flesh – to whom that old-fashioned word 'wicked' could be reasonably applied. But there are many other prisoners who, one might argue, are victims themselves – of poverty, of poor parenting, of drug addiction – and who have ended up here, in part, because of the family and area in which they grew up; most of the 10,000 prisoners who pass through the prison each year come from the most impoverished postcodes in Glasgow.

Though it looms large in the legend of the city, the prison remains a mystery to most citizens. Unless you live in the north-east of Glasgow, you might never in your life see even the brooding exterior, except perhaps for the blunt chimneys and barbed wire glimpsed from the motorway and soon forgotten. To walk freely inside its yards, halls and cells is a rare privilege that feels rather like visiting a national monument. As governor Derek McGill puts it, 'This is not just a prison. This is Barlinnie.'

McGill is a silver-haired 57-year-old whose navy pinstripes set him apart from his staff of 350 uniformed officers. He has come through the ranks, however, and is far from aloof. For 18 months he has been in charge, and is as proud of his position as the 'Guvnor' mug on his desk suggests. He finds Barlinnie endlessly fascinating. 'Right,' he says, 'are you ready for a wee walk about?'

Most of the prison population is held in five four-storey halls, the thick sandstone walls darkened and pitted with age. At the front of each block is a tall, arched window; above each main entrance is a painted crown. Inside, the brick walls are painted white, and the first impression is one of space and light; long vanishing points and a blue sky visible through the high glass canopy.

The reception area is as hectic and cramped as the halls are airy. There are seventy-four prisoners leaving the prison for court appearances. Prisoners yet to be processed stare sullenly through the windows of the claustrophobic holding cubicles, known as 'dog boxes'.

A prisoner walks forward and has a metal-detecting wand swept over his body. Brian – a 37-year-old with pale jail skin, short dark hair and hollow eyes – is a veteran of the search process. He has been in and out for years. This time he has been charged with serious assault. 'I'm in for defending my property,' he says with stale defiance. 'I was attacked in my house, but because I've had three previous convictions, here I am.'

How does Barlinnie now compare with how it used to be? 'Too cushy,' he says. 'Too easy for the cons. It used to be that you respected the screws.'

Brian is against having television in the cells. Some prison officers consider telly the best thing that ever happened in Barlinnie because it pacifies the prisoners, making them less likely to harm themselves and others. However, TV has also had a huge impact on the literacy of prisoners, which has knock-on effects with regard to rehabilitation and future employment. 'I couldn't read or write when I first came in here,' says Brian. 'If I'd had the telly back then, I would never have learned. I've managed to get a bit of intelligence about me now; not that you'd think so, with me still coming in and out of here at my age.'

The majority of Barlinnie inmates have been charged with or convicted of thefts, breaches of the peace, drugs offences, sex offences and assaults of varying seriousness, with a little over half serving sentences of between one and four years. The prison also holds, in a small segregation unit, or – colloquially – the Wendy House, a few prisoners unable to mix with the general population, including high-ranking gangsters. Barlinnie's intelligence unit helps officers decide which halls are the most appropriate to house particular prisoners; mortal enemies, rival gang members and those owing drug money to affiliates of dealers are kept well away from each other. It is similar to deciding where to seat bickering relatives at a wedding reception, albeit on a much large scale and with much bloodier consequences.

The familial metaphor is apt. Incarceration in Barlinnie is dynastic. The prison has been home from home for three generations of some families. One prison officer says his father worked here for 35 years, locking up the fathers and grandfathers of the prisoners now in his custody. There is a dismal sense of destiny about it all.

Most prisoners are in their twenties. Just boys, really, in prison-issue jeans and red sweatshirts. Their cells, which measure about two metres wide by three and a half long, have bunks and glossy girly posters and are strongly redolent of teenage bedrooms; the small window, high on the back wall, is curtainless, but prisoners improvise with T-shirts and pillowslips, creating bands of red, white and blue or green, white and orange, depending on footballing allegiance.

Many of the prisoners, perhaps most, will have been working up to Barlinnie, having first spent time in Polmont Young Offenders Institute. This is a grim post-industrial echo of the apprenticeship system. The young cons here are apprentices no longer; they are journeymen criminals whose scars mark their fraternity with that particular guild. That's one of the first things you notice here – the scars.

They zig-zag across faces unmarked by age, and carve their way through short hair like contour lines on a map. One lad has a thumb stitched where his nose should be, having lost it to a samurai sword.

New prisoners arrive daily with cuts and bruises, but it is possible to get hurt in Barlinnie itself. In the last three years there have been two serious and fifteen minor prisoner-on-staff assaults, plus 53 serious and 56 minor prisoner-on-prisoner assaults. Weapons have been fashioned from sharpened forks and screws; a favourite piece of Barlinnie hardware is a toothbrush with two razor blades pressed into the melted plastic. 'You can tell a jail slashing,' says McGill, 'because you get a great big thick scar on your face, too wide to stitch properly.'

Barlinnie's atmosphere is a curious mix of tension, resentful boredom, melancholy, and gallus gallows humour. 'Haw!' shouts one young prisoner, Paul, trying to attract the attention of a passing officer. Paul is serving 27 months for assaulting a policeman and is eager to discuss a healthful change to the dinner menu. 'What's happenin' wi' thae square sausages? Thae links are gonnae kill folk.'

Not all exchanges are so amusing. In D Hall at lunch-time, a prisoner called James, a tall man with longish dark hair, becomes very angry all of a sudden. 'You've no got a fuckin' warrant to hold me,' he screams. 'I know what happened to my family and girlfriend in here. You're gonnae get me murdered.' He is bundled into his cell and the door locked. D Hall holds prisoners with mental health issues. Mostly, they are not so ill that they can be sectioned, but not well enough to be safely out in the community, so here they remain. The governor points out one disturbing, shambling figure in particular. 'He set himself on fire a couple of weeks ago, and when they went in to get him out he attacked two firemen.'

Stevie Geddes, an officer in E Hall, says the job requires constant vigilance. Many old hands among the staff were young officers at the time of the 1987 riot, and though the Barlinnie regime is now far less confrontational, the memory lingers of how quickly disorder can escalate. 'We deal with some of the most violent people in Scotland,' says Geddes. 'There was a member of staff assaulted in C Hall yesterday. We've had officers with broken jaws and all sorts.'

Violence is commonplace in Barlinnie, only the severity varies. Anything can cause a fight; the illicit trade in merchandise, for example, inflates both the price and perceived worth of items that, outside of prison, would be considered disposable. 'A tenner bag of heroin in here is worth £60,' Geddes explains. 'The going rate for a mobile phone is £1,000. A Mars Bar to you and I is 40p; in here, it's high stakes.'

Drug use is rife. Prevalence testing suggests that 82 per cent of those admitted to Barlinnie are on drugs; on release, 10 per cent fail a test for illegal drugs. Narcotics get into the prison in various ways. A small bag of heroin may be passed from mouth to mouth during a visiting time kiss. Less romantically, a drug user attending court and believing that he is going to be sent to Barlinnie will often hide a mobile phone and as much heroin as possible up his back passage, a part of the body known to prisoners as 'the bank'.

Packages containing drugs also come over the perimeter wall, sometimes fired by crossbow or catapult, during daily exercise; if the prisoner for whom it is intended is lucky, he will be able to lift it before the officer notices. There are also prison officers who will bring drugs and other items into Barlinnie – either because they are well paid to do so, or because they are too frightened to say no. McGill loathes such betrayals – 'I don't like it when they sell us out for the other side' – and has taken measures to toughen up security screening of staff.

A daily ritual at Barlinnie, a sort of profane communion,

is the dispensation of the heroin substitute methadone. Prisoners who have a prescription before coming to prison continue to receive it inside at the same dosage. Barlinnie is the biggest single-site dispenser of methadone in Western Europe – four hundred or so prisoners receive it every morning, adding up to more than 15,000 pints of the green liquid each year. Prisoners are brought to the waiting room of the clinic ten at a time and each in turn goes up to the hatch to receive his dose from the nurse. After swallowing, each prisoner must also drink a cup of water. This is to prevent them from holding the drug at the back of the throat then subsequently hawking it up to sell – a practice known as 'the methadone spit'.

Talk to any random selection of prisoners in Barlinnie and the chances are that most will have become involved in theft or violence because of their addiction to drugs or alcohol or both. What you hear again and again is that prison, for chronic addicts, is a safe place. They can detox, get fed, stay alive for a while longer.

'Jail saved my life,' says David, 47, serving three years for head-butting a drug dealer. 'The only time my ma could sleep at night was when I was in here. She knew I wouldn't be found with a needle in my arm.'

Big Mick, 42, used to be a security guard, but since his mid-thirties, when he split from his wife and children, has been lost in drink. He has had seventeen sentences for shoplifting in the last seven years. This time he is in for four months. He finds it impossible to stay sober outside prison. 'I see the pain it is causing my ma and da, but the only time I can stop is in here.' When he is released, he intends to commit further crimes – and get caught – so he is sent to Barlinnie again. He is not the only prisoner who admits to this strategy. Statistics show that around 90 per cent of those prisoners currently inside will return in future. Some hardly get further than the three off-licenses at the bottom of the street.

The last prisoner to commit suicide here was on his 50th stretch and was only 32. 'I think he'd just had enough,' says the Governor. 'They cannot break the cycle of offending. People blame the prison service for that, but we deal with them as best we can. I think we do a great job. Look at what we do with work, with prisoner programmes, getting people off their drugs, getting them to put on weight again. By and large, they turn their life around when they are in here. But what we don't do is go out the door with them.

'I know people will talk about a 90 per cent failure rate because the prisoners keep coming back, but it's not my failure rate, or the Scottish Prison Service's failure rate, it's society's failure rate because there's not enough outside the prison walls.'

Barlinnie is in many ways a microcosm of society, and its members have the same everyday needs – both physical and spiritual. There is a church in the prison grounds, a barber, a dentist and a gym. Services are held every Sunday and 250 haircuts are given each week. The widespread use of methadone, which dries the mouth and encourages tooth decay, is one reason why the dentist, Dr Kieran Fallon, is often described as the busiest man in the prison. The kitchen, meanwhile, serves up 1.5 million meals a year, including porridge, of course, and is staffed in large part by Chinese and Vietnamese migrants caught during police raids on cannabis factories.

The prison laundry, too, is staffed by inmates, specifically the sex offenders. The mainstream prisoners would not tolerate their food being prepared by the 'beasts' of the jail, but find it acceptable that they wash and iron their clothes. Also, according to the governor, they are simply very good at the job; there is, apparently, something in the psychology of a sex offender that makes him neat and fastidious. Seeing these pale, plump, watchful, hateful, sad-eyed men folding bedsheets is just one of the many remarkable, troubling things about Barlinnie.

The prison has been open for more than 130 years. Built to hold 1,018 prisoners, it has rarely done so, and is almost always massively overcrowded. There are, at present, around 1,500 prisoners in Barlinnie, most of them sharing cells built for single occupancy. The population is seasonal. Christmas and summer are relatively quiet. From August onwards, the number increases rapidly, and last year reached its highest ever level – 1,786.

When Low Moss prison opens on the outskirts of Bishopbriggs next month, it is likely to offer Barlinnie some brief respite, but McGill does not believe it will be a long-term solution. 'Judges know when Barlinnie's not full, and all of a sudden remand numbers increase,' he says.

The 2008 Scottish Prisons Commission noted that high prison populations are more likely to 'drive reoffending than reduce it' and favoured community-based sentences over short jail terms. The result is that Barlinnie now has far fewer prisoners serving less than six months, but the prison actually has more prisoners altogether. It would appear that remanding a prisoner in custody, awaiting trial, is being used to take troublemakers out of communities for up to 140 days, without imposing the politically difficult short sentences. The significant downside is that there are so many – right now, around 550 – men being held in prison for quite long periods without having been tried for any crime.

Overcrowding is a problem because it means a large proportion of the prison population cannot access work placements, education, or many of the rehabilitative programmes that are supposed to help them change into useful members of society while inside. According to the most recent inspection, on average 70.4 per cent of the population is locked up in cells instead of being on purposeful activity. Prisoners can spend up to 23 hours a day locked up with a cell-mate – or 'co-pilot' – they loathe. Physical fights in these circumstances, prisoners say, are a daily occurrence.

What, then, is the future of this Victorian jail in the 21st century? The chief inspector of prisons, while noting that the institution is well led and run, and drawing particular attention to the excellent care prisoners – often frightened and despairing – receive during their first night in custody, has called for its redevelopment as soon as possible. McGill himself believes that by 2020 the present buildings will have fallen out of use and a new prison built nearby. Barlinnie's own long stretch is, it seems, coming to an end.

'It would be sad to see it demolished completely,' says the Governor. 'There's a huge amount of history here. You could imagine them running tours. This could be the Alcatraz of Glasgow. I think even the prisoners would be sorry to see this go. Places like Polmont don't have any atmosphere. Barlinnie has got a lot of life.'

A lot of life and, despite the odds, a lot of love. By 5.00 pm, there is a long queue for visiting. It's almost all women: dolled-up wives and girlfriends; sorrowful mums and grannies. One lad catches the eye – maybe six years old, cute in his crewcut and good clothes, walking round in slow, bored circles, heel-to-toe, swinging a key for the prison locker, familiar already with the rules of visiting. How many birthdays, you wonder, has his father missed, and how many to come? And here's the most dreadful question of all: will that wee boy, too, one day end up here or in whatever prison replaces it?

Barlinnie, every groan and dirty stone of it, has a habit of weighing down the mind with such fatalistic thoughts. So, as fascinating as it has been, it is a relief to finally leave the prison and walk out into the cold dusk, a half-moon rising high and pure and free above those grimly iconic chimneys.

The Fortieth Lambing of Bert Leitch

BERT Leitch, a sheep farmer on Mull, loosens the flaps of his deerstalker cap and ties them under his chin. 'Right,' he says, bending once more into the wind, 'let's ca' on.'

This simple phrase, often on his lips, expresses so much about the man and his way of life. It speaks of the urgency of the lambing season; the thrawnness necessary for the job; the eternal, cyclical nature of the work. Leitch is 71. A Fifer, this is his 40th year on Mull, his 40th lambing on the island, though he has worked with sheep since 1956. Under his watch, many thousands have been born. He has, too, seen many die. Those lost during their births, others lost to the crows and snows, avian predators and climate being pitiless killers of lambs. Shepherding is life and death in the raw. A calling not a career.

'If your sole aim in life is to make money, you would never entertain the likes of this,' he says. 'Never. The time you put in, and the return you get, and the disappointments you get, you'd be daft or damn near it.'

Leitch is a short, stout man with grave blue eyes which, like the rest of him, are always on the move. He leans on a crook as he walks the hills of his 2,000-acre farm, snagging lambs in a quick sweeping motion with the curved horn handle. He is accompanied at all times by a dog. Today it's the turn of Cap, an amiable, keen, lushly-coated Collie. When Leitch wants to attend to a particular sheep he sends the dog to round it up, barking sharp, gruff commands – 'Away to me!' meaning go right, or 'Come by!' meaning go left – in a voice that expresses his absolute dominion.

The lambing season, on Oskamull farm, began just after

mid-April and will go on until towards the end of May. Leitch has 450 Blackface ewes – he pronounces the word in the traditional Scots way as 'yowe' – and the vast majority will lamb during this period. Most will have just one lamb each year. They orbit the hill, each ewe and lamb, like a planet and its moon.

Male or 'wether' lambs are sold for meat at about five to six months old, and the top price Leitch got in Oban last year was around £30 per animal. The market for lamb has picked up considerably over the past three years following a long period of decline. Showing 'richt smart lambs' in the sale-ring and being paid well for his effort gives Leitch a buzz. But there are also huge costs, especially as he lives on an island; the rising price of fuel, especially, smoulders away at the margins. The best of his new ewes he will keep for breeding.

Leitch's hands are rough, red and blunt, yet deft and sensitive enough to reach inside a ewe then identify and rearrange the head and limbs of a lamb presenting in the wrong position; 'guddle aboot till you find a leg,' is how he describes this procedure. He makes quick work of lambing. It's over in less than a minute, the animal sliding wet and yellow from its mother. He wipes the mucus membrane away from its nose and mouth, and presses the ewe's face towards its lamb – 'C'mon, girl' – in the hope of encouraging bonding. He also squeezes the ewe's teats till milk begins to emerge.

There's a sort of rough tenderness, a gentle decisiveness to his actions. He is breeding and raising these animals in order to profit from their eventual death, yet he has a kind of instinctive affinity with them, an understanding or 'kenning' as he puts it.

He is regarded within Scottish farming as 'a sage-like figure' full of sheepy wisdom. He is a modest, plain-spoken man, always keen to deflect praise, but it becomes clear very quickly, when spending time with him on the hill, that he has his own country philosophy. There is an unwritten Tao Of Bert collated from his own stoic experiences – 'You aye lose a puckle beasts at lambing' – and the gnomic aphorisms of other shepherds: 'This yowe hasnae enough milk to grease the hinge of a spectacle.'

It is half-past six in the morning when I walk out with Leitch to the lambs. His land is rough, rocky and steep; pasture pocked with clumps of brittle heather and new bracken emerging in crook-like fronds. There can be few sheep in Britain with a better view. Ben More is an ancient kingly presence wearing an onyx crown of cloud. To the west, Staffa and Iona are warm with sunshine, pearls on the tide. Leitch has a strong empathetic sense of those who walked these hills before him, pointing out the abandoned village of Corkamull which lost much of its population during the Clearances to make way for sheep farming. It is a rickle of stones.

Leitch walks his land every day during the lambing season, examining every gully, hollow and ridge. Most of the ewes will lamb quite naturally and without problems. The fear, though, is that he might miss a ewe having diffi-culties by simply not seeing it. But no matter how good his vantage point, he can never achieve a perspective superior to the hooded crows, his sworn foes, for whom lambing season is an annual feast. 'Those beggars there,' he says, pointing at the birds with his crook, 'they'll watch for a yowe lambing and then take the tongue of the lamb if they can. And if the yowe cowps they'll take her eyes.'

Hoodies are not the only predator, though they are the most numerous. Leitch says he also loses lambs to ravens and sea eagles. This last point is controversial as the white-tailed sea eagles, Britain's largest bird of prey, were once extinct in this country, but, having been reintro-duced, are now an important tourist draw for Mull. 'The RSPB will tell you they only eat dead or sickly lambs, but that's nonsense,' says Leitch. 'A sleeping lamb – that's just

61

convenience food for a sea eagle.' They are protected by law and Leitch therefore cannot shoot them. 'But it comes very close to it sometimes.'

It's intensely cold on the hill in a strong wind, but a mercy that it's dry. Wet weather is the worst, even worse than snow. It seems to wear the sheep down. And when the burns are in spate, it's common for lambs to drown while trying to follow their mothers across water too fast and deep. 'Bloody sheep,' says Leitch. 'They can find lots of ways tae dee.'

In the byre, in a pen beside its mother, there is a dead lamb. It was 'hung', meaning it started emerging from the ewe head-first with its legs tucked back behind and became stuck. Leitch was too late getting to it. 'You curse yourself. You think 'What the hell did I miss that for?' But you cannae be everywhere at the one time.'

So he has a dead lamb. He also has a live lamb without a mother. To fix these two problems, Leitch performs a 'twinning'. He lifts the limp damp corpse from beside the keening ewe, lies it on a rusty oil drum and with a small knife removes its head and front legs. He cuts into the abdomen and rubs blood on the head of the live lamb, which bleats a little at this indignity. He then skins the lamb, and holding the live one between his knees, pulls the gory fleece over its head as if it were a new jumper. He puts the lamb in the pen beside the ewe. She sniffs this newcomer. She licks the blood. She seems to accept that the lamb is hers and suffers it to drink her milk.

'It's keen to sook,' the farmer says with quiet satisfaction, 'and her mothering instinct's strong. There's no going to be a problem with this yin.'

Of such small miracles, a lambing season is made. Of traditions and rituals. To see Leitch twinning the lamb is to see an old, old skill, a thing handed down. It is not just a lifetime's experience but the experiences of several lifetimes. Leitch learned how to do this in the 1950s from 'auld Sandy Lean', a shepherd in Fife, but who knows who Lean got it from, and who before him? Lambing is said to be worth more than £600 million annually to the UK economy, but its true value, I believe, is as a trove of these practical yet in some ways rather mystical skills, and as a means of keeping people in these remote areas, working the land and raising families of their own.

Leitch and his wife Chris brought up three children here. His granddaughters – Eilidh, five, and Kate, three – are delighted, at this time of year, to have the opportunity to bottle-feed orphan lambs. Though Leitch is now in his seventies and has suffered health scares in recent years, he has no thoughts of retiring – 'Whit wid ah dae?' He has seen too many men go into decline when they stop work.

Rather, he will continue to walk the hills, in the sleet and smirr and the snell wind, past the abandoned crofts and tumbledown dykes, all those old ghosts, with the smell of smoke and blood and dung and the sea in his nostrils. He will walk and work because stopping is not in his nature. 'Right,' he says, 'let's ca' on.' And we do.

Glasgow Central

"WALK this way," says Paul Lyons, "and I'll tell you another tale."

Lyons is in his late forties, lives in "the people's republic of Clydebank", and has been a railwayman for the past 15 years. It is a job which defines him. He works as a customer services assistant at Glasgow Central, one of those bland modern titles that tells you very little about the man doing the job. What Lyons does, in fact, is help elderly and disabled passengers to and from the trains, but he is also an evangelist for the station, its unofficial historian and tour guide. He carries with him at all times a heavy freight of collective memory dating back to the station's opening on August 1, 1879 and continuing to the present day.

He can tell you about the time, in 1932, when Laurel and Hardy arrived at Central and were met by a crowd of 40,000 whistling the stars' famous theme tune; or he can tell you how, more recently, he himself gave a lift on the mobility assistance buggy to David Soul, of Starsky and Hutch fame, and they ended up singing Silver Lady together as they arrived in first class. More importantly, he can express very well what this grand Victorian station means to the city and the people who use it.

"This is not just a railway station," he says. "It's part of the fabric of Glaswegians' lives and souls. It's a microcosm. People die in here. People have gave birth in here. You get wee snapshots of people's lives, and then you never see them again. This is a city within the city."

Central is beautiful. A "cathedral to the iron horse" built in 1879 in blonde sandstone, dark wood, girders and glass. Honeyed evening light slants in through tall arched windows, as it has done for more than a century, giving the passengers on platform 15 the look of a chosen people, even though all they have chosen is a cheap day return to Troon.

The station covers more than two square miles, and seen from above resembles a pair of skyscrapers lying as if fallen amid the spires and rooftops of the city. Central has the largest glass roof in the world, some 48,000 panes; maintaining and replacing these is a ceaseless job – the Glaswegian equivalent of painting the Forth Bridge. Up there, in the company of gulls, one can admire the glass and steel, the vistas and vanishing points. Look north and see the spires and domes of the city. Look south, beyond the wide brown Clyde, to the suburbs and, beyond them, to the hazy moors. Look down and see the "throat" of the station, the name given to the area just south of the platforms where the 14 lines narrow and bunch, and on which swans have been known to land, mistaking it for water.

Central is a starting point or destination for some 40 million people each year, and there are approximately 1,300 train movements each day. The tannoy is ceaseless in its poetic incantations: Priesthill, Nitshill, Barhill, Carluke, Carstairs, Cardonald, Kilmaurs, Kilwinning, Kilmarnock. From the moment when the grand Victorian gates – now restored to their gold and green pomp after years in glossy mourning for the death of Prince Albert – open at 4am to when they shut at half-past midnight, there is always something going on.

The station functions as an emotional barometer of the city. Often, you can judge Glasgow's mood from just a few minutes on the concourse – scunnered, heads down on dreich winter mornings; buzzing and boozy, full of reckless joy, on electric summer nights. It is all about life – folk hurrying, thronging, experiencing that keen sense of belonging that comes with living and working in this city. The staff get to know the familiar faces. The drag queens and druggies, the commuters and cosplay kids, the guy wearing a sarong and rigger boots who keeps a cat in a harness on one shoulder.

Up in the Comms Room, the team monitor CCTV. Before the July 7 bombings of the London Underground, Glasgow Central had seven cameras; now there are more than 200, and every inch of the station is scrutinized at every moment. This, of course, is helpful when it comes to investigating and prosecuting crime, including football-related violence; following one post-match brawl, a man's ear was found lying on the concourse. That makes the station sound like a dangerous place, which isn't fair. Such incidents are simply the inevitable consequence of such enormous numbers of people passing through each day. One veteran worker still shudders at the memory of the hordes of pink-stetsoned women on the ran-dan, travelling to and from Mount Florida, when Take That played Hampden for three nights in 2011. "I'd rather have a football crowd," he says.

Walk out on to the concourse and talk to people. You won't look far for a story. Something akin to the population of Dundee passes through each day on their way to work, to home, to meet friends and lovers and bitter enemies, to commit crimes and adultery and suicide, and sometimes, now and then, just to spot trains.

An old gentleman in a check tweed jacket, a rolled newspaper in his pocket, falls over near the Gordon Street entrance and cuts his head above the right eye. On the other side of the station, his wife is frantic looking for him, knowing he has dementia, knowing that he'll be anxious and confused. When, finally, they find each other – "What have you been doing to yourself?" she mock-scolds – all that worry and relief is expressed in the gesture performed here hundreds or perhaps thousands of times each day since the Victorian age: a simple hug.

Sitting by the departures board, waiting for the Ayrshire

service which will take him to see his son, James Ginnitty has time to tell his tale. He is 76 and dapper – shirt and tie, Clark Gable tache, feathers in his trilby. The eye is drawn to the chunky gold, silver and diamond rings he wears on each finger, and from there to knuckles which appear strangely flat. He comes, he explains, from a family of street-fighters and worked in the late 1950s as a bare-knuckle boxer, touring Britain in the fairground booths, taking on all comers. If anyone could go three rounds, they got three pounds; if they knocked him out they got a fiver. "They seldom went three rounds, I can tell you that," he says. "I made sure they didnae." In 1959, after a ferocious fight, he became champ of Appleby Fair. He lives, these days, on Mull and likes to sit and play the accordion beneath the Tobermory clock.

There is, too, the secret wildlife of Glasgow Central. The family of foxes with a den by the tracks; the swallows nesting on girders; the otter that got loose here once, and the ferret; the pigeons, scabby doos docile on account of having their feet melted by the overhead wires. There was once rumoured to be a penguin hiding underneath a train on platform nine, which subsequent investigation revealed to be a guillemot. Most venerable of all is the 86 year old tortoise, Derek, an honoured resident of Milngavie who makes frequent journeys to Euston on a seat of his own, unfailingly travelling first class.

Much of Central is unseen. Its subterranean areas attract conspiracies like a magnet attracts iron filings. Websites are full of fevered speculation about secret passageways, abandoned Victorian villages still intact, a mysterious portal known as Door 24, and an old boilerhouse where, in 1929, a businessman is said to have strangled his wife for the insurance money.

"So," says Ross Moran, the station manager, "this is the way into the secret tunnels. The rumours are true – they do exist. It's a labyrinth down there."

We are standing in a bright underground corridor, and Moran has just unlocked and opened a door. He clicks his torch. The beam probes the darkness uncertainly. There is a ladder leading down into what looks, through the mirk, like an abandoned platform; all rust-pitted pillars and bricks clarted in the coal dust from trains that ceased running long ago.

"I'll show you," he says, putting a foot on the ladder. "Come on ..."

Moran is still in his thirties, young to be in overall control of such a place. Yet it's clear that he regards himself as a privileged guardian of the station. His office overlooks the concourse and he has a grand view of the famous clock suspended from the roof, a landmark which has served as a rendezvous for generations of couples, its mechanism no doubt outpaced by the fast-beating hearts of those waiting below. He had at one time intended to become a writer, and only thought of the railway after the funding was pulled for his PhD in baroque poetry. Yet for anyone with an appreciation of plot and character, the station is more rewarding than any literature course.

He leads the way across the uneven, rubble-strewn floor where tracks once lay. We're in a sort of brick vault with rooms leading off to one side, their function now forgotten. Stepped pyramids, suggestive of Aztec ruins, form the base of unseen pillars high above. There is a smell of earth, the sound of trickling water, the rumble and grind of trains moving overhead. Once, this whole area would have been busy with commuters, but has been abandoned and sealed up since the Beeching axe fell half a century ago. "It just goes on and on," says Moran, pointing his torch into a tunnel. "We don't know how far it might go."

Hidden underground, too, is the area from which the night mail used to leave Glasgow for the south of England. It was this service, on August 8, 1963, which was targeted by the Great Train Robbers, resulting in the theft of £2.6

million and – many believe – the eventual death of the driver Jack Mills who was coshed on the head with an iron bar. Paul Lyons recalls working in London in the early 1990s and noticing railwaymen spitting on the ground as they passed an elderly flower seller who had a stall outside Waterloo station. This old man was, it turned out, Buster Edwards, the most famous of the robbers, and the rail workers spat at him to express their contempt. "That drove home to me the family ethos of the railway," says Lyons. "If you pick on one, you pick on all of us."

There is a tremendous sense of solidarity among the staff. You might have thought all esprit de corps would have been lost following privatisation, but in fact the atmosphere is not at all corporate and bland; it is more like that of a shipyard or steelworks in its mix of black humour and rough camaraderie. Spend time on the concourse and that becomes apparent very quickly. They love a story here, stories offering a kind of buffer against some of the darknesses of the job. "D'ye mind the time ..." someone will say, and that will be them off.

They all remember, for instance, the night a drug addict gave birth on platform fifteen; she'd been hanging about for ages, resisting encouragement from staff to go to hospital, desperate to score one last time. Next thing, she was shuffling down the platform with the baby crowning, and it was just lucky that a driver, arriving on a train from Ayrshire, was able to step out of his cab and deliver the child. "So," the punchline goes, "if you ever meet wee ScotRail MacPherson, you'll know where he was born."

There was the time, too, some years ago, when a guy, unhinged, climbed the fire escape and threatened to leap off. It was a huge stooshie. The police were called and, eventually, the man's girlfriend talked him down. "Then, a week later," you're told, "he cut her head off." A pause. A sniff. A stoic sip of tea. "Should've let him jump."

This is a place with skeletons in its closet – literally. Ask

69

Stevie Gardiner nicely, and the maintenance supervisor might lead you into the paint store where, in a narrow, upright, wooden box, he keeps a skeleton, coming apart and discoloured with age. This rickle of bones is one Central's sorrowful mysteries. A small, dirty label on the pelvis indicates that this specimen has its origins in Maison Tramond, a Parisian supplier of anatomical parts, most likely early in the 20th century. It appears to have at one time belonged to a doctor based on the sixth floor of the hotel adjoining Central and working in occupational health for the railway. The station, though, is a place that never lets the facts get in the way of a compelling tale, and there is, therefore, some speculation that these are the mortal remains of a hotel chef who threw himself from the seventh floor after a chambermaid spurned his advances.

Whatever the truth, the skeleton suits Central; it is a fine memento mori for a building that has seen its share of death. The station is a living place, but it feels, sometimes, haunted by memories. Would it be too fanciful to imagine, among the hordes of commuters, the ghosts of travellers past? The hundreds of men who, the following year, left from platform one to fight in the Spanish Civil War, fists held high, singing the Internationale. The wives and mothers and sisters who came here, in 1919, to meet returning soldiers, and those unlucky ones who found their husbands, brothers and sons in the temporary mortuary downstairs; a room which, even now, feels uneasy and chill. Laurel and Hardy. Rudolf Hess. Queen Victoria. JFK. All the famous and infamous dead who once passed through this place, and all the millions of unknown passengers whose journeys gave it life and purpose.

Paul Lyons, at four stately miles per hour, processes across the concourse at the wheel of a blue mobility buggy, taking an elderly lady and her cases to her carriage. It brings to mind the time he met a tearful middle-aged American off the train; she had travelled from Texas to meet, for the first time, her fiance (they had got together online) at his "ranch in the Gorbals" and had just been put in the picture by a fellow passenger. Lyons, as he approaches platform one, passes grafters, shirkers, nuns, junkies, pickpockets, cops and a fellow dressed as a pirate. He passes James Ginnitty and – who knows? – maybe the restless shade of Benny Lynch, who, at 9.35 pm on January 20, 1937, arrived on platform 11 from London as the new flyweight world champion and was greeted by a crowd of 15,000; within a decade he would be dead of malnutrition brought on by drink.

Lyons passes through the station he loves, through its 135 years of history, and knows that this place will still be standing after he and the rest of us have joined the long narrative of its past. "When I first started working here I thought it was just a railway station," he says. "But this place is Glasgow's best kept secret. The stories of the city are the stories of Central. And here endeth the lesson."

Karaoke at the Horseshoe Bar

'THIS,' says Raymond, 'is where the magic happens.' He gestures towards a tiny stage in the corner of the pub, maybe eight feet by five and raised just a couple of inches off the floor, within staggering distance of the ladies loo. It would not rival Caesar's Palace for glamour. Yet this, indeed, is where the magic happens – seven nights a week at the Horse Shoe karaoke.

The Horse Shoe Bar is one of Glasgow's iconic pubs, and the karaoke an institution within it. Raymond Fitzpatrick has been a compere here for most of his adult life, and next year will celebrate his 20th anniversary. That's two decades of cuing up backing tracks for every Chrissie Hyndland and Dusty Springburn keen to tell the listening tipplers about the brass in their pocket and the windmills of their mind. He loves it, Raymond. Just look as he rolls up a trouser leg and reveals the proof of his devotion – a tattooed horse shoe with the melody to Robbie Williams's Angels running through it.

Robbie is just one of the celebrities with whom Raymond has sung over the years. They did Take That hits. A bigger thrill, though, was duetting with Ally McCoist, a personal hero, on Joe Cocker's Unchain My Heart. He remembers, too, Kerry Katona getting up and doing Summer Nights. 'She warned me she was rubbish,' says Raymond, 'and right enough, she was.'

They have high standards at the Horse Shoe. Some great singers come here. Not famous. Ordinary folk with extraordinary voices. Raymond is no slouch himself. You want to hear his Paolo Nutini.

This is also a place where the karaoke dead are remembered and honoured. The name Willie Wales still rings out. 'He must have been well in his seventies and he used to do My Way, the Sid Vicious version,' says Raymond. 'He was a legend in Glasgow for it.'

And did Mr Wales sing any other songs? 'Oh, he did. I'm Too Sexy. What a showman.'

The karaoke starts at 8.00 pm, except on Sundays – the most popular day – when it's 5.00 pm. On the night I visit, the town's hoaching with works nights out. They come piling into the Horse Shoe on the stroke of eight, loosened ties and party frocks, drouthy for vodka and Irn-Bru. 'Right,' says Raymond, 'let's get this show on the road.'

First up is Sally Loy. No messing about. Straight in there with Don't Stop Believin'. Sally is 45 and from Auchinleck. She came up on the train with her friends, work pals from Tesco, but if you'd told me she flew I'd believe you. Sally is a wee ball of energy. Bobbed hair, floral dress, shiny black boots. She has a brilliant, throaty, fags 'n' bevvy voice, giving it, 'Just a small town girl/Living in a lonely world ...' She plays air guitar during the solos and bends into Raymond's face to deliver the line, 'Some were born to sing the blues.' She is quite astonishingly good.

Afterwards, having a smoke outside in Drury Street, Sally says she's been into Journey since she was sixteen – 'That's my most favourite song and band in the world' – though she also has time for Meat Loaf. So is Don't Stop Believin' her party piece? 'If I've got a wee drink in me, aye. That stops the nerves kicking in.'

Sally clutches my arm. 'See the Glee version? I hate it. Hate it.'

Back inside, Pat McGuire, a Horse Shoe stalwart in his fifties, is explaining the appeal of these nights. 'A lot of people knock karaoke, right? But in these times, with people not working or struggling, this is their wee five minutes of fame. It makes their week.'

Pat first came to the Horse Shoe towards the end of his first marriage. His second wife wasn't really into the karaoke so his visits lessened. But now that marriage is over too, so he's back and giving Space Oddity laldy. He's keen on respect, Pat. He remembers the days when a performance would be received in silence and applauded at the end. Now everyone gabs away, and he doesn't like it. Women, he feels, cannot handle their drink. 'They should mibbe just have a Sweetheart Stout or a wee sweet sherry at a funeral.'

Pat's other quirk is that he doesn't like to sing songs that other people sing. He used to do Hoochie Coochie Man, but now a guy called George has started singing that, so Pat gives it a bye.

There is no shortage of singers. People keep coming over to Raymond and handing him slips of paper with their name and chosen song.

Sometimes, he says, they can be waiting hours to perform. 'I tell people don't wait till they're drunk to put their name down, because by the time I call their name they might need helped up on to the stage.' It is vital to achieve a perfect alcoholic equilibrium – half-cut to avoid anxiety, but not so plastered that the performance is impaired. Needless to say, not everyone gets this balance right. One young woman – a swaying vision in polka dots – performs a profane version of S Club 7's Reach, of which the best that can be said is that we now know how Jerry Sadowitz might have covered it. She wanders off into the crowd, still singing and swearing, and Raymond has to reel her in using the microphone lead like an angler landing an especially tricky trout.

Next up is Teresa. She's a social worker from King's Park, 47 years old, mad for The Beatles, the young Paul McCartney tattooed on her right leg, but here tonight to sing Lily Allen's It's Not Fair, which she does brilliantly. The lyrics, lamenting bad sex, have the mild-mannered, golf-jumpered fellow in the front row fair spluttering into his pint. Teresa sings It's Not Fair for the craic, but also because she reckons the many women in the audience will relate. 'I am married 28 years, separated three, and I've had two relationships,' she tells me. 'That song says something to about 70 per cent of females who've been to bed with men who are rotten. The other 30 per cent are very lucky.'

Which brings me to John Binnie. He is 73 years old, a retired baker, dressed immaculately in double-breasted pinstripes, hair slicked back, gold watch and shoes shining. Mr Binnie is Mr Karaoke. On Friday evenings he tours six or seven pubs and clubs, including the Horse Shoe, favouring each with a song. On Saturday afternoons, he visits the Grant Arms in the hope of finding a hen party to entertain. Sunday afternoons see him at the Old Ship Bank on the Saltmarket, where senior citizens of both sexes perform the hits of the fifties and sixties to live keyboard accompaniment. 'I don't drink and I don't smoke,' he says, 'but give me a microphone and I'm away in another world.'

Mr Binnie is, perhaps, the most extraordinary live performer I have ever had the fortune to witness.

His signature song is Bad Case Of Loving You, which he knows backwards, meaning he doesn't need to read the scrolling lyrics, leaving him free to bump and grind, strut and frug in the direction of those female members of the audience whom he judges will not mistake him for – in his own words – 'an old pervert'. His pièce de résistance is delivering the line 'No pill's gonna cure my ills' while yanking, from his jacket pocket, a blister-pack of Viagra. This gesture is met with shrieks of delight from the crowd and when the song ends Mr Binnie returns to his seat, a conquering hero.

'These are no' just for show,' he confides, indicating his little blue pills. 'I've got a girlfriend. It doesn't all stop at 23.'

Some place, the Horse Shoe karaoke. Not at all like The X-Factor. For one thing, the repartee is very different. 'The

Beatles!' Teresa shouts from the audience, hoping Raymond will break the habit of a lifetime and play a song by her favourite group. 'Naw,' says Raymond. 'The Beatles are pish.' You don't get that with Louis Walsh.

Also, and this is important, unlike a TV talent show, the karaoke does not feel in any way fake. The emotion is real. The people singing these songs do so because they love them.

At one point Raymond duets with a man called Lex Crawford, an accountant suited and booted straight from his work, on Don't Let The Sun Go Down On Me. Here are two men pushing forty, everyday guys, standing in the corner of a pub, by a sign advertising pies, and you could swear – if you shut your eyes – that it really was Elton John and George Michael. The whole place is swaying, hands in the air, a tear in many an eye. It is, undoubtedly, A Moment and a great example of the transformative power of music. As one of the punters puts it: 'If you sing well at the Horse Shoe, you feel like a superstar.'

There is a theory that karaoke suits Scotland because it is a contemporary version of the old tradition of doing a turn at Hogmanay. Maybe so. Certainly, everybody gets a turn tonight. Buxom Debbie, newly graduated, doing La Isla Bonita. Big John singing Bad Company. Don from Uddingston celebrating becoming a grandad with a heartfelt version of Mr Brightside.

Best, though, to give the last word to Raymond, for whom karaoke is not just his living but his life. It is after midnight and he is in philosophical mood.

'What would I be if I wasn't a karaoke compere?' he muses. 'Probably a virgin.'

The Hawick Common Riding

THE bells of St Mary's are striking six as the Drum and Fife Band marches into the hopeful morning light, playing the Hawick anthem Teribus, martial beats echoing in empty streets, raising rooks from gables. It is the duty of the band to waken Hawick and to alert its folk, known as Teries, that today is the Common Riding, the loudest, proudest day in the town's calendar.

In truth, everyone knows already. Hawick is decorated in the Common Riding colours of azure and gold: flags strung across streets and hung from balconies; shop windows tricked out with ribbons; pansies in planters blooming in the approved livery. Even the climate has obliged with a honey sun in a pale blue sky.

The Common Riding takes place each year on the first Friday after the first Monday in June. Dating back to 1514, it represents both the capture in battle of an English flag by the youth of Hawick and the ancient custom of marking the boundaries of the common land. There are similar festivals throughout the summer in the Borders towns and elsewhere, each a spectacle of pageantry and a booze-up, but Hawick is first and so has a particular air of abandonment and joy.

'It will never be forgotten in this toon,' says Ronnie Nichol, a giant of a man, steam rising from his bald head as he removes his band cap. 'Things are changing all over the country, financially and in every other way. But this will always go on.'

At this, his friend and bandmate Ian Anderson nods with great certainty. But what makes them so sure their

77

tradition will endure? 'Because fathers sing Teribus to their sons instead of lullabies,' says Anderson.

Nichol has been in the band for 37 years, Anderson for 33. That's the way things go in Hawick. You find a role and stick at it. Yet there is no sense of dry obligation. Rather, these men and many other Teries take enormous pleasure in participating in the ritual.

'Whatever high point you have in Glasgow it can't touch this,' Anderson explains to me, a Glaswegian, with gentle pity. 'If you're a Celtic fan and they won the European Cup six times in a row then that might come close. But it wouldn't be the same.'

There are ceremonies within the ceremony. On the Kirkstile, at the foot of the church, a large group has gathered. Some wear tweeds and golden waistcoats. Others wear bowler hats and carry riding crops. Some have beer on their breath and whisky on their mind. A wee girl in pyjamas waves down from a window. It is quarter past six in the morning.

In the midst of the crowd stands Mike Aitken, a 50-year-old joiner in his eleventh year as Song Singer. It is he who leads the songs throughout the day. For the moment, he must perform his other task – distributing snuff from an old ram's horn to those brave enough to fight for it. A cry goes up – 'Let's have it, boys!' – and suddenly Aitken is at the centre of a writhing, struggling, grunting scrum, all hoarse curses and builder's bum. Men fall to the ground, heads smacking stone. Someone loses a shoe. Occasionally, a burly figure emerges, grinning broadly, their fingers dark with snuff dug from the horn.

Afterwards, Aitken has blood on his neck and battered brogues. 'That was pretty coorse the day,' he grins. 'That's as rough as it's been. The word on the street last night was a bunch of Denholm boys were coming up to pinch the horn. There was fifty quid to whoever got it from us. They did their best but the horn's still oors.'

The tradition, after the Snuffin', is to retire to the pubs for the day's official beverage – rum and milk. 'Have a wee taste,' offers Graham Bennett, 44, standing outside the Exchange Bar. 'It's not bad after you've had a couple.' Bennett is visiting from Musselburgh. 'I was Honest Lad in 1986.' The places that hold Common Ridings send envoys to each of the others. Often these men introduce themselves as Coldstream or Kelso and so on, rather than giving their names. Where they're from is, today, more important than who they are.

Inside the Exchange, it's rammed and they're singing Up Wi' Auld Hawick. A group of friends, old mill girls, are swaying with their arms linked, bellowing it out. 'Where are you from? Scotland On Sunday? We'll still be singing come Sunday,' says Helen Ford, 69. 'This means everything to us. I can't explain it to you. It's in your blood.'

Ford has a glass of rum and milk in front of her, but her pal Merle Campbell is on the gin and soda. It's only seven in the morning. Too early yet for rum, she reckons. Her fingernails are painted blue and yellow.

Only one year did she miss the Common Riding. She was in Germany and listened on that day to a tape of the old songs. 'Oh, the tears were streaming down my cheeks. It was heart-rending.'

At 8.25 am, we get our first glimpse of the Cornet, the young man chosen to lead the riders as they travel on horseback around the boundaries of the common land. He also carries the flag, representing that captured from the English all those centuries ago. It is a tremendous honour. You are the toast of the town, a hero and heart-throb; Mr Darcy for the day.

This year's Cornet is Michael Davidson, 25, who works in forestry. This is the most important day of his life. He first rode out when he was seven years old on a pony called Rupert. Today, he sings the Old Common-Riding Song outside the town hall, reading the words from inside the top hat which he holds in front of him, then it's on to his horse, Storm, and away through the streets.

Some 329 horses are taking part this year. Each horse and rider is cheered by a crowd of several hundred as they canter out from a vennel. The band are at the front with oak leaves on the brims of their hats; then comes the Cornet in his green tail-coat and white breeks. The visiting dignitaries from other towns are also on horseback. The four men from Jedburgh, splendid in their Balmoral bonnets are particular favourites with onlookers. One dashing fellow wears a burgundy sash which identifies him as The Linton Whipman.

At the sight of the Cornet and riders, none cheers louder than Charles Whillans, known as Chuck or Mr Common Riding, a small jovial man in a blazer. At 87, he is the oldest living former Cornet, having discharged that duty in 1948. He hopes, he says, to have his coffin draped in the blue and gold flag; though, of course, his many friends in Hawick pray that day is far off. It was Helen Ford who pointed him out to me. Whillans is the first Cornet she remembers; he visited her school in his green tailcoat when she was five. Now both are old but seem young. 'Here's my Common Riding kiss,' she says, pecking his cheek. 'Thanks bonnie lass,' he replies.

One important stop on the journey of the riders is The Hut, an old barn at St Leonards farm, a short distance outside town, with Rally Roond Oor Cornet written above the door. This event, at which songs are sung and toasts given, is arguably the emotional highpoint of the day. It is men-only. The proceedings are piped out by tannoy to the assembled womenfolk picnicking on the grass.

The principal ladies, among them 23-year-old receptionist Kirsteen Hill, the Cornet's Lass, sit in their finery on benches beneath the branches of an ancient oak, having travelled here by stretch limo. 'I'm right proud for Michael and happy that he's got to fulfil a lifetime dream,' says

Hill. She doesn't seem bothered at having to remain out here, wrapped in her official Cornet's Lass blanket, while her boyfriend is warm indoors.

She might even be better off. The Hut is a hot, crowded, beery place with red-faced, damp-eyed men crammed together, elbow to elbow, jowl by jowl, banging on the tables and singing lustily. They alternate spoonfuls of curds and cream – known as 'soor dook' – with more rum and milk. One young man stumbles out and embraces his mother. 'Don't go back in just yet,' she tells him. 'The longer you stay out here, the less drink you'll have.'

Eventually, proceedings at The Hut are over and the riders make for the Moor Racecourse, where most of the townsfolk have set up a makeshift camp of gazebos strung with gold and azure bunting. It is Agincourt meets T in the Park. The revelry will go on until dawn. 'This is the best party in Scotland,' says one woman, and she may have a point.

The Common Riding is certainly vastly more enjoyable than, say, Edinburgh's Hogmanay, perhaps because it is in no way geared towards tourists or the media. It is by the Teries for the Teries. Though the locals are very welcoming, the Common Riding would happen if no-one from outside town was here. Indeed, its very insularity is the key part of its identity; it is about boundaries, about the community that holds you in its sweet embrace. It is not narrow parochialism, it is big-hearted local pride.

Steph Reith, a local woman here with her husband and teenage children, sums it up. 'A day out of Hawick,' she laughs, 'is a day wasted.'

The Naturists of Loch Lomond

IT seems an ordinary room, if a little old-fashioned, with floral prints on the walls and a view over Loch Lomond. On banquette seating, four men and four women, aged from their 50s to late-70s, are enjoying tea, scones and a chat. They are wearing the casually robust clothes of Scots on holiday in their own country. This could be the clubhouse of a local history society or some sort of church group.

Look closer, though, and two signs reveal the truth. 'As this is a naturist club,' says the first, in stern black ink, 'uniform is the norm (weather-permitting). We are not a clothes-optional club.' The law having been laid down, the second sign limits itself to matters of etiquette: 'Nae Bare Bums Oan Seats.'

The Scottish Outdoor Club has been promoting naturism – known formerly as nudism – since 1938. Founded on Fenwick Moor, near Glasgow, the club moved to its current base, Inchmurrin island, in Loch Lomond, a decade later. It has a membership of about thirty, down from 100 in its heyday, and they stay in wooden chalets arranged around a clubhouse on a south-facing hillside. The naturists rent this fenced-off, eleven-acre space from the family who own Inchmurrin. They are welcome to visit the rest of the island, including the hotel, but for this they must put on clothes – or, to use the jargon, go textile. Nakedness is known among naturists as being in uniform.

SOC members visit here most weekends during spring and summer. A boat ferries them from Balmaha on a Friday evening and picks them up again on a Sunday. I was met at the Balmaha boatyard by Colin, a slender 69-year-old. He was fully dressed and wearing a lifejacket. Colin isn't his real name. 'My son is in a sensitive job,' he explained, 'and I don't want to cause him any embarrassment.'

Naturists often worry about being misunderstood and ridiculed. It can cause problems at work or within families. One man on Inchmurrin has fallen out with his brother over it. A woman says that her strait-laced son would love her to give it up. During the Glasgow Fair holiday, the naturists can hear the commentary from passing tour boats – 'And here yer comin' up tae the nudie bit. Get yer binoculars oot.'

For years it was the norm for naturists to use first names only or nicknames. It wasn't the done thing to ask where someone lived or what was their occupation. These days, though they are more relaxed, there is still a reluctance to be named in public. 'People get funny ideas about naturist clubs; that we're all swingers and so on,' says Colin, steering the boat past a small island that is home to a colony of shags. 'But nothing could be further from the truth.'

British Naturism, the organisation for naturists in the UK, has 12,000 members. Naturism is twice as popular, per capita, in Britain as in the United States, but we lag behind much of Europe. The reasons are climatic and cultural. Simply put, it is not often warm enough to take all your clothes off outdoors. Also, we are the country of saucy seaside postcards and Carry On films; Britain blushes and titters at the thought of nakedness.

In Scotland, where it is colder, naturism is even less widespread. 'The Scots are very narrow-minded, except when they're drunk,' says Marion, a 77-year-old naturist from East Kilbride. 'There's a Presbyterian thing that, actually, you shouldn't be enjoying yourself at all.'

The SOC is one of two naturist societies in Scotland. There is a society called Sunnybroom, based in the countryside west of Aberdeen. In Glasgow, you can swim naked at the Western Baths on Sunday mornings. There are also a number of unofficial naturist beaches around the coast and an officially designated one – Cleat's Shore, on Arran. But Inchmurrin is the hub of naturism in this country, the kit-off capital of Caledonia.

I arrive on a typical spring morning – unseasonably cold, with the threat of rain. It's early in the season, so there are only eight people here today, and not all of them are undressed. 'I've not got mine off,' says Frances, who is 79 and from South Lanarkshire, 'because my leg is out in a rash.'

The nudity is very casual. It just sort of happens. I'm sitting in the chalet of Alice, a friendly woman in her fifties who is a tremendous cook, when Colin daunders in, clad only in black socks and Ugg boots.

'Have you got your towel, sweetheart?' asks Alice, who is dressed. For hygiene reasons, the naturists carry towels and sit on them while visiting.

'Somebody told me,' says Colin, 'there was apple pie on the go.'

'Oh, for God's sake!' says Alice. 'It's just oot the oven.'

Colin takes a piece of pie and looks at it askance. 'This is naked without a bit of cream.'

Alice resumes the story she was telling. 'Once, I was really depressed, and I went away with my husband for the day. He was fishing and I stripped off. Aw, it was so beautiful in the sun. It was like a weight coming right off me.'

Colin nods. 'I had a very stressful job, but never needed to go to a shrink. You just come here and the birds are singing. It's so relaxing. We're not fanatics. You've maybe seen in the papers this joker who keeps getting arrested for walking the streets naked. He's a bampot and he doesn't do anything for naturism.'

The 'bampot' in question is Stephen Gough, the so-called Naked Rambler, whose nude hikes from John o' Groats to

Land's End have resulted in jail terms. Public nudity is not a statutory offence in Scotland, but those going naked may find themselves charged with breach of the peace. Nakedness is not, per se, a sexual act, so an indecency arrest is less likely. Gough is in Perth prison, serving 21 months for breach of the peace and contempt of court after refusing to put on his clothes. Many naturists dislike him and regard his actions as harmful to their own image.

There is a schism within naturism between those for whom it is a lifestyle to be enjoyed privately within designated areas, and those for whom it is an ideology. Most of the Inchmurrin naturists belong to the former camp, though one couple who own a chalet – Mick and Diane Goody, from Cambridgeshire – have travelled through London on a mass naked bike ride and sailed naked down the Thames. They believe that people should have the right to go without clothes on all Britain's beaches and in public parks.

I ask Colin if he can explain the appeal of naturism. After all, he would experience tranquility on Inchmurrin even if he kept his clothes on. So what added value is there in nakedness? It is, he suggests, to do with equality and togetherness. 'When people are dressed, others look at them and put them in a pigeonhole. Here. when everybody's naked, you don't know whether they are a lawyer or a binman.'

He stands and lifts his towel from the couch. 'I'm going to put my clothes back on because I need to use my chainsaw.'

Alice rolls her eyes. 'We've had eejits here that's used a chainsaw with flip-flops on and nothing else.'

Chainsaws loom large on Inchmurrin. All the relaxation is underpinned by a great deal of work. Often the birdsong is drowned out by the buzz of logs being sawn for the sauna. The chalets and clubhouse require constant maintenance – roofing, painting, guttering etc – and there is always grass needing cut, hedges trimmed and brambles cleared. There's a fair bit of heavy lifting too. Once, years ago, a man carried a piano to the clubhouse on his back. These days, the Friday evening journey up the steep hill from the shore is aided by two dumper trucks, the luggage loaded into their giant shovels.

Walk around the sites and the irony is obvious: nature, if left alone, would soon reclaim this place from the naturists. The rain and sun take their toll on the wooden buildings, and the vegetation threatens to overwhelm them. On the front of one unoccupied chalet, a painted yin-yang symbol is fading into nothingness. This is one reason why the Scottish Outdoor Club is having open days, today and on 30 May – without new blood, people who are able and willing to take on some hard work, the club could eventually fold. Colin is blunt. 'It's getting too old. If we don't get some younger members it'll die out.'

Everyone here would be sorry to see that happen. This place means a lot to the naturists. Some of them have been coming here for almost 50 years and have enjoyed it in the company of children and grandchildren. The 1960s, 1970s and even the 1980s were, of course, more innocent times. These days, many people would be, at best, uncomfortable with the idea of naked children in the company of naked adults to whom they are unrelated. British Naturism has a written child safeguarding policy and advises all affiliated clubs that they should appoint child protection officers who have been checked by the Criminal Records Bureau.

Though there are no children on Inchmurrin now, everyone says that it is a great place for them to play and hopes that, one day soon, new families will join. 'My daughter was carried up here in a carry-cot when she was three weeks old,' says Doug, the 65-year-old club chairman. 'She virtually grew up on Inchmurrin, and from the time she was three you could let her wander about in the knowledge that people would keep an eye on her. It was so easy and natural.'

His daughter, Emma, is now 25. She describes her childhood experiences as a pleasant mixture of liberty and security – free to roam around and explore a beauty spot, she also felt that the adults were a sort of extended family who would make sure she was safe.

Didn't she feel odd, as she got older, being unclothed around her parents? 'Because I went from such a young age, it never crossed my mind that it was strange,' she says. 'It was normal that you might see your parents naked and they might see you naked. There was nothing embarrassing about it at all. I don't have children, but if I did I would be happy to take them to Inchmurrin.'

Can she say how growing up in that way might have shaped her? 'One of the things is that because you don't rely upon hiding behind clothes you realise that fashion isn't the be-all and end-all. So that's quite liberating.'

Early and frequent exposure to naked people of various ages has had a further influence. 'I've had conversations with university friends and what I view as normal body image is quite different from most of them. I was more accepting of different body shapes and knew that everybody didn't have to look like the models you see in newspapers and magazines.'

As the afternoon warms up and more people strip off, and bottles and boxes of wine are opened, the pleasant lifestyle of Inchmurrin grows more apparent. Alice, now naked, reveals how she copes with the blight of midges – a liberal application of body cream mixed with eucalyptus and citronella.

Then she tells a story about the first time she went nude, while on holiday in Yugoslavia, and found herself drifting helplessly out to sea on a lilo. A German man swam to the rescue, but dragged her to safety on a 'textile' beach and she had to run past the gawping tourists. But despite this fiery baptism, she is now evangelistic about the unclothed lifestyle. 'I love being a naturist,' she grins, 'and I do quite a lot of my housework in the scud.'

For her, it's to do with confidence. 'I was awfy self-conscious years ago. I worried – was I too fat for my swimming cozzie or too skinny? On a textile beach everybody's going, 'Aw, look at the state o' that!' But on a naturist beach nobody looks at you twice.'

The reason the naturists give for living their lives this way are various. Some are pragmatic: exposure to sunshine and air helps relieve eczema, says one man. Most speak vaguely of relaxation, escapism and especially freedom. Alice says that revealing your body to others results in emotional intimacy – 'You can't hide. So you're more honest.'

So what sort of people are naturists? 'We don't get many working-class people in naturism, and that's a great sadness,' says Michael Farrar, chairman of British Naturism. 'Middle-class people may feel more need for release from the bonds of civilisation.'

Those I meet on Inchmurrin are mostly retired, but in their day worked as engineers, cooks, businessmen and lorry drivers, among other professions. 'It can attract people who are very orthodox, and this is maybe their little bit of eccentricity,' says Doug.

What about politics? Is there a general liberalism? 'I wouldn't say that,' he laughs. 'Folk accuse me of being more right-wing than Attila the Hun.'

A woman sitting fully clothed beside her naked husband tells me, 'Any Sunday we're not here we're in church.'

It's interesting how conventional the naturists seem, and how intolerant of unconventionality. 'We've had one or two come up that hill who are right weirdos,' says Laura, a woman in her sixties from Renfrewshire. 'A single guy came over and it turned out he was one of these people that go walking naked over the moors. He appeared in the clubhouse wearing a denim mini skirt.'

'He had it on in the sauna for a while,' says Colin, 'and he was told, 'Get that off or get out.' There was another joker, who drank solidly and ended up falling off the jetty when the ferry came to take him away.'

They are careful about who they let join. Prospective members are invited for a one-day trial. The number of single men given membership is strictly limited, and you will not be allowed to join if you are one half of a married or long-standing couple and your other half doesn't want to come. 'We could fill this club with married men whose wives are not naturists,' says Laura. 'But we would end up with three times as many men as women, and the women would feel intimidated.'

Why do they get so many more enquiries from men? 'I can only assume that in some cases it could be sexual,' says Colin.

The naturists are absolutely insistent that there is nothing sexual about what they do, and that people do not look at each other in a lustful way. Occasionally, two naturists will begin a relationship, but these assignations sound pragmatic rather than romantic. 'You see what you're getting,' says Marion. 'There's no mystery.'

What about male arousal, though? Men are not really in control of what goes on down there. So what's the protocol? 'There was one guy that came here and Dougie had to speak to him about it,' says Laura. 'What we find is that it doesn't happen with true naturists. If it happens, then you are here for the wrong reason. Let's face it – you look at the women in this club; we've got no page three girls. We've got nobody that's going to turn anyone on.'

Colin, gallant, demurs. 'Well,' he says. 'It depends on your taste.'

The first naturist site in Europe, Freilichtpark, opened in Germany in 1903. The first in the UK opened in Essex in 1926. Naturism was suppressed by the Nazis but boomed in Britain throughout the 1930s. By the middle of that decade, reports of naturists were appearing in the Scottish press. Nudists, declared the Sunday Mail in 1935, had been spotted, through binoculars, in a field near Hamilton, dancing to a gramophone. The Glasgow Bulletin, three years later, reported that 'a sun-bathing and naturist club' was to be established in the St George's Cross area of the city, catering to those visiting the Empire Exhibition.

While domestic naturism flourished for decades, the pendulum has now swung back towards Europe. The availability of information on the internet, together with cheap flights to the continent, has meant that those interested in naturism can easily experience the lifestyle on the beaches and in the resorts of France, Spain and other countries where, unlike Scotland, sunshine is the norm. That's why the Scottish Outdoor Club and other UK societies are struggling for members. 'But it's a wee paradise over here,' says Laura. 'Folk don't know what they're missing.'

After more than 60 years, it would be a shame to see this place go. But Inchmurrin, undoubtedly, has an elegiac feel. On my way off the island, I pass Alice's chalet. She's visible through the window, vacuuming the rug, listening to Flower of Scotland at high volume, her bottom poking out beneath her cardy. And I can't help wondering about Alice and all her fellow Scottish naturists – when will we see their like again?

Ladies' Day at Musselburgh

THERE may be the sound of thundering hooves, of cursing bookies and the echoing whack of whip on rump, but I really couldn't say. This is Ladies' Day at Musselburgh Racecourse and all I can hear are women. Let me qualify that. All I can hear are women, all I can see are women, all I can smell are women. Perhaps Musselburgh, on every other day of the racing calendar, is distinguished by the good, honest reek of horse dung; today, however, the air hangs heavy with Fake Bake.

Ladies' Day was introduced at Musselburgh six years ago to encourage women to become regular race-goers. Whether that has succeeded, I do not know, but as a one-day wonder it is a phenomenon. There are 8,000 people here today, the vast majority of them female, intent on the good time to end all good times, and dressed with appropriate fabulosity.

The stalwart punters – crag-faced men in bunnets, their fingers inky from the Racing Post – appear to be an entirely different species, never mind gender, from these exultant glamazons. There are so many false eyelashes that, laid end to end, they would stretch up the road to Harvey Nicks in Edinburgh, and so many false nails that they would reach all the way back down again. There is enough spray-on tan to paint the Scott Monument orange, with enough left over for Greyfriars Bobby.

Preparations begin early. Some women keep savings accounts to help them afford their Ladies' Day outfit. Others have an early start on the day itself, rising at dawn to do their hair and put their face on. 'We were in the shop from quarter to six getting ready for this,' says Jane Killen, one of a party of hairdressers and beauticians from Prestonpans. 'We come here every year without fail,' says her pal Nicola Scott. 'It's a brilliant day. We love the atmosphere, we love the people, and we love the beverage.'

Ah, the beverage. Musselburgh Ladies' Day runs on booze. Wearing heels and getting wellied, that's what it's all about. Magnums of champers sell at 75 quid a chuck. There are also mojitos, rum punch and something called a raspberry mule, a cocktail which could equally describe the footwear of many here. The atmosphere – dressy, brassy, messy, sassy – feels like a wedding. Dearly beloved, today we are gathered to celebrate the coming together of gin and tonic. Arlene Stuart, 43, sums up the mood: 'I've drunk my body weight in champagne. I've eaten about five pies. I'm feeling good.'

All around, people are knocking it back as if Alex Salmond were about to introduce prohibition. A girl in a pink tutu and shoes that would grace an S&M dungeon accessorises with a big glass of rosé. Another young woman negotiates the steep stone steps down through the stand from Freddie's Bar in a thigh-squeezing dress and four-inch heels while carrying a bottle of Prosecco and seeking advice on her mobile about who to back in the fourth. 'Irish Boy or Rothesay Chancer,' she asks. 'Which ay them is a guid horse?'

The great trick at Musselburgh is smuggling in your own drink so you don't have to pay bar prices. Security search all bags, but it seems there are ways of beating the system. I hear about one group of nurses who decanted white wine into colostomy bags and strapped them to their thighs. There is also a rumour going around that some enterprising soul hid a bottle of pinot noir inside a hollowed-out baguette. 'Oh, aye,' confirms a seen-it-all security guard when I ask about this. 'That's been tried. But you can tell by the weight. Mind, they'll try anything and everything.'

'There was a woman came in today with jelly,' laughs his colleague. 'But I smelled it and it was pure alcohol.'

All the confiscated bevvy is poured away, which will be scant consolation for those whose unopened bottles of Moët and Stoli are dumped into big black bins. Peering into one of those is an eye-opener. There's a bag of wine wrapped in tin foil which someone tried to pass off as roast chicken. Best of all is a tube of Pringles with a bottle inside, some crisps on top as camouflage, and the top sealed shut. Amazing. Here is the innate Scottish ingenuity and enterprise of which we are rightly proud.

The gates opened at 11.00 am. There was a great cantering to get in and bag the best picnic spots. At Wallyford, the nearest railway station, the platform was mobbed as racegoers made for the shuttle-bus. 'And we're off!' shouted one of the lairy lads up the back. 'C'moan driver, pit the fit doon!' Further up the bus, where the women sat, fascinators poked up above the backs of seats like the quivering crests of exotic birds. The lads were less exotic. In shiny suits and skinny ties, diamond studs in their ears, they looked like Poundland Krays.

'Is Kieren Fallon here the day?' asked one.

'Naw,' said his mate. 'This is the poor man's Ascot.'

Is that true? Maybe so. But it's the wrong way to look at it. Musselburgh Ladies' Day is, in fact, a very rich experience. It has no pretensions to be anything other than what it is – exuberantly vulgar and big-hearted hedonism. It is classless but pure class. Sure, Ascot was attended by Bruce Forsyth, but Musselburgh has 'Bruce fae Fife' – 21-year-old Bruce Gregory from Lochgelly, here on the ran-dan with a party of pals. 'I'm just a plumber,' he says. 'But next week I'll still be bevvyin'. First time in a suit – here we go!'

Jenny Kohler, 44, actually lives very near Ascot but is here today as part of her sister's birthday celebrations. 'Musselburgh is much better,' she says. 'You go to Ascot and all the ladies are in their posh frocks and posh hats, but by the end of the day they are covered in their own puke. And you queue half an hour for a wee.'

Hats are important at Musselburgh, too. There is a competition for the best one. 'Just give me the medal now,' says Louise Morrison, a young nurse from Dalkeith, brimming with confidence. She has converted a black topper into a sort of merry-go-round using the octagonal lid from a tin of Quality Street and some toy horses 'borrowed' from her 10-year-old nephew. 'He doesn't know I've drilled holes in them.'

Morrison faces strong competition from a group of thirtysomething friends from Edinburgh, each of whom has created a hat based on a different song. Lesley Scott, 37, is wearing a Napoleonic bicorn representing Waterloo by Abba. 'We have two others in our party,' she says. 'Strawberry Fields Forever and Knocking On Heaven's Door. They are at the bar, but you'll be able to identify them. They are very large. The hats that is, not the ladies.'

It isn't only women who have made an effort. Some of the men are equally eye-catching. One chap has a sporran so fluffy it must surely be Pomeranian. Then there's Harry Crombie, 27, an estate agent from Edinburgh in a slim-fitting white suit and matching top hat, hoping to be crowned Musselburgh's King of Style. 'I came in second place last year,' he says. 'I enjoy the admiration of all the adoring ladies.' In the end, however, he loses out to a man wearing his grandfather's old tweeds.

With the focus very much on fashion, it is easy to forget there is racing going on. The jockeys and horses in the parade ring are watched by a pretty thin crowd. These are not the fillies we are here to see. Yet the races themselves get everyone going. Many of the women swap their heels for pumps, the better to leap up and down in support of their chosen horse. Chipolatas go flying across picnic rugs when Red Kestrel comes in at 7/1. One of the bookies, 57-year-old Cumbie Bowers from Glenrothes, resplendent in trilby and pink jumper, takes a moment to reflect on the day's punters. 'Mostly it's daft women,' he says. 'But that's the kind you want.'

As the racing ends at around half past five, most people begin to leave. The steps of the stand drip with spilt fizz. Chalk-faced young women teeter-totter to the portable toilets, betting slips tucked into their cleavage. Outside, a little way down the street, there's a punch up between lads from Niddrie and Tranent; one, with blood polka-dotting his shirt, is sick on the pavement. Teenage girls from the Loretto boarding school, demure in long kilts, look on aghast.

Back inside, as the Saltire flies from the roof of the stand, Louise Morrison, the nurse from Dalkeith with the merry-go-round hat, wants to have a word. 'Next year we're going to have my hen do here,' she says. 'So look out, we'll be back!'

The Last Voyage of
Jimmy McFarlane

THE last voyage of Jimmy McFarlane begins at a little after nine on a sunny morning in Glasgow. It will end – after 12 miles, six hours, two bottles of whisky and several fish suppers – in Bowling, where the dark sluggish canal empties, glistening in its sudden rush, into the Clyde.

Jimmy is the skipper of the Wee Spark, a working replica of a traditional puffer, but run on diesel and one-third the size. A retired fitter/welder, Jimmy built the boat twelve years ago with the late Archie Rennie, a retired joiner. Ever since, the Wee Spark has been a heartening sight on the Forth and Clyde Canal. But now Jimmy, a spry, wry, twinkle-eyed man in his early seventies, is navigating those waters for the last time. He is heading west to Bowling basin, where, not without sadness, he will tie up the Spark and sell her. 'You can't keep a boat like this on a pension,' he says.

Her hull and funnel painted red and black, her name inscribed with evident pride in gleaming white capitals, the Wee Spark is hell of a smart. The cabin is a cosy wood-lined space complete with coal stove and kettle. Six portholes show the banks slide past. Jimmy and his pals – Hughie, Alan and Alex, all men of a certain age – are amusedly impatient of land-lubbing journalists who climb down into the cabin while facing forwards. 'There's a rule, son,' I'm told. 'Never turn yir back on a ladder or a wummin.'

The Forth and Clyde Canal runs from Grangemouth to Bowling, the cinched waist of Scotland, connecting the two firths. Construction was completed in 1790. During

Scotland's industrial age, the canal transported timber, clay, coal and sand. But in 1963 it closed, becoming dirty and derelict. July 6 and 7, 2012 will mark the 10th anniversary of the reopening of the lowland canal system, with celebrations taking place at the Falkirk Wheel.

Untying the boat and giving two jaunty peeps on his steam whistle, Jimmy sets off from the Applecross Street basin. The engine keeps up a staccato tick, like a gigantic grandfather clock, as we glide towards a horizon of spires. The canal is flat calm, reflecting tower blocks and tenements. Bald tyres arc, Nessie-like, above the surface. A line of lilypads resembles the tracks of cloven hooves. Every few yards we pass another Buckfast empty bobbing in the water, leaving one to wonder what desperate messages might be found in these particular bottles.

Jimmy points out areas of the canal, unremarkable to the casual viewer, which were important to heavy industry, and which have, too, their own sombre unwritten history. 'This basin we're going into now is where Broonlee's sawmill kept the hardwood logs,' he says. 'This is where aw the kids used to get drooned.'

He is tremendously keen on Scotland's waterways and on puffer lore – 'Let me introduce you to the ship's Bible,' he says, bringing forth a well-read copy of Neil Munro's Para Handy Tales. He has lived his whole life on or around the canal. When he was first married, he set up home in a ketch in Bowling basin. His grandfather was one of the last bargees with a horse-drawn boat. 'And it's just as well the horse knew where it was going because Auld Geordie was usually three sheets to the wind.'

It takes us an hour to get to Maryhill, where there is a system of locks and mushroom-shaped pools. Alongside the Wee Spark, waiting to go through the first sluice gate, is the Peccadillo, a beautiful green barge transporting a gallus cargo – a party of women celebrating a 50th birthday. One of them, removing her cardigan as the day warms up, is treated to a rendition of The Stripper from the Spark. The lock-keeper, leaning down, speaks to this lady – 'You're gonnae gie these men here a heart attack.' Hughie, though, is blithe about the danger: 'Awready hud wan,' he shrugs.

Bev Schofield, skipper of the Peccadillo, whose constant companion on board is Richey, a dachshund in a life-jacket, is worried about the lack of vessels on this stretch of water. 'It's great that I've had the Forth and Clyde to myself for ten years,' she says, 'But the fact that there are not enough boats moving means that ultimately the canals are going to close up again.'

It does seem true that most of those who enjoy the water do so from the land – as joggers, cyclists, dog-walkers and fishermen. So, at Maryhill Locks, I disembark from the Wee Spark and explore the life of the canal path, walking westwards.

You could spend your whole life in Glasgow and never see the canal. It is a hidden part of the city. On the M8 at Port Dundas, traffic roars eastwards, most of the drivers unaware that, just to their left, pike lurk in a deep pool, lit by harpoons of sunlight slanting into the water. These pike are infamous, growing ever larger and more ferocious with every angler's account. They eat voles, I'm told; ducklings, cygnets, poodles. The canal is hoaching with roach, pike and perch, and is rumoured to be restocked, now and again, with carp and trout. 'But ye cannae eat anythin' oot ae here,' the fishermen say. 'Deid bodies and everythin' in here, man.'

The canal has trees on both sides and for long periods you would not guess you were in a city. But occasionally a land-mark looms up – multi-storeys, CCTV cameras, an Orange Lodge gaudy with bunting – to remind you of the urban reality. A heron flies south over the Anniesland gasometers. 'You forget that you're in the middle of Glasgow,' says Tracey Bridges, throwing bread to the ducks with her young sun-bonneted daughters. 'Oh, look, there's a dragonfly.'

You meet all sorts on the canal: a recovering alcoholic who comes here to fish rather than sit in the house and drink; foot-sore field officers from Historic Scotland surveying the banks for erosion and intent on a particular ice-cream parlour in Kirkintilloch; two Jehovah's Witnesses handing out pamphlets by a wall on which is scrawled this righteous text – 'Fuck the Maryhill polis'. Here and there, tied to fences or laid next to the locks, are bunches of fading flowers, tributes to those who have lost their lives in the lonely water.

In Drumchapel, as the canal curves past pebbledashed low-rises, a group of young men, neds from central casting, are packing up their rods and the remains of a carry-out. They have an air of drunken befuddlement and a minimalist sartorial approach best summed up in the phrase 'Glaikit, nae jaikit'. They are here daily, landing eels and then attempting to kick them across to the opposite bank. 'Listen, mate, I'll gie it tae ye straight,' says one who introduces himself beerily as Clarence. 'We jist get fuckin' full ae it and fish.'

A small blue boat, low in the water, with complicated apparatus attached to the bow, comes chugging past. This is a harvester, bound for Dalmuir, cutting away the weeds that can tangle round rudders. The pilot of such a craft is privy to the sunken underworld of the canal. 'You name it, we've found it,' he shouts over to me. 'Shopping trolleys, motors, motorbikes. See the weight in a three-piece suite when we bring it up? Murder.'

The sounds of the canal are birdsong and ice-cream chimes. The smells are cut grass, honeysuckle and the occasional whiff of hot fat as you pass close to a takeaway. A grand place to eat on the canal is McMonagles, 'the chippy boat', a ship moored where the water passes under Argyll Road in Clydebank. Vessels can tie up alongside and collect fish suppers from a hatch. It is also a favourite with the local swans, which have been known to chap the window with their beaks until served a portion of chips. The seagulls, too, know all about the chippy boat and are an ever-watchful presence. John McMonagle, the owner, did try to deter them by stationing two owls on guard duty, but these sentinels were stolen and the gulls continue to lay siege to the bankside tables.

A familiar figure on the Clydebank path is 48-year-old Phil Toye, known as Boxer, a great enthusiast for his town and the narrow channel that runs through it. During the 1970s, he and his pals from the Linnvale scheme would nail together wooden palettes from the whisky bond and stage Viking battles with kids from Whitecrook, the housing estate on the other side of the water. The canal for him was and is a kind of magical realm. 'Because of the warm water from the Singer factory,' Boxer recalls, 'you didn't need to go to the fairground to get your wee goldfish in a bowl. You could just take wan out the canal with a net.'

In late afternoon sun, I arrive at Bowling, the basin drowsy in the heat. The name of one moored barge, Dungraftin, is strongly suggestive of easeful retirement. Jimmy McFarlane wakes things up a bit, though, as the Wee Spark arrives in her final berth, and his neighbours, the residents of houseboats, come out to greet him. Jimmy is the sort of man for whom banter is a personal philosophy, so if he is downcast about the end of this final voyage, he chooses not show it.

'Is that no' a lovely colour?' he says, raising a glass of Auchentoshan, which he takes, of course, without water. 'I'll keep drinking to your health until I ruin my own.'

Showfolk

IT is a gloomy spring morning, low cloud drooping like a drowsy eyelid over Kirkcaldy and seeming to almost touch the tallest of the fairground rides. The Links Market spreads for nearly a mile along the Esplanade. Although it has taken place annually since 1304, the fair has the cloistered atmosphere of an independent principality: a neon Vatican; a Monaco fuelled by pokes of chips rather than poker chips.

From across the Firth in East Lothian, the fairground must look like a town in its own right. Its spires and weather vanes are those white-knuckle rides that draw crowds of teens – the gleaming white Air, thirty metres high and topped by a globe, and the terrifying swooping pendulum 2Xtreme with its crowning star. At the bottom of the latter ride, a stern notice warns: 'All riders must have natural legs from the knees upwards.'

The Links Market marks the beginning of Scotland's shows season. There are about 800 people working on approximately 200 attractions. Afterwards, like seeds from a dandelion clock, they disperse in a hundred different directions, spending the spring, summer and autumn touring 'the run' of fairgrounds, from Dumfries to Hawick to Burntisland to Nairn, which they and their families have visited for generations. This great migratory loop begins and ends in Glasgow, home to the majority of Scotland's estimated 4,000 showfolk.

Travelling shows are part of the texture of Scotland's summer. They go with cut grass and light nights and the fretful, headachey feeling of close weather and a threatened

101

electrical storm. No-one who grew up in a Scottish town, especially a small town, will be unfamiliar with the excitement of waking up to see the shows have arrived in the local park. It is a seasonal ritual. You may not notice the first swallow, but you will not miss the waltzer.

'It's the highlight of the showman's year, the Links Market,' says Philip Paris, chairman of the Scottish Showmen's Guild. 'It's the largest fair in Scotland and everybody looks forward to it.'

Paris, like most showmen, is the umpteenth generation of his family in the business. His great-grandfather Felice Parisi was an Italian immigrant who, according to legend, helped build the Forth Bridge then started travelling around the fairgrounds with a fish and chip cart. On the maternal side, Paris's family are Codonas, the so-called 'royal family of the fairground'; one esteemed member is said to have performed a Punch and Judy act for King George III.

It would be wrong to assume that showfolk, because of their itinerant lives, have no sense of rootedness. On the contrary, most seem familiar and proud of the intricacies of their family trees and speak with great confidence and ease about what are extremely tangled and interconnected genealogies. More, they feel very much part of Scottish society, not remote from it, and are always keen to point out the patriotic contributions showmen have made, such as clubbing together to pay for a Spitfire, 'The Fun Of The Fair', during the Second World War.

They are intensely pragmatic people grafting in a true family business. Everyone mucks in. You see wee girls working the microphone, encouraging punters to roll up and try their luck on the hook-a-duck. You see boys who haven't started shaving but whose welding skills would put a Clyde shipbuilder to shame. The wives and mothers have it toughest, combining domestic life with most of the accountancy and admin work. As one puts it: 'If there wasn't any women in our business, there wouldn't be no business.'

Showmen refer to the hyperbolic patter they use to attract punters to their rides as 'telling the tale'. Meeting them, and asking about their lives, it's notable that many tell the tale about their own backgrounds in a similarly polished style. David Wallis, a 66-year-old showman, is here with his Ice Maze. 'Born in Liverpool, travelled the world,' he says. 'I left school at 14 and went on the road to the university of life. I'm the fifth generation of my family in this business. I have four married children and ten grandchildren all in the business. So we're into our seventh generation of travelling showmen. It's a proud way of life and a labour of love. How many other professions can boast that they take money off people and send them away with a smile on their face?'

Twenty minutes is how long it takes to walk sharply and in a straight line from one end of the Links Market to the other. But no one walks sharply and in a straight line at the shows. There's too much to take in. The smell of frying onions and burnt sugar. The chug and clank of cash pay-outs. The teasing spiel of the showmen: 'There's fun and laughter on the inside, fellas,' and the inevitable, time-honoured: 'Screamifyouwannagofaster!'

Then there are the sights. Not the obvious flashing lights and whooshing swoop of the rides. But the little things you notice if you're paying attention. The showering arc of sparks as a jug-eared, gel-haired ned flicks a fag out into the night from the entrance of the puggies. A show-woman in a gold lamé top chewing her nails inside the paybox – a rusting fairytale toadstool that has seen better days. Behind the ghost train, three plump and gloomy teenage girls eat chips 'n' cheese as, beside them, a giant Igglepiggle doll – a prize from one of the stalls – lies on the low wall, unloved.

Walking round, you meet some fascinating people. Fred Wheatley is 83, swaddled against the cold in leather cap and green anorak, and describes himself as 'the last of the performing showmen'. Here with his Outer

Limits, a funhouse he built in 1964, Wheatley is known as The Professor on account of both his mechanical know-how and his mental store of fairground lore. He grew up in the days of sideshows, when the rides were not so dominant and punters would queue at boxing booths, shooting galleries and peep shows. He himself performed a magic act, wearing evening dress, walking up a ladder of swords in his bare feet, and faking his own beheading in a guillotine. He also travelled with performers that might, though it's not a pleasant term, be considered freak show acts.

From a 21st-century perspective, the idea of people being paid to exhibit their own physical oddities seems depressing and perhaps even immoral. But Wheatley was born and raised in that culture and sees things differently. His parents had sideshows and so did his paternal grand-mother. 'She had a girl called The Pig-Faced Girl who was about 14 and came from King's Lynn,' he recalls. 'A lovely girl, a good talker, with a wee snout. She had been locked up in an attic so nobody could see her. Her family were ashamed of her. So my grandmother went to ask her would she like a job.

'When she started travelling with my grandmother she felt as happy as could be because she met people and lived with them and ate with them and talked to them. She died at the age of 20 in Blackpool. She had gone out to a shop in the rain and caught pneumonia.'

That era, though within living memory, seems impossibly distant from our own. Fairgrounds now are still predicated on the same principle – displaying the attractions to best effect in order to part the public from their cash; 'the front of the show gets the dough', as David Wallis puts it. But the emphasis now is on the rides. It is high-risk big business.

One large new attraction debuting at Kirkcaldy is reputed to have cost over £1 million to manufacture. You have to be confident of pulling a crowd if you are going to invest that much money. The Links Market attracts an estimated 150,000 people over six days. Although that sounds like a healthy number, few fairs are as popular as Kirkcaldy, and the economic situation seems dire for showmen at the moment. As a class of workers they are, perhaps, a bit like the farmers – never happier than when grumbling about money. A quote painted in silver on the cab of one show-man's truck sums up the often Eeyore-ish conversational tone: 'It was better than this last year.'

Having said that, they do appear to be genuinely up against it. Rising fuel costs are especially crippling as they use huge amounts of diesel to transport rides and run generators. Then there is the fact that the public, strug-gling with their own household budgets, are spending less than they once did. There are also fewer fairgrounds with every passing season. Councils, concerned the shows may attract anti-social behaviour, are increasingly reluctant to grant permission. Showmen, for their part, often struggle to afford steep licensing fees.

Even the Links Market, though busy, has a slightly elegiac end-of-days feel – a melancholy base note detect-able beneath the sound of blaring pop music and The Blue Danube played on a pipe organ. A number of showmen express their fears for the future of the business and their mixed emotions – relief tinged with disappointment – that their children have chosen another line of work. 'For the first time in history,' says Alan Ingram, 51, a fairground enthusiast visiting from Glenrothes, 'there is a chance that the travelling fair as we know it could die out.'

* * *

Dalmarnock on a muggy week day is a brown and red landscape of high brick walls, warm and crumbly to the touch. Behind these are the showmen's 'yards' – gated communities in which, typically, there are several mobile homes converted into chalets. The showmen tend to tour fairs in smaller caravans, which they wagons, but retain chalets as a base.

These homes look substantial and well kept, some with diamond-pane windows and porcelain figurines on windowsills. Babies air in old-fashioned Silver Cross prams. Parked up near the chalets are various fairground rides undergoing maintenance. A boiler-suited man up a ladder screws a coloured bulb on his Spider-Man waltzer. The smells of this place catch the back of the throat – hyacinths, hops and the stink from the sewage works.

Although there are similar yards in Stirling and Edinburgh, the east end of Glasgow is where an estimated 90 per cent of Scotland's show families spend the winter and any downtime between fairs. Yet you could live in Glasgow your whole life and be unaware that this – a town within the city – was here. Dalmarnock is the district with the highest concentration of showfolk. They are thought to constitute a third of the local population. Swanston Street, Shore Street, Strathclyde Street, Cotton Street – that's where you'll find them, hemmed in between the railway line and the Clyde.

The look of the area is a strange mix of post-industrial and chintzy-suburban. There's a strong sense that this is where objects usually in motion come to rest: flitting lorries, black cabs with their bonnets up, Super Whippy ice-cream vans parked on vast lots.

There's a surreal sort of beauty to this part of the city, if you look in the right places. One place is the yard of 60-year-old Melvin Thomas in which he stores his collection of vintage fairground equipment – everything from wooden wagons to the hoopla used by his grandfather.

Though the fairground culture is intensely pragmatic and tends not keep objects that have outlived their usefulness, Thomas values the heritage. His father died when Thomas was in his early twenties and the collection seems to be a way of retaining a closeness to a parent lost too soon. 'It's total sentiment,' he says. 'And it's keeping me poor.'

Some of the yards are protected by CCTV. Though it is uncommon, it is not unheard of for there to be trouble with the local community, in particular from neds who confuse showfolk with gypsy travellers.

There is a clear distinction between the two groups, showmen insist; they are not an ethnic group and their travelling is for business reasons, rather than from any inherent cultural disposition towards being nomadic. It used to be that showmen would refer to themselves as travellers, and some still do out of the hearing of 'flatties' – outsiders – but there has been a deliberate shift in public language to emphasise their own identity. Not that they have anything against gypsy travellers, they say, but they feel it is terribly unfair that they should experience bigotry by proxy.

Rodney Johnstone, a 42-year-old showman, lives in Govan. He does not allow his sons, Kieron, 15, and Rodney, ten, to leave the yard unaccompanied or to mix with the local children. 'We've had people throwing stones and calling us gypsies,' he says, 'and we've had lorries set on fire and dogs shot with air rifles. That's why we have cameras now. At Kilmarnock last week one of the stalls had its shutters ripped off and the prizes taken out.'

For the showfolk, for the most part, the yards are a safe and supportive space in which you live near relations and people you have known your whole life. It is, says one showman, a self-contained culture not unlike an old-fashioned pit village in which it is common to use the terms 'Uncle' and 'Aunty' as tokens of respect and familiarity even if those addressed are not actually blood relations. You are never stuck for a babysitter in the yards, and people tend to look out for the elderly.

Florence White, Aunty Florence, lives in a yard not far from the Dalmarnock cluster. She is 74 with blonde bobbed hair and glasses, and can trace her family back to lion-tamers and female boxers. She is sometimes known as Florence Matchett; her great-grandfather, inviting wagers at his boxing booth, would say: 'And I'll match it!' – a spiel that became the family surname.

Her father John, also a showman, served during the Second World War as the driver of Field Marshal Montgomery, a position he acquired thanks to his considerable mechanical skills. 'There's a lot of brains in our business that never get used,' says Aunty Florence.

It is certainly true to say that the showmen are enormously resourceful and creative people, though many have had very little education. One showman in Kirkcaldy, Gilbert Chadwick Jr, 46, admitted he could barely read or write, but he is one of the world's most accomplished creators of ghost trains – an achievement that requires great imagination, engineering nous and an eye for the market. His intelligence and artistry are almost tangible.

Until relatively recently, it was usual for children from show families to leave school at fourteen. Their educational experiences tended to be poor. They would move school every time they moved town, a fortnight here and a fortnight there, and it was common for children of all ages to be bundled into the one classroom and spend the day drawing pictures.

Now, however, thanks to work by education liaison officers from the Scottish Showmen's Guild, children enrol at a base school near where they winter. During off-season they attend school as normal, but while on the road they travel with special work packs and are assessed regularly by teachers at the base school.

The pervasive idea that parents care nothing for their children's education, preferring them to work in the business, is nonsense according to Leslie Broughton, 44, a show-woman from Glasgow whose own teenagers are schooled by teachers sent out to the fairground by individual local authorities. 'I've fought for their education all the way,' she says. 'A lot of the schools think, 'They're here for a week, so it doesn't matter. They're all stupid anyway'. That's a lot of people's attitude towards our kids. But I want them to get an education. This business might not always go on, so you want them to know something else as well.'

It's hard to say what the future does hold for the travelling fairs. Part of their appeal is their transience, the way they vanish, leaving behind little more than flattened grass and the lingering perfume of candyfloss and diesel. But it would be a tremendous loss to our society if this fascinating, misunderstood and still rather mysterious culture did disappear for good.

Like the swallows, like sudden lightning, Scotland's summer would be a sadder season without the shows.

The Waterloo

'OH, Yeah,' says Mark, a fortysomething with close-cropped hair and a collarless leather jacket, 'you can get a lumber in The Waterloo, if that's what you're after.'

The Waterloo is Glasgow's oldest gay bar, some say the oldest in Scotland. A framed sign proclaims that this pub has been 'serving the gay community for over 30 years'. Many of the regulars will tell you that, in fact, it's been closer to half a century.

While many long-established pubs have their stalwart clientele, the fact that there are far fewer gay bars than straight ones means that the same people drink in them for decades. You get all sorts in The Waterloo. 'Polis, binmen, judges, priests,' I'm told. 'We even had a monk come in one time. We get a lot of clergy of all denominations. It's a kind of haven for them.'

Plenty of married men, too, especially since the public toilet on St Vincent Street closed. 'It was known as The Palace of Light because the sun would shine down through the translucent pavement tiles,' a man called Charlie tells me. 'It was just a scabby underground toilet, but by God it went like a circus.'

To someone walking in for the first time, The Waterloo looks like a regular old-fashioned boozer. Dark wood bar. Deep red walls. The big windows are topped by stained-glass panels showing the crests of the regiments that fought at Waterloo. It would be easy to miss, at first, the small rainbow flags behind the gantry, or the bucket of condoms in the corner, or even – if you were engrossed in the puggy – the young guy with his white T-shirt pulled up and

knotted above his stomach, standing at the bar and swaying louchely as Karma Chameleon plays on the jukebox.

Melanie Lyons, a 31-year-old nurse from Stranraer,
didn't even realise it was a gay bar the first couple of times
she came in. She loves it, though. 'I wish there were more
places like this. It's nice to visit a pub where you can be
yourself.'

She is one of very few women in The Waterloo. It's
mostly men, and mostly older men. 'The chickens call
this place Jurassic Park,' someone laughs, 'chicken' being
slang for a young gay man. There is a real mix of different
types. There's a skinhead in bomber jacket and big boots;
an old chap dressed for the Old Course in white bunnet
and pastel V-neck; there's Craig, out celebrating his 40th
birthday, who has that fine Scots phrase, 'Whit's fur ye'll
no' go by ye', tattooed in Latin across his chest.

At one end of the bar there's a group of sombre-suited
men with grey handlebar moustaches who bring to mind
a pod of pleasantly bevvied walruses. In the middle of
the floor, a small, mild-looking man in a lilac tank-top is
grinding his hips to Lady Gaga.

'I've got two daughters who come in here and they absolutely love it,' says Alan Larkin, a stocky, silver-haired man
in a purple gingham shirt. 'I was married at 21 and lasted
five years. That was when I was a closet poof. I couldn't
handle being gay. I worked in the shipyards in Greenock.'

The Waterloo has its share of characters. There's Robert,
for instance, The Human Jukebox; give him your date of
birth and he'll tell you what was number one when you
were born. 'Was it the theme to Van der Valk?' he says,
quite correctly, when I tell him mine. Then there's old
Jimmy with his boxer's nose and missing front tooth. Gay
bars aren't the best places to find a sexual partner, he tells
me; he's had more luck in the bookies'.

'You get a lot of transvestites coming in here as well,'
says a gently-spoken man who introduces himself as

111

Randy Andy. 'There's one auld guy, he's about 80 years old and hackit as sin, and he dresses up as an 18-year-old lassie – long blonde wig and a mini-skirt up to here. He's got a boyfriend who must be about 70 and wears a string vest. They sit in the corner kissing and cuddling. And he walks through the city, from here to Delmonica's, right along Argyle Street, dressed like that. Oh, the dog's abuse he's had, but he gives as good as he gets.'

The transvestites tend to visit in the quiet afternoons. Mostly, they get changed and made up in the toilet then sit, dressed as women, with a pint and the Sudoku till it starts to get busy. They then change back and leave for their normal lives.

Betty Hutton was The Waterloo's most famous transvestite, named after the star of Annie Get Your Gun. A framed portrait behind the bar shows a somewhat Les Dawsonish figure. His younger boyfriend was known as The Wean. Stories about Betty are legion. He was an intimidating figure, feared and beloved in equal measure. One man, telling of the time Betty threw a glass of gin in his face, recounts the incident with the proud reverence of a born-again Christian recalling their baptism.

'Betty Hutton was amazingly, fabulously terrifying,' says Mark Swift, a drag artist who DJs at The Waterloo as Cheri Treiffel. 'Imagine Desperate Dan in a Crimplene dress, Nora Batty tights, terrible wig, Hilda Ogden lipstick, stubble still showing through, and just the foulest, dirtiest, evilest mouth you've ever heard in your life.'

The Waterloo has a traditional frontage and occupies the corner of a six-storey red sandstone building. Regulars make a point of using the entrance on Wellington Street. The Argyle Street doorway is known, I'm informed, as 'the poofs' door' and is the correct province of ingenues and newbies. There is an unofficial hierarchy within the pub that determines who stands where. The end of the bar closest to the toilets is the most prestigious spot. At the other end of the bar and the other end of the social spectrum is 'Compost Corner' – considered fit only for those in the most advanced stages of decrepitude.

Many who come to this part of town will do so by walking beneath the Hielanman's Umbrella, through its characteristic miasma of exhaust fumes and chip fat. Most of Glasgow's gay bars and clubs are clustered further east, around the Merchant City. The Waterloo is a remnant, a revenant of an earlier era when the scene was more underground and based around the city centre.

The names of those long-gone bars still ring out among the punters here: The Duke Of Wellington where you were greeted by a hostess known as Titsalina Shagnasty; Madame Gillespie's on Argyle Street where the barmen wore togas; and – most of all – Vintners on Clyde Street. 'When that place closed, I stood on the other side of the river and gret my eyes out,' Randy Andy recalls.

Although nobody wants to go back to the dark ages when homosexuality was against the law, which didn't change till 1980 in Scotland, some of the older men remember that the danger made everything much more exciting and engendered a closeness among those on the scene. This, too, was in the pre-Aids glory days; during the 1980s, punters from The Waterloo were attending a funeral most weeks. 'We lost a helluva lot of good friends,' one man in his fifties tells me.

Back in the early to mid-1970s there weren't any gay clubs. When the pubs shut at 10.00 pm, you either went on to a house party or you attended one of the very occasional dances put on at the Langside and Woodside Halls. These were licensed by the old Glasgow Corporation. You had to smuggle in a hipflask if you wanted a drink. Kissing and bodily contact were forbidden, a rule enforced by elderly commissionaires in green uniforms. Things have moved on a lot since then, but there is still a great deal of prejudice and thus a need for gay bars. You hear stories of men forced from their homes by abuse, or of getting spat at, abused or attacked in the street.

Standing outside The Waterloo, blowing fag smoke at the drizzle, Cheri Treiffel is a vision. More than six feet tall in red platforms, psychedelic trouser suit and pink wig, she also has an impressive decolletage achieved by wearing a bra three sizes too small. Mark Swift has been a drag artist since 1985. The Waterloo is his local. His ex-partner used to say they should never go there. Not their sort of pub. When they split, Mark took a taxi straight down here and fell for the place. For the forthcoming Royal Wedding theme night, he is considering dressing as the Queen Mother.

A passing ned, daundering past, notices Cheri and looks aghast. 'Hello, lovely!' says Cheri to the ned. 'Aye,' says the ned. 'You wish.'

Cheri shouts after him: 'I don't do fucking charity work!'

Back inside, it's dark and the disco lights are on. It's that transcendent, transient moment when everything seems to come together – the music, the laughter, the company, the drink. There's a sense of connection in the room. It feels, in a way, like a family occasion. 'It's not that different from the heterosexual world,' says Keith, taking a musing sip of Stella. 'I mean, do you know what we do here on Sundays? Bingo. What a bunch of outrageous deviants, eh?'

As I leave for the night, Cheri Treiffel is playing Candi Staton. In Compost Corner there's an old man singing along.

'Young hearts,' he sings, 'run free.'

He has tears on his cheeks and looks like he means every word.

Ye May Gang Faur and Fare Waur

I DROVE through the darkness and I drove through the dawn, mist lying thick on golden fields of oilseed rape, and I came at last to Stracathro Services, off the A90 just north of Brechin.

Well, I'm calling it Stracathro, but regular travellers on this stretch of road will know it as Ye May Gang Faur And Fare Waur – the phrase painted in huge black letters right across the front. Meaning 'You might go further and do worse', it is a slogan at once modest, defiant and dryly funny, unusual perhaps for a transport café, though certainly in keeping with the character of the rural north-east.

Stracathro offers 24-hour parking and fuel, food and drink between 6.00 am and 9.00 pm, and thus attracts a devoted clientele of long-distance lorry drivers from across the UK. Over the course of a year, some 24 million litres of fuel, six tons of bacon and 72,000 eggs are consumed. The smells of Stracathro are diesel, dust and the cheerful aroma of proper fry-ups.

'Whit're ye efter?' asks Wee Alan behind the counter.

'Kinahgetarollwibaconandtottysconeplease?' the driver's reply, happy in the knowledge that their desired order will arrive soon after and they can get back on the road.

The café is a remarkable building; long, low, flat-roofed and pebbledashed, saltires flying from rusty flagpoles. Daffodils on the grass verge tremble in the slipstream of northbound traffic. Inside is a throwback, unchanged since the 1960s; Formica tables, fold-back leatherette seats, squeezy bottles of brown and red sauce, and silver bowls of sugar. The owner, Pat Melville-Evans, 61, recalls that when she was a teenager the Kinks stopped by en route to some gig somewhere and she gave the group pony rides. Such is the anachronistic nature of Stracathro that it would be little surprise if the young Ray Davies were to walk in even now and order a mug of sugary tea. He might be thrown a little, though, by the plate of rowies bronzing beneath hot lamps.

What you see instead of pop stars is a constant stream of truckers. At a little before 7am, Ian Willis, 63, walks into the café with his damp silver hair slicked back and quiffish, a towel and toilet bag held beneath one beefy arm. He arrived last night from Cumbria and by 8.30am must be at the harbour in Aberdeen with his load of concrete pipes. He has been a driver for forty years and is away from his home in Dumfries for most of the week. He sleeps, like all drivers, in his cab. 'You're pushing against the clock all day long, unfortunately,' he says. 'Gone are the days when you'd go into transport digs and you could have a leisurely stroll up to the wagon in the morning. Noo, you're oot your bed, straight into the seat and away. That's just the way of the times, really.'

This elegiac tone is common among long-distance drivers. They pine for a vanishing golden age before precise delivery deadlines and satellite tracking; when they had more freedom to choose their own pace and route without the boss knowing where they were at all times; when it was safe to pick up hitchhikers and everyone used CB. What you also hear from many drivers is an awareness of the personal costs of the job – 'I missed my kids growing up.'

There is a strong sense, too, of a looming demographic crisis within the profession. Most of the men stopping at Stracathro are middle-aged or approaching retirement. In almost twelve hours, I meet only one driver in his twenties. 'Once our age group finish, there's no drivers left,' says Geordie, 55, from Peterhead. 'There's no young ones going into it. No incentive for them. It costs three grand for your licence but then nobody'll take you on without two years' experience.' This, of course, is potentially a massive problem for the proper functioning of British society as we rely so heavily on food and other goods being transported around the country by road. Geordie gives a despairing grin. 'It's a dying trade,' he says.

Still, there is something undeniably romantic about long-distance driving. The trucks themselves are fantastic beasts, growling into the dusty car park, the stoor clearing to reveal the home towns emblazoned across the fronts – Wick, Forres, Dundee, Keith – as well as the names of wives and children painted delicately in sentimental fonts. Often, too, the vehicles are expressions of patriotism: tartan valances; nodding Westies on the dash; airbrushed thistles and lions rampant and extracts from Amazing Grace. The very flies squashed black and scarlet on the windscreens seem to add something to the psychedelic pomp of the cabs.

The drivers, for all their natural pessimism, have a real appreciation for the aesthetics of the job. One speaks of the beauty of early mornings on quiet roads through the glens; another of his joy at being able to see over the hedges and watch farmers at work; a third recalls how, just the day before, the sun was shining and he had the windows down while listening to first Frank Sinatra and then Metallica at high volume. He breaks off from this reverie, however, to explain that the reason the pigs are squealing so loudly in his trailer is that, 'One's horny and he's trying to jump another which isn't taking kindly to the idea.' Lorry-driving is rich in bathos.

There are few places like Stracathro left, the drivers complain. The old-fashioned truck stop with heaped plates and decent showers and plenty of room for vehicles is a thing of the past. Most modern truck cabs are fitted with microwaves and fridges, and many haulage firms will not pay overnight parking fees. It's all to do with saving time and money, but it can make for a lonely life of stale sarnies and lay-bys. Stracathro, therefore, is a beacon and

117

sanctuary, the hub of a working community, though not without its dark side. Service areas, perhaps as places of transience and apartness, tend to be favoured spots for suicides; one driver was found hanging in the back of his truck, another from a nearby tree. There are also two or three prostitutes working the parking lot – 'We look the other way,' says Pat Melville-Evans. 'Just so long as it's not causing trouble for us or the customers.'

Melville-Evans is an extraordinary woman, a force of nature involved with the running of Stracathro from the age of nine. That was in the days when it was nothing more than a wooden cart selling milk, potatoes and eggs at the side of the A94, which was the main road between Dundee and Aberdeen before the present dual carriageway was built. It was Pat's grandfather, the owner of Clearbank Farm, who had the initial idea, but it was her late father, Captain Evans, known as Auld Cleary, who seems to have seen the potential and pushed for expansion.

It was he who arranged for Ye May Gang Faur And Fare Waur to be painted on the facade in what seems to have been a typical gesture by a great old character. He wore two monocles, despising spectacles, and hurtled up and down the A94 in a Rolls-Royce which he had fitted with the number plate from Clearbank's first tractor. He enjoyed wearing plus-fours to posh restaurants and would simply count out banknotes from a bulging wallet if any maître d' complained. A naval man, he had been a war hero, as had his wife; Pat thought it normal, as a child, that both one's parents should have won the George Cross.

'He died as he lived,' says Pat. 'He was 75 with a 28-year-old mistress in London. He went down one day and attended in full dress uniform the Admiralty dinner in the House of Lords. He stayed overnight then came home, had Sunday dinner with his family, and had a heart attack the next day. You couldn't beat that as a way to go, could you?'

With her splendid farmhouse and stable of 60 horses, which she breeds for top-level eventing, Pat Melville-Evans could, no doubt, get by fine without a transport café. But she loves the place, which she regards as a real-life soap opera, and considers herself its guardian rather than owner, resisting all calls to make it look more contemporary. Much of the excellent food comes from her Victorian walled garden, home to a 150-year-old fig tree of which she is especially fond. She does occasionally consider such radical changes as adding a bit of lettuce to the sandwiches, but customer feedback – 'Can ye no' get a fuckin' cheese piece here ony mair?' – has taught her to exercise caution.

She remains a hands-on boss, sharing an office with a Jack Russell bitch called Dude whose hatred of tanker drivers can be placated only by chewing on a Nokia mobile, an object Dude finds enormously soothing. Earlier this year, Pat was joined in the business by her 24-year-old son William, recently returned from four years as a professional polo player in Argentina, and it is hoped that he will continue the family tradition of filling truckers' tanks and bellies for many years to come.

Stracathro Services is, without doubt, an unsung Scottish landmark, a sort of Forth Bridge or Maeshowe in greasy spoon form. Unesco ought to hurry up and declare it a heritage site. We need colourful, characterful places like this, it seems to me, in order to save us from the bland homogenous corporate culture which is always threatening to engulf our society. 'We have a phrase,' says Pat, "Only at Stracathro,'' – and it's very easy to see what she means.

Up-Helly-Aa

IT is 7:15 pm when the street lamps of Lerwick go off, pitching the Shetland capital into instant darkness.

The only light is from the clock face of the turreted town hall; the spotlit flag flying on top – a raven on a scarlet ground – informs the local people, as if they did not know, that tonight is Up-Helly-Aa. Since 1873, the fire festival has been held on the last Tuesday in January. It is the highlight of Lerwick's year and surely Scotland's greatest, weirdest spectacle.

All is black. The crush of bodies on the roads and pavements is sensed not seen, as is the feeling of poised anticipation. Then, in the split-second of a camera flash, strange figures become visible. Flash! A giant puffin. Flash! A burly shepherd crammed into a skimpy dress. Flash! A man wearing a Tommy Sheridan mask. A grandad in drag speaks urgently to his wife: 'Quick, tak my photo so I kin pit it on Facebook.' These are just four of Up-Helly-Aa's 959 guizers, split between 47 separate squads. The men in costume will spend the next hour or so processing through the town, most carrying a large flaming torch.

Suddenly, there is a huge bang as a firework is sent up to signal the start. Dozens of distress flares, hissing like angry cats, turn the scene an unearthly incandescent pink. Marshalls use these to light the torches, and in an instant the air is full of fire and paraffin reek.

The procession moves off, led by the Jarl Squad, fifty men dressed as Viking warriors. They pull behind them a nine-metre replica galley with a dragon's head prow, built in secret over the winter and revealed to the public for the first time that morning. Within the ship, wreathed in smoke, torchlight reflecting from the mirrored scales of his armoured breastplate, wearing a silver helmet plumed with great arcs of raven feathers, sits Up-Helly-Aa's most esteemed figure – the Guizer Jarl.

In ordinary life he is John Hunter, a 37-year-old lifeguard at the local swimming pool, but Up-Helly-Aa has little to do with ordinary life, and so Hunter is effectively king for a day – hailed, honoured and cheered wherever he and his galley pass. Early that morning, the Jarl Squad had stopped briefly outside the home of the Goudie family. As a heavily pregnant young woman cheerily distributed drinks – 'Who wants gin? Gin! Gin! Gin!' – her mother, Pearl Goudie, offered Hunter some food. Afterwards, as the Vikings advanced down the street, she regarded the leftover crust as if it were a holy relic: 'The Jarl,' she declared, 'et that sandwich.'

The Vikings have been touring Lerwick since dawn and will continue to do so until 8am the following day. But right here, right now – the fiery procession – is the crucial moment. The crowd roars the Guizer Jarl on, and he and his squad roar back, raising their axes in acknowledgement of the 5,000 spectators who have come out to celebrate both their Norse heritage and the community itself.

John Hunter uses the word 'kindred' to describe his feelings about Up-Helly-Aa and it's true that, despite the huge scale, the festival is a sort of family occasion, uniting old and young in a sense of belonging. The Guizer Jarl has memories of Up-Helly-Aa going back to early childhood. His late mother Kathleen loved the festival. She died before her time in 2002. Hunter has honoured her memory by having her portrait painted into The Bill, the ceremonial placard erected in Lerwick's Market Square on Up-Helly-Aa day.

Though Up-Helly-Aa is full of delicate personal resonances like those, it is undeniably a grand public event.

Fire as far as the eye can see. Wind whips and stretches the flames. The heat from the torches is intense. To brass band tunes reminiscent of VE Day, the guizers march into the King George V park, circling like a fiery maelstrom around the Viking ship in the centre. 'They'll burn the galley in a peerie minute,' a mother tells her daughter, holding the restless infant on her shoulders. Peerie is the Shetland dialect word for little. A good few folk tonight have had a peerie dram, for instance. In the morning they will have a muckle headache.

Watching from his bedroom window, golden light flickering across his face, is 76-year-old Allan Anderson, a retired and widowed postman who was Guizer Jarl in 1971. He has two children and four grandchildren, and says being Jarl was the highlight of his life. 'Up-Helly-Aa is far more than just an excuse for a drink, isn't it?' someone asks. 'Oh my, yes,' Anderson replies. 'It *is* a brilliant excuse, though.'

Although the Jarl Squad are the icons of Up-Helly-Aa, their bearded, snarling images beamed around the world, the majority of guizers dress in costumes which, though always eye-catching, are rather less magnificent. 'A good mix of satire and vulgarity,' is one guizer's summation. Often the disguises are topical, hence Tommy Sheridan, due for sentencing the following day. Sometimes understanding them requires a deep local knowledge. A guizer with a rubber quiff and inflatable guitar might be taken for Elvis if you didn't know the costume was a reference to Showaddywaddy, who performed at the local leisure centre many years ago.

The most common aspect of the guizing is cross-dressing. Not for nothing is Up-Helly-Aa known as Transvestite Tuesday. 'I had a man in to try on a pair of tights and he had shaved his legs for the occasion,' Inga Scott, owner of local fancy-dress shop The Stage Door, said earlier. 'I'm the UK's biggest seller of extra-large fishnets.'

'And,' said Mandy, the shop assistant, 'we've sold oot ah fake boobs.'

The cross-dressing no doubt has something to do with the fact that women are not allowed to form a squad and take part in the Up-Helly-Aa procession. But Scott just laughed when asked whether she feels oppressed. 'It doesn't really bother me. It's a tradition and you get used to it. Up-Helly-Aa is like a man's wedding day. He can be waiting years for it. It's probably more expensive than a wedding, actually.'

Up-Helly-Aa was once a modest affair. Costumes were make-do and mend. But with the coming of North Sea oil, Shetland grew rich and the costumes became increasingly sophisticated. It wasn't unknown for the Jarl Squad to import bear and wolf skin for their capes.

This year's squad have settled for rabbit. But they have not skimped on the intricately carved helmets, shields and weapons. A Jarl Squad suit can cost over £1,500, or £900 for a child's version. It is an expensive business. Having been elected at a mass meeting, men know they are going to be Guizer Jarl fifteen years in advance, and they spend that time saving. One former Jarl is said to have bankrupted himself.

It would be surprising if money is in John Hunter's thoughts as he surveys the scene inside the park through eyes red with smoke and emotion. He climbs down from the galley and a triumphant bugle sounds (this is such a well-loved noise that many locals have it as their mobile ringtone). On the final note, the guizers surrounding the galley hurl their torches on to its deck. The moment feels dangerous, vivid, wild. They sing The Norseman's Home then turn and leave, happy that the ritual has been observed for another year. Within a short time, the park has emptied. A constellation of sparks flies upward from the galley. It's a clear, cold night and the stars are out. The Plough hangs over Lerwick, bright and sharp like a Viking axe.

Though the aesthetics of Up-Helly-Aa are Norse, the festival was developed in the late Victorian period by a group of bright young socialists who wanted to give an aesthetic overhaul to the town's festive celebrations, which until that point had centred around hauling burning tar barrels through Lerwick's narrow streets in addition to such occasional pleasantries as firing a cannon full of dead cats.

The 1870s were years in which islanders were becoming increasingly interested in their Norse heritage. Shetland was colonised by Norsemen in the ninth century and didn't become part of Scotland until 1468. Ask Shetlanders whether they feel Scandinavian or Scottish and many reply thus: 'Baith.'

Shetland does seem a place where identity is in flux and the usual social and cultural divisions have been eroded. In Lerwick's masonic lodge, at lunchtime on the day before Up-Helly-Aa, young men in Celtic tops sank pints; sinking pots at the pool table, 30-year-old Ryan Wright bent over his cue, the sleeves on his Motorhead T-shirt riding up to reveal his name inked in Viking runes and a tattoo of a burning galley. The stereo played Scottish country dance music and Dixieland jazz. A jar of pickled eggs sat on a pub table, and round the table a group of men were eating and drinking, enjoying a break.

These were the 'torch boys' – the men charged with making the 1,153 torches for Up-Helly-Aa. Kay and Flossie, two middle-aged women dressed as nuns, had popped round to the lodge from the Happy Haddock with thirty fish suppers to sustain the hardworking crew.

There is a kid-on rivalry between the torch boys and the galley boys who build the ship. Really, there's a great deal of mutual respect. Up-Helly-Aa is run by volunteers. There is a huge amount to do. Planning for each festival begins in the preceding February. Work begins on the galley and torches in October.

Up-Helly-Aa enjoys much continuity, both in the ritual itself and in the people who run it. There are some highly esteemed men, tribe elders of a sort, who have performed the same role for many years.

Lowrie Shearer is 69, has been making torches for 44 years, and hopes to continue until the half-century. Jim Nicolson is 77 and has steered the galley through Lerwick's streets every year since 1963; he looks regal and mystical in his horned helmet and white beard. Roy Leask, 58, has been involved in building the galley since he was 15. He knew James Smith, a boatbuilder known as Boatie Jeemie, who established the template for the present galley in 1949, the first Up-Helly-Aa following the war. The skills Leask learned from the old men of his youth, he now passes on to a new generation of keen boys, and so it goes on.

Up-Helly-Aa is altogether remarkable, and some of its most remarkable sights can be seen in the halls – the buildings in which hostesses stage parties following the procession. Typically, food is provided but you bring your own drink. Bands play strip-the- willow and the like, breaking off as each Up-Helly-Aa squad arrives and performs their act.

In Bell's Brae Primary School, the walls of the assembly hall are lined with Jarl Squad shields going back to the 1920s. It is around midnight and the party will go on till breakfast. There are prim older ladies and gentlemen seated around the edge of the dancefloor. Among the young women it's all handbags and gladrags, Lambrini and cutty-sarks. A twentysomething's gold dress rides up to her waist as she is lifted on to the dancefloor by a man in a white bodystocking.

The atmosphere isn't horribly drunken, though, or especially sexual. It's quite tender in a way. Watching people of all ages dancing to Wild Mountain Thyme, it becomes clear that the true tradition of Up-Helly-Aa has nothing to do with Vikings but rather is to do with the generations of Shetlanders who have a clear sense of belonging to this place and have certain values in common – kindness, empathy and an enviable capacity for joy.

No sooner does that thought occur, though, than a squad turns up and performs, to rapturous applause, a dance routine to Fight For This Love, led by a plump 21-year-old man dressed as Cheryl Cole in peaked military cap and buttock-revealing leotard. It's a vision that, combined with heat, lack of sleep and neat whisky, can leave an outsider disorientated and confused. A good time, perhaps, to heed the advice John Hunter, the Guizer Jarl, had offered during an earlier conversation.

'Up-Helly-Aa's just Up-Helly-Aa,' he said. 'You don't ask any questions. You just get on with it.'

The Fishermen of Dalmarnock

'SEE the Clyde?' says Tony. 'It learns ye patience. At another river ye'll maybe catch fish regular. But ah've sat here for fourteen hours and had nuthin'.'

Tony Dickson is 39. He doesn't have a job at the moment ('No for want of tryin'') but worked previously as a removal man ('Every job was a three-up. Naeb'dy lived on the ground floor') and he spends his Thursday evenings fishing the River Clyde. He's here tonight with four pals and his daughter, Ellie, whose job it is to fetch maggots and dig for worms. Ellie has a pink rod and has already, at five years old, established a reputation as a keen and lucky angler. She gets the first fish of the night. 'There ye go,' says her dad, holding up a small silver fish with orange fins. 'A wee roach. Well done, hen.'

He takes it off the hook and throws it back in the water. 'They say that women have a pheromone and that's how they're better at catching fish,' he observes. 'A lot of fishermen used to rub their wife's knickers on the line.'

In truth, few women venture down here to the river at Dalmarnock Bridge in the east end of Glasgow. Chas Owen's mother came by once with a plate of mince and tatties for her son, a driver-labourer in his early forties, but that's about it. Thursday night fishing is a masculine ritual.

A few miles south, at this precise moment, Benedict XVI is celebrating Mass in Bellahouston Park. The Pope is known as a fisher of men. But these men in Dalmarnock are more interested in fish. You might think that the Clyde would be too dirty for fish to survive. In fact they are thriving. It's said that there are more than 30 species in the river. Chas Owen reels some of them off: 'Sea trout, brown trout, roach, dace, perch, eels, barbel. But ye cannae catch any salmon at this bit.'

Catching a salmon in the Clyde, as it flows sluggishly through Glasgow, is like trying to hail a taxi on Renfield Street at 3.00 am on Saturday. They just go speeding past. So those few souls who fish in the city are stuck with coarse breeds and the odd trout, which assumes legendary status. 'My biggest fish was a five pund brownie,' says Chas. 'It was April Fool's Day, 2007. A Sunday. At ten to twelve. I'll never forget that.'

Those most remarkable catches – their weights, species and who caught them – are commemorated by being scratched into the galvanised steel of a shelter the men have built on the broken wooden pier from which they fish. It's made from scaffolding poles and plastic tarpaulin. One side is left open so they can keep an eye on their spinning rods, leaning against the railings, line trailing in the water. They are alert to the merest twitch that might indicate a bite. 'Are ye in?' they shout when a fish is hooked. Then there's a great rush to see if it can be landed.The shelter is a real boon, especially in the Glasgow rain. For ages they tried to get by with a tarpaulin arranged on branches, but neds kept setting that on fire and chucking the chairs in the water. There's no way they can burn the steel, though, and the bench, these days, is nailed down.

'Therr the Pope therr!' someone shouts as another fisherman arrives. 'The only Pope we'll see the night.' John Paul Clark is 36, nicknamed the Pope for obvious reasons, even though he is of the other persuasion. He's wearing a T-shirt which says 'Dear God, thanks for the booze, birds, fags and football.'

The fishermen of Dalmarnock assemble here on Saturdays, too, the radio tuned to football. It is traditional, whether gathering on an evening or weekend, to have a few drinks. Cans of lager and a bottle of Buckfast are shared round. There's Irn-Bru for those who need to be up early working. Ellie is pretty generous with her Maltesers.

There's always something going on here. Once, they prevented a woman from throwing herself into the water. That was dramatic, but mostly time passes in animated conversation. A favourite topic is whether, if they could catch enough eels, a Chinese restaurant might swap them for a free meal. The biggest thing I see them catch, though, is a passing rowing boat.

I walked here, along the north bank of the river, passing over and under several bridges. First came Victoria Bridge, which links the Gorbals with the city centre. There's a litter of dirty syringes down by that bridge and a rusty iron hoop once used to moor boats that no longer sail. Across the road is the Briggait, the old fishmarket now home to artists' studios. On the facade, Glasgow's coat of arms – the bird, tree, fish and bell – is a reminder angling goes right back to the city's origins, when Govan was a fishing village.

These days, the Clyde is in some ways incidental to Glasgow. Though it bisects the city, it is not much used. A lot of effort and money is going into regenerating the waterfront, but I spent an hour walking along the river and hardly met another person. It's beautiful, though, especially in early autumn. Golden leaves fall twisting through the blue air. The water is brown but glitters in the sunlight, reflecting in dappled mackerel patterns on the low underside of Rutherglen Bridge. Down by the water, among the brambles and hogweed, you could almost forget you were in a city.

There's a distant sound of sirens and ice-cream chimes. Occasional waves of stink flow from the brewery and sewage works. Further east, a long, tall concrete wall is covered in graffiti which mixes stern imperatives ('Fuck the polis') with bold declarations – 'Wee Mo is sexy'.

Eventually, Dalmarnock Bridge comes into sight – a 19th century structure of cobwebby cast-iron. East of the bridge, you need a permit to fish. But within the city boundaries it is free. Even in those areas where a permit is required, however, it is relatively cheap. You'll pay £65 to fish salmon for a season in the Clyde. You might pay that much or more for a day's fishing on the Tay. 'It's an affordable price for the working man, and the Clyde, on its day, is as good a river as any,' says John Blair, 38, who runs riverclydefishing.com. The website offers information on all aspects of angling on the Clyde, but also functions as a cheerleader for a river which has plenty of detractors. 'People will say, 'You got a salmon out the Clyde? That's manky. I widnae eat that.''

In fact, the fishermen of Dalmarnock do not eat their catch. 'We know what's in the water,' says Chas. The Clyde is much cleaner than it was; at one time this stretch of water was purple with chemicals and full of stolen cars. But in heavy rain it's common for a sewage pipe to overflow. So they release those fish they land.

Recently, John Blair was fishing near Uddingston and hooked a 20lb salmon 'like a slab of silver'. It snapped his fly line and pulled it into the water. That's a line he could ill afford to lose, so he took off his waders, dived in and swam for it. 'That's how daft us Clyde boys are,' he says.

The Dalmarnock men have been fishing here and hereabouts since they were children. They learned at the knee of a local fishing guru called John Flannigan, known as John Trout, in whose honour they compete each year for a memorial shield.

Twenty-five years ago, it was common for the local boys to fish and explore the countryside. Paul Smith, a 37-year-old with colourful lures stuck to his fishing hat, recalls that in his early teens he'd sit out by the river all night with a rod bought from a catalogue. There were swimming trips, too, and expeditions into a nearby area known as 'the valleys', where base camp would be established at the foot of a pylon. Paul and his pals would see deer and foxes, shin up trees for birds' eggs, and plunder crab apple trees. Great bags of fruit would be brought back to the scheme and used as projectiles in mass battles. Thus, in the mid-Eighties, Dalmarnock got its five-a-day.

It's fascinating to hear these stories. The idea of lads growing up in the east end of Glasgow being immersed in the countryside is not familiar. Paul and the others look back on it as a kind of Eden before the fall. 'Drugs came in badly when we were fifteen, sixteen,' he says. 'Smack tore the scheme apart. Half a dozen o' yer closest crowd became junkies. It's sad tae see. They're no' like the person ye knew.'

These fishing nights provide a sense of that community they knew growing up, a community that is largely gone. A number of the men talk about fishing as a kind of escape. A few hours away from wife and weans and the pressure of work or not having work.

Dalmarnock is changing. A lot of it has been demolished to make way for the Commonwealth Games. Other areas, including 'the valleys', are being developed as part of the Clyde Gateway regeneration project. So whether you land no fish or forty fish in one night, the point of coming here is the same – a reconnection with a place still recognisable as where you grew up. Those uncatchable salmon swimming upstream are following a similar impulse.

'It's like coming back home,' says Paul, downing his beer as the moon rises, 'to oor ain wee place.'

Kingussie vs Newtonmore

'SHINTY?' says Ronald Ross, 'It is an addiction here and a way of life.'

He should know. If shinty has an icon it is undoubtedly Ross, the so-called 'Ronaldo of the Glens', the only man in the game ever to have scored more than 1,000 goals. Without him it is unlikely that his club, Kingussie, would have become – according to Guinness World Records – the most successful team in the history of world sport, winning the league in every year between 1987 and 2005, then again between 2007 and 2009. It was a period during which their great rivals, Newtonmore, could do little beyond consoling themselves in the bar of the Balavil Hotel, where whisky and old photographs of the great teams of the past offered sepia comfort.

Now, however, Newtonmore are in the ascendant. They won the league last year and could still defend that title. 'Kingussie and Newtonmore is similar to the Rangers and Celtic thing, but without the religion,' Ross explains. 'The two places are just three miles apart. They've got a great history and tradition and so do we. They want to win and so do we. It's not a friendly rivalry. It's very competitive. You don't ever want to lose to them.' He grimaces. 'That can be a nightmare.'

It is a fine day in Newtonmore when I visit. The air is warm and smells of bonfires. The Monadhliath mountains are hazy blue humps. The only sounds are the sarcastic caw of crows and the answering meh of Blackface sheep. The main street of the small Highland village, 15 miles south of Aviemore, is deathly quiet. So many are away at the shinty.

Today, Newtonmore are hosting Kingussie at their ground, Eilean Bheannchair, known to all as the Eilan. Kingussie, in their famous red and blue, play at the similarly fortress-sounding ground the Dell. This is the first so-called Badenoch derby of the season, the latest bout in a grudge match that has been going on since the 19th century, and everyone – players and fans – is well up for it.

What is remarkable, given that the combined populations of Kingussie and Newtonmore number around 2,400, is that there are some 1,000 or so people here today; the Glaswegian equivalent would be an Old Firm match attended by approximately 240,000. Were this a cup-final, the attendance would swell to more than 3,000. You'll see a crowd like that in Inverness next month, when the two teams play for the Camanachd Cup, shinty's most coveted prize. The Badenoch sides last met in that final in 1997, when Kingussie beat their rivals 12-1 – 'The worst day of my life,' one Newtonmore veteran recalls with a groan.

The Eilan is little more than a shinty pitch and a clubhouse. No grandstand, no terracing. The crowds, many of them in Newtonmore's blue and white, stand right up at the side of the field. 'You don't wear red in this village,' someone explains. The atmosphere is pleasantly informal. The great thing is to park your 4x4 right behind the goal and lean on the front bumper, drinking beer and casting aspersions at the visual acuity of the referee.

There are whole families here. Some of the women, during lulls in the action, dip their heads like sandpipers into the pages of Grazia. A group of teens, drinking Strongbow on a small green hill beside the clubhouse, exchange banter in what a visitor, overhearing, might take for the melodious old Gaelic tongue – 'Geez a can, ya nugget.' Amongst the older men, a bottle of Dalwhinnie, won in the raffle, is passed from hand to hand.

Kingussie go 1-0 up after half an hour, plunging the home crowd into gloom. No one is cheered by the scenery around the pitch; they are too used to it. But it is beautiful – a landscape of fir-cloaked slopes and old Scots pines. When the big Newtonmore keeper wallops the ball, you'd swear it was going to land somewhere near the peak of looming Creag Dhubh.

Shinty balls are small and hard, made of cork covered in leather. At one point, it goes flying off the park at speed and dents a silver Skoda. 'It's all right,' someone laughs. 'That's a Kingussie car.'

It is a hard, hard game, shinty. What you don't get when you watch it on television or YouTube is the bang of caman on caman, the distinctive curved wooden sticks; the clash of the ash, they call it. 'Turning your back is not something you do. You have to stand your ground and take the hit,' says Newtonmore's Norman Campbell later. At 32, the defender – known as Bandy – is a veteran and one of the most highly regarded players in the sport. 'When you see footballers rolling about it's quite embarrassing,' he continues. 'I've had teeth knocked out, my jaw broken, a wrist broken. Some boys get really bad injuries but they always come back to play. Gordon Macintyre from Oban got his eye knocked out at the Dell, and he was back within six weeks.

'As a youngster, you are taught to toughen up by the older guys and by your family. I can remember being out in the back garden with my father and I'm in tears because he's giving me knocks to the shins. That builds the determination and commitment into you.'

Standing near the Newtonmore goal, leaning on the iron rail, is Cameron Ormiston. He turned 82 the day before and looks well on it. 'I was born in that farm up there,' he says, pointing towards the hillside, 'and I walked through the top goals here the night before I was born. My mother was carrying me at the time.' The idea behind this ritual was that the boy would be a shinty player, and so it turned out; he played for Newtonmore, which was ironic as he came from Kingussie stock. 'My father played for Kingussie and my grandfather. It's him that sits on top of the Camanachd Cup. A man called Jock Dallas.'

Shinty is dynastic. There seems to be a shinty gene, a phenomenon perhaps best summed up by Kingussie's stirring town motto: 'Follow closely the fame of your fathers'. Ronald Ross and Newtonmore's Rory Kennedy, for example, are cousins, and can both trace their bloodline back to the great shinty-playing family Sellar, which has been a force in the game since the early 1900s. Minto Sellar, Ross's maternal grandfather, played on the Newtonmore side that won the Camanachd Cup in 1931. Ross's father, Ian, won the cup with Kingussie in 1961. And Ross himself was in the cup-winning side of 1991. It is a standing joke in Newtonmore that Ross inherited his shinty skills from their village and everything else from Kingussie.

The great untangler of these twisted genealogies is Rob Ritchie, chieftain of the Newtonmore club, and perhaps the game's most enthusiastic stalwart and historian. At 68, the retired policeman and builder is still a big strong man, with bright blue eyes and powerful arms. In shinty he is a tradition-bearer, or seannachie, a keeper and teller of tales. He used to play the game, but excelled as a heavy athlete. Two years ago he became the world champion caber-tosser in the over-sixties category. On the side of his truck, parked at the side of the Eilan, he has his initials and a silhouette of himself wearing a kilt and throwing the hammer.

In a footwell of his vehicle are two old camans. 'That's possibly the oldest club in shinty,' Ritchie says, lifting one. 'It's made of birch. I meant to get it carbon-dated. It's a couple of hundred years anyway.' Quickly, as if reciting a school lesson, Ritchie sums up the history of shinty in the area. The first recorded games between Newtonmore and Kingussie took place in 1888, he says, though it's known that shinty was played informally in the area for many

decades, and perhaps even centuries, before that. The rules
– twelve players in each team, 90-minute matches etc –
began to be formalised in 1893.

The teams were amalgamated for two seasons, in 1926
and 1927, but this is considered a distasteful memory now
in both villages, similar to the way contemporary France
feels about the Vichy government. The rivalry has improved
the quality of shinty on both sides, everyone agrees, each
team whetting the other's edge. Between them they have
dominated the sport.

Kingussie won the very first Camanachd Cup in 1896,
and have gone on to win on a further 21 occasions. Newtonmore, however, are the record-holders. They have won
it 28 times, though they were last victorious in 1986. In
Badenoch, shinty is more religion than sport. When, in
1961, Kingussie won the cup for the first time since 1921,
the club president announced, 'We have been in the wilder-
ness for 40 years but today we have reached the Promised
Land!'

Today's match ends in a 2-2 draw. Norman MacArthur,
the Newtonmore manager, known as Brick for his stocki-
ness, is unhappy. 'I'm gutted,' he groans. 'Our full-back
got booked for dangerous swinging. I mean, come on.
Shinty's about dangerous swinging.'

Driving away from the Eilan, Ritchie nods his head
towards some kids kicking a football. 'Look at these wee
ones,' he says. 'From the age of four or five we never went
anywhere without a shinty club in our hand. And if any
of the old timers saw you with a football, they'd pick it
up and put a knife through it. Oh aye, that was strictly
forbidden.'

Times have changed. These days, with the success of
Ross County and Inverness Caledonian Thistle, local boys
can dream of making it in professional football. Shinty is
an amateur sport, which is part of its great charm, but there
is no money in it; most of the Kingussie and Newtonmore

players work in the building trade. However, shinty is still the dominant sport in the area, and they initiate players young. It is thought that to become a top-level player you ought to start at no older than seven. 'I don't know anyone over twelve years old who has picked up a stick for the first time and become a decent player,' says Brick MacArthur.

The teams work with local schools to get kids playing. Unlike football, there is no culture within shinty of signing players from outwith the catchment area of the club, so it is vital that new blood keeps coming into the sport. The clubs keep a close, anxious eye on talent in the primary schools, worrying about what its lack might mean for the strength of the first team a decade hence. At the moment, MacArthur is concerned that Kingussie's primary school players are miles ahead of Newtonmore's. Meanwhile, in the Kingussie camp, they bemoan the fact that many more boys seem to be born in Newtonmore than to families in their own village.

Fraser Coyle, the 35-year-old owner of the Balavil Hotel, has come along to today's match with his two sons. James, at nine months, is resting in his buggy. But two-year-old Joe has a little caman and is knocking a ball around. 'Joe and I play in the garden nearly every day,' says Fraser. 'Every day I ask him what he wants to do and he says, 'Go and watch the big boys playing shinty.'

'My family first moved to this village when I was seven, and I remember one of the first people that came into the hotel was Rob Ritchie with a couple of sticks for me and my brother. It's a great community we have here. I've got close friends in Kingussie and they always say they don't have what we have here. I know I'm biased, but that seems to be so.' He gives a grudging laugh. 'Och, I'm sure there's a load of nice people in Kingussie too.'

Kingussie is the slightly larger of the two villages. They are separated by the Allt na Fèithe burn and it takes just two minutes to drive between them. Yet the rivalry is real and not confined to sport. 'I've known cases where families see Kingussie as the enemy in everything,' says Brick MacArthur. 'They'll say, "You're not going to work down there. You're not going to work for that Kingussie bastard."'

'Well, it's historical,' explains Joe Taylor, chieftain of Kingussie shinty club, with a mischievous twinkle in his eye. 'Kingussie was the earliest place. Newtonmore in Gaelic is the new town on the moor. It was built by people who were rejected by Kingussie. They weren't suitable to live in Kingussie. So they were sent to live in Newtonmore. Kingussie is the capital of Badenoch. It was a planned town, whereas Newtonmore just grew up. When I worked in Newtonmore I cycled from Kincraig every day. One Monday morning, I was cycling along the main street to go to my work, and the wee boys were going to primary school with their shinty sticks in their hands. One said, 'See that man on the bike? He's a Kingussie supporter.' Well, they literally stoned me along the street. I had to put my head down and pedal like anything. So, as a result, I'm for anyone who's playing Newtonmore.'

The stories of trouble between the two sides are legendary. Tales of drunken punch-ups and high jinks, ancient and modern, are recounted with a mix of disapproval and glee. There was the time a referee was rewarded for a controversial decision by being thrown in the River Spey. Then there was the occasion when the Kingussie team bus, driving through the rival village to jeers from the doorsteps, stopped just long enough for one of the players to disembark and belt his cousin, a Newtonmore man, on the jaw.

Much of the mythology is recounted in the singalongs of shinty songs, led by folk musician Davy Holt, in the thronging bar of the Balavil Hotel following Newtonmore victories. The most popular is an adaption of the Jacobite anthem Sound the Pibroch, demonstrating the depth of the sport's roots in the history and emotional landscape of the area. As Joe Taylor puts it, 'Shinty is the last true remnant of Gaelic culture that remains here.'

This, surely, is what is most important about shinty in Badenoch – it gives meaning and joy. It is the glue that binds the community. And at a time when many Highland villages are struggling with depopulation, it has offered young men and their families a reason, an obligation almost, to stay. 'Definitely,' says Bandy Campbell, who works as a machine operator. 'There were things that I did fancy doing, like the army, but there was only ever one stumbling block – it was never women or anything else, it was always shinty. Playing for Newtonmore is everything to me.'

He has a son now himself, Brodie, just 11 months old but already the owner of a caman and a knitted hat in blue and white. Bandy hopes that the boy will grow up to be the fifth generation of Campbells to play for the Newtonmore team. Certainly, he plans to raise him in the true faith. And so it goes on.

'Long after other teams have stopped,' says Rob Ritchie, 'they will still be playing shinty in Kingussie and Newtonmore.'

Thistle vs Rose

A STRANGER visiting Scotland for the first time and keen to get an idea what the place looks like could do worse than stand in the centre circle at a few of the country's 150 or so junior football grounds. Beyond the terracing, the visitor would see high flats and Highlands, coast towns and ghost towns, cash-strapped streets and snow-capped peaks. Around Barrfields Park, home to Largs Thistle, the hills are thick with whins the same gold as the team strip.

From the vantage point of Prestonfield, the ground of Linlithgow Rose, you can make out the steel-steepled palace in which Mary, Queen of Scots was born, and the post-war semi that was the birthplace of Alex Salmond. You learn a lot about Scottish culture and values from junior football, and the first lesson comes in through the eyes.

Junior football is not, despite the name, a game for youngsters. It is played by men, real men who work through the week, typically as joiners, brickies, mechanics and other grafters, then spend Saturday afternoons playing hard, attacking football. They are watched from worn, phlegm-flecked terraces by passionate, obsessive crowds, which are often greater in number than those attending third and even second division games.

Linlithgow Rose and Largs Thistle will today meet in the final of the Scottish Junior Cup at Kilmarnock's Rugby Park. It is the most coveted prize in the junior game, and the subject of a great Scottish novel, *The Thistle And The Grail*, published in 1954. When Robin Jenkins described these cup ties as a 'mysterious masculine sacrament', he

140

wasn't indulging in hyperbole. There is a devotional aspect to junior football.

Take the Auchinleck Talbot centre-half who, at dawn on the day of a cup final, visited his father's grave to pray for success. Then there was the loyal committee man who, when his club won the cup, took the trophy home and photographed each of his thirteen grandchildren sitting by it, as if it was a sliver of the one true cross.

Tommy Scouler, the 75-year-old kit man with Largs Thistle, regards the cup final as a personal second chance at glory; as a player with Greenock Juniors, he missed the 1960 cup final due to injury. So when Largs won their semi-final, the years fell from him in a kind of miracle. 'Ah wisnae even limpin',' he says. 'Ah threw ma stick away.'

At a time when Scottish professional football is withering for lack of money, it is refreshing to spend time in the pure-hearted world of the juniors. The typical player gets about fifty quid a week. Some clubs pay more, others less, some pay nothing at all. None of these men are in it for the money. It's about love of the game. This passion finds a deafening echo in the cries of a crowd, each member of which will have paid around a fiver to get in. Every time the ball is won, the home fans let out an orgasmic roar; a ball given away is greeted by a frustrated wail that suggests coitus interruptus. Over ninety minutes, this is tantric football.

Prestonfield. Saturday afternoon. Linlithgow Rose are at home to Dundee's Lochee United in the second leg of the Scottish Junior Cup semi-final. Rose are 1-0 down from the first match and the 1,400-strong crowd is tense. Linlithgow have won the cup on three previous occasions – 1965, 2002 and 2007 – and are regarded as one of the leading junior clubs. But things aren't looking good.

'We're nervous,' admits David Archer, 45, a Rose fan sitting before the game in the social club next to the ground. It would be wrong to think that, because junior

141

clubs are small, the pain and joy of following them is at all diminished. For the fans, defeat hurts just as much as it does for Scottish Premier League supporters. 'More so,' says Martin Brown, 39, wearing a maroon replica top, 'because instead of it being a team from sixty miles away, it's a team from just over the hill that have beat you.'

Junior football is played in regional leagues, pitting town against town, village against village. Bad-tempered local derbies are common. 'It can feel like the longest drive home in history,' says Brown, 'and it's just a few miles.'

Standing by the social club bar, members of the Linlithgow Reed Band, splendid in scarlet jackets and black peak caps, have drams in one hand, drums in the other. They are preparing to take to the field and perform the much-loved club song, Hail The Gallant Rosey Posey, which is played to the tune of Battle Hymn Of The Republic.

'If the Rose win today, Linlithgow will be empty on the day of the final,' explains Alex Grant, the 71-year-old cornettist. 'Everybody will be there. When they win the cup, we play on the open-top bus that takes them through town.'

Rose, in the end, do win. The game is one long act of faith. Linlithgow concede an early goal, but equalise from a penalty shortly before half time. In the second half, the resurrection is complete – they score three.

At the final whistle, Danny Smith, the talismanic centre-midfielder, has tears in his eyes as he runs over to hug his sister and niece. Later, walking into the social club to huge cheers, he winks at the doorman – 'Do ah need to sign in?' The answer, of course, is no. The man is a hero.

The air smells of beer and bridies, victory and reheated hope. A Lochee fan downs a scunnered pint and heads for the bus, leaving his blue and white scarf where it lies. 'You're very welcome to that,' he says. 'I never want to see it again.'

* * *

Danny Smith is 32, lives in Denny, and works as a coach-builder. He looks older than his years – tough, like Richard Harris in This Sporting Life. He sits in his front room and talks movingly about what Linlithgow Rose and its support means.

'You see your superstars of football?' he asks. 'Well, I've lived that dream, but on a different level. For a working-class guy like myself, it's been amazing.'

Smith has been with Linlithgow Rose for twelve years. As a teenager, he had hoped to make it as a professional, but that didn't work out so he joined the juniors. The best junior players carry within them a perfect mixture of humility and pride; humility because they have accepted they are not, in general, as talented as the pros; pride because, despite their limitations, they continue to do their best for club and community.

'My level's junior football,' says Smith. 'At seniors, I could be ordinary; at junior football, one of the best. I realised early doors that Rose was a special club and I could make something of my time there. The supporters appreciated me because they could see that I was going out on a Saturday and giving it everything I had. We've got a real special bond. It means the world to me.'

Part of that bond is the result of the fact that Smith has sustained many bad injuries while playing for Rose. Junior football can be very aggressive. Smith has broken ribs, a foot and his right leg. The second time he broke his leg, the bone snapped and he lay on the pitch for forty excruciating minutes, waiting for an ambulance. 'I was 29 and everybody thought that was it for me. The papers said my career was in tatters, and I thought that myself.'

It was a miserable period; he was off work for four months and suffered a number of infections. But, after almost two years, he returned to training. 'I got a right hunger inside me to play again. I didn't want to be remembered for breaking my leg and that being the end. It was the start of a new journey.'

One Saturday morning, the Rose manager named him as a substitute in a game against Tayport and he came on in the last ten minutes to tumultuous roars. Danny Smith was back.

'I've proved to any doubters that are out there that I can still do it. I've won well over twenty trophies with Linlithgow, but this cup final means more to me than them all put together.' He plans to retire as a player at the end of this season. 'I feel I've got one last big medal in me. I want to go out on a high.'

Smith has become a sort of holy martyr for Rose fans. The man willing to take the pain. Yet he's an icon they can touch, an idol with whom they can share a joke or drink. 'If you're a professional football player, you don't have a relationship with the fans,' he says. 'You maybe sign something and walk on. To me, the fans are more like friends.'

There is an intimacy in junior football between supporters and club. Much of the angst in professional football comes when supporters feel alienated by the club they love. The juniors clubs are run by fans on an unpaid, voluntary basis. Often, these volunteers have a relationship with the club as long and deep as a marriage. 'I've only been on the committee for 46 years,' says one man at Largs Thistle, dismissing himself as an dilettante.

Davie Roy, the club secretary at Linlithgow, has held that position since 1959. Before George Best, before The Beatles, he was helping the Rose to bloom. He's 77 years old and cuts the grass yet.

Football can transform people, elevate them. The players spend all week doing ordinary jobs; come Saturday they have the opportunity to shuck off anonymity and achieve momentary greatness. The footballing life can also, despite the evidence of the tabloids, be personally exalting.

'The junior game has changed my life around so much,' says James Marks, the 27-year-old striker with Largs Thistle. In his late teens, having moved to Greenock from the United States, he fell in with a bad crowd and became, in his own words, 'a ned', wasting his days with fights. 'I was running the streets, getting bad press in the local papers, I was going to court quite a lot.'

He was approached, at this time, by Sandy MacLean, now manager of Largs Thistle but then with Greenock Juniors, who had heard he could play football. Marks would be allowed to play with the team, he was told, but he had to clean up his act. 'Ever since that, I've worked hard, and I've not been in one bit of trouble. I don't run about with the same crowd, I train twice a week, and I keep my head down. My wife says that junior football has saved me.'

Winning the cup would be, for Marks, a glorious symbol of his redemption. 'It means everything,' he says. 'It's the biggest game of my life.'

* * *

Just as junior football can transform individual lives, it can shape and change whole communities. Take Auchinleck Talbot, one of several teams based in what were once thriving mining villages in the Ayrshire coalfield. It's no exaggeration to say that Talbot was built on coal. Nearly half the squad that won the Scottish Junior Cup in 1949 were miners, and the following year 12,000 tons of pit slag were dumped round the ground, Beechwood Park, to form an ersatz terrace. Football culture in those days was more bing than bling.

Since the pit closures, Auchinleck and nearby Cumnock – home to their hated rivals, Cumnock Juniors – have struggled for employment and meaning, but the football provides an identity and focal point these places would otherwise lack.

'What does the club mean to me?' says John Davidson, 50, sitting in the Beechwood Park social club before a game. 'It's part of the family. You've got your weans and you've got Talbot.'

During a mid-week match against Irvine Meadow which yields three goals and ten bookings, the fanaticism of the Auchinleck support is evident. Sitting in the stand, having chosen a seat with great care to avoid the pigeon mess, there's much entertainment in listening to the fans shouting at their team. 'Keep the heid, Talbot!' one man cries. 'Play fuckin' fitba! It's no a hoat spud yer kickin'!'

This is tough love. The devotion of the fans has been repaid in so many victories it's arguable that Talbot are the greatest junior club of all. They certainly know about winning the Scottish Cup, having lifted the trophy more often than any other side. They won it five times between 1986 and 1992.

'Willie Knox was the man that done that,' explains Jim McAuley, a 50-year-old whose fandom is such that he named his dog after one of the players. 'Willie Knox is a god in Auchinleck.'

Willie Knox is 71 and lives a life of quiet obscurity with his loving wife Sheila down a cul-de-sac in his home town of Kilmarnock. At weekends he helps out as 'gofer' at a local boys' team, carrying the balls and corner flags. Yet Knox is regarded by many as the best junior football manager to ever stalk a touchline. Some say that, in his way, he was the equal of Bill Shankly, Jock Stein and Matt Busby. Yet he had no interest in managing a senior club, preferring to keep close to his roots and inspire a community for whom he had great love and empathy.

As manager of Talbot between 1977 and 1993, he won 43 trophies, taking the team from nowhere to the dominant force in the junior game. His greatest achievement was to lift the Scottish Cup for three years in a row, a feat that has never been equalled. His cup runs took place at a time when Auchinleck and much of Ayrshire were depressed and divided by the pit closures and miners' strike. Whole families had been torn apart as some men chose to cross the picket line. Footballing success, in this context, was a healing force. What's remarkable is that Knox intended it to be so.

'What goaded me on was that in Auchinleck there was nothing,' he recalls. 'The pits was shut and there was nae work at all. When I started we were lucky if there were 30 people coming to the games, but see by the time I finished up? You're talking about 2,000, maybe more. We had to win the cup to unite the village. That was very important for me 'cos my dad was an ex-miner.

'When we won the cup that first year, we went back to the village and the scabs and the guys that had stayed oot on strike aw got drunk thegither.'

Knox is not physically a big man, but he has presence and authority even now. As a player he started his professional career at Raith Rovers beside Jim Baxter before joining Third Lanark in the late 1950s; the near-mythical Glasgow club were then managed by Bob Shankly, a man from whom Knox learned many of his later managerial skills.

As a manager, Knox was known for his sang froid. In 1986, with Talbot 2-0 down to Pollok in the Scottish Junior Cup final at Hampden, the gaffer was in the dug-out, calmly eating an egg piece. His composure proved justified when Talbot went on to win 3-2.

Under his regime every player was paid the same. He himself got £20 a week, but a retired miner once gave him a ton of coal for his fire with the proviso – 'As long as you keep winning for Talbot'. Money was never important to him. When he received a cash prize at an awards ceremony he spent it on a park bench in memory of a local Labour councillor. 'I've made nothin' oot o' fitba',' he says, 'but I've made a lot o' guid friends.'

147

Unquestionably, Willie Knox embodies the values of junior football – egalitarian, community-minded, loyal and thrawn. Most likely, some of those values will be on display today at Rugby Park. Largs versus Linlithgow, Thistle against Rose, west meets east – all opposites, but the teams and players are united in a desire to excel and to display the true spirit of a game which, though seldom beautiful, is always a sight to behold.

'For 90 minutes all hell breaks loose,' is how one fan described the cup final. He might have added that afterwards, if you win, you're in heaven.

At the Berries

BY the time I arrive at West Haugh Farm, it's a little after seven, the sun has been up for three hours, the mist has lifted from the fields around Blairgowrie, and another day of the berry harvest is about to begin.

It could be a scene from another age, and indeed another country, as hundreds of pickers pull into the farmyard on bicycles, sleep clinging to them like pollen, and greet each other in their native tongues – mostly Polish, but also Czech, Slovak, Romanian, Latvian, Lithuanian and Bulgarian. Swallows, tiny stunt pilots, fly joyously around the red brick chimney of the old jute mill.

'What's the estimate for today then?' asks Peter Thomson the farmer.

'It's 3,800 trays,' replies Eddie Christie, who is the farm foreman, or to use the old Scots word he prefers, the grieve. That number of trays translates to around one million strawberries. Imagine that in a single day. The season lasts from the end of May until mid-October, but right now, early July, is its peak.

Christie is a whip-thin man of 64 with Billy Fury's hair, Samuel Beckett's face and Robbie Shepherd's voice. He started picking berries at the age of sixteen on a farm in Marykirk, finding himself a vocation and a wife, Ann, into the bargain. He prides himself on being able to estimate, by close examination of the crop, how many trays of strawberries and raspberries will be picked each day. It's important work. Underestimate and the fruit may go unsold. Overestimate and Tesco, Sainsbury's and the like will not receive the amount of fruit they were expecting, news they would not take well.

'It's an absolutely brutal business,' says Peter Thomson, who is 56. 'The supermarkets have got zero tolerance.' They take a 40 per cent cut and will impose hefty fines for fruit which they reject as not meeting their standards. Growers, therefore, have a horror of mould and root rot, and insist that the pickers handle the fruit with infinite gentleness. 'There are two ways to pick a raspberry,' Christie explains, demonstrating, like some Doric tai chi master, the finger-curl and the three-finger-pick. 'The criminal thing is squeezing it. If you break the drupelets, you're crying out for a juicing in the punnet.'

Thomas Thomson, which is the name of Peter Thomson's firm, harvests around fifty million strawberries and a similar number of raspberries each year. The industry as a whole is worth £130 million to the Scottish economy. It is a big business. High pressure and high stakes. And yet in truth it is difficult to get a real sense of that as you walk around the farm. The view across the Strathmore valley to the Sidlaw hills is gorgeous. The air smells of honest sweat and is filled with the electronic burble of unseen skylarks. The berries taste sweeter and juicier than their shop-bought kin. The fruit has the heat of the day in it, and something of the languid, erotic, narcotic quality of Edwin Morgan's poem Strawberries.

Within this bucolic setting, the polytunnels appear futuristic, alien. They protect the fruit from the cold and the rain, extending the growing season and improving the quality. It's quite trippy inside them – stifling, hushed; the only sounds are the drowsy drone of bees and music leaking from the iPods of the pickers.

Przemek Uzieblo, a 27-year-old in baseball cap and knee-pads, has downloaded a show from a Polish techno station and is listening to it through his phone. Others favour Macedonian metal, Bulgarian folk or the power ballads of Whitney Houston. Rusu Florin-Dragos, a 24-year-old Romanian student in a blue Nike T-shirt, has recorded his college lectures and listens to those as he works.

The farm employs 400 pickers, putting them up in caravans and cottages on site. Most are students, but you get entire families travelling 'to the berries'. There are picking dynasties. The Mazurs, the Bulas, the Zelkas, the Blazinskas. Mothers and daughters, husbands and wives, fathers and sons.

Inevitably, with so many young people living and working together so closely for so long, romances blossom. Last year, Jamie, one of the supervisors, learned Slovak specifically so that he could woo a beautiful young picker called Iveta. 'Working here,' says Fiona Caldow, the senior supervisor, 'you definitely don't need to watch soap operas.'

The pickers are suntanned and strong. Neither peely nor wally, they could never be mistaken for Scots. Some of the women have that solid, muscular, unstoppable look familiar from field athletes of the Soviet era.

There is a misconception that the industry employs so many eastern Europeans rather than locals because they will work for low wages. In fact, they earn at least the Scottish Agricultural Wages Board minimum of £5.96 per hour. There is the opportunity to make more than this, however, as workers get paid according to the weight of berries they pick. Anyone picking so few berries that they would, if paid by the kilo, earn less than minimum wage is likely to be sacked before too long as they are, in effect, costing the farmer money. The real reason so few Scots work as pickers, according to growers, is that they cannot or will not work fast enough to justify their employment. They find the work too hard or quit on the grounds that they would be better off on benefits. Scots, sad to say, are too soft to pick soft fruit.

It was not always thus. Raspberries have been grown

commercially in Scotland since the late 19th century, beginning right here in the Blairgowrie area. Indeed, Peter Thomson's family have been in the berry business since 1905. And for most of that time, the picking was done by Scots, especially Dundonians. It was part of the Dundee summer. Each morning, the so-called 'berry buses' would visit housing schemes, such as Fintry and Kirkton, and transport hundreds of local kids and adults to the berry fields of Blairgowrie, Alyth and Kirriemuir. Child labour laws mean that youngsters are no longer allowed to pick berries, but as recently as the 1970s, boys and girls were expected to do so in order to pay for their new school uniforms.

It was harder graft back then as well. New varieties of raspberry have been bred without thorns, but it used to be that your arms would get shredded at the rasps. And there were no polytunnels to keep you from getting burnt or soaked. Mind you, the rain was rather welcome as it would increase the weight of your raspberries and you'd get paid more. 'Another thing folk used to do for that was to piss in the pails,' says Christie.

Back then, with parents and children working together, it was a chance for poor families to earn much-needed extra income. The money is just as meaningful now for pickers from countries where wages are low. Sirbu Florin, a 30-year-old from the Romanian city Iasi, lies back in the sun during the half-hour lunch break, muscles flexing beneath his minotaur and magic mushroom tattoos, and explains why he is here. 'My country offers me nothing. I want to live better. In one month in Romania I could make £150.' He is in sales and marketing. 'Here, if you are a good picker, you can make £70-£80 a day. But you must concentrate. Just you, the strawberry, and nothing else.' After the berries, he is going tattie-howking.

The undisputed King of the Pickers is a 28-year-old Pole called Woijeich (pronounced Voy-check) Mucha.

The supervisors speak of him with a mixture of amusement and awe. 'Woijeich is a machine,' says Caldow of the man known as The Combine or The Fly. 'It doesn't matter whether it's strawberries or raspberries,' says Christie, 'he's the fastest at both. He just loves picking fruit.'

I catch up with Woijeich among the rasps. He is wearing a brown hoody and orange baseball cap. Attached to his thick leather belt is a slim blue rope tied at the other end to a metal sledge; he drags his trays of fruit behind him as he passes along the dreels. Christie said that good pickers have fast hands and fast eyes; Woijeich clearly has both these qualities and then some. He can fill a punnet in less than a minute. His hands are a blur as they plunge into the bushes. Watching him pick berries is like watching Ali fight, like watching Neo in The Matrix; he seems to exist in a different temporal plane. He once picked ninety trays of strawberries in one day. His record with raspberries is seventy. Most pickers are doing really well if they reach fifty. 'Sometimes I am faster,' he says, glaring at the bush as if it were his mortal foe. 'Today berries too much green.'

By the time I leave West Haugh Farm, it is late afternoon, the hour of sore backs and dry throats and cravings for cold beer. The berries picked today will soon be on sale throughout Britain. It is one of the sadnesses of supermarket logistics that a housewife in sultry Slough, selecting a piece of fruit from the fridge and biting into its cool tart flesh, will never know that it ripened to the sound of skylarks and Polish techno, and that a genius called Woijeich plucked it from the plant.

I'm glad I know. It's been a beautiful day. I'd like to remember these people, their stories and these strawberry fields forever.

Whatever Happened to the Castlemilk Lads?

IT is early 1963 and a group of schoolboys are standing on a green hill in Castlemilk, Europe's largest housing estate, having their photograph taken. They jostle in front of the camera, crowding into the frame, anxious to be in the picture. One stands on tip-toe, leans his chin on another's shoulder, and stares straight at the lens, defiant.

The photographer, a handsome young man, would stand out anywhere in Glasgow, but at more than six feet tall he towers over these youngsters. He must look curious to them – black beard, Russian hat, dark cape, eyes and hands that are never still. Nevertheless, he has an easy manner, asking about school and football.

The boy at the front, the one with sticky-up hair, is called Charlie. He supports Celtic, as does the photographer. Charlie has an interesting face – tough but vulnerable, with something in his eyes that suggests he has seen things in his thirteen years that no one of that age should witness. When the boy's gaze is snagged, suddenly, by something to his right, the photographer knows that this is the moment and takes the picture. Click.

Oscar Marzaroli died of cancer in 1988, and so it is impossible to know for sure what he felt when he first developed this photograph and saw the boys begin to materialise in the darkroom. We can guess, though, that he must have realised he had created something special.

He called his picture The Castlemilk Lads and it has become iconic, appearing in books and on the sleeve of Deacon Blue's Chocolate Girl single. The Scottish National

154

Portrait Gallery in Edinburgh uses the photo prominently in its advertising; Charlie's face hangs on a banner outside the grand sandstone building.

The faces of the boys, then, are famous, but they themselves remained unknown. Marzaroli did not take their names. He did not wish to intrude beyond taking the photograph. Yet, as the poet Edwin Morgan put it in 1984, 'It is impossible not to wonder what the Castlemilk Lads are like today'. And as the years have passed, this instinct has grown ever stronger. Are they alive? Have they had good lives? Whatever happened to the Castlemilk Lads?

* * *

Last year, I decided to find out. I put up posters around Castlemilk; forlorn notices of the sort one might make for a lost cat. One day a message was left on my phone by a woman called Emily. I think, she said, you are looking for my brother.

Charlie Gordon is 63. He lives with his wife in a suburb of Birmingham, a city that has been his home for the whole of his adult life. He left Scotland at eighteen and went down to England to work as a labourer. He had been involved with one of the Glasgow gangs, the Cumbie, and served short sentences for fighting. He never used a weapon, he says, but was once hit on the back of the head with an axe.

You would never know now, to meet Charlie, that he was involved in all that. He's friendly and funny, a grandfather five times over, a burly man with a Brummie accent, though sometimes, as he talks about the past, his native Glaswegian emerges. He had a heart attack in 1999 and his health hasn't been great since – 'Every day is a bonus for me' – but you can still see the wee boy in him. His silver hair still sticks up. He could never do anything with it. When he takes off his specs, it is possible to make out the small scar above his left eye, visible in Marzaroli's shot, which he got when he threw an empty cider bottle into a midden and it bounced back and cut him. 'I've got scars all over the place,' he says. 'You had to in those days, growing up in the Gorbals.'

He was born in 1949 and spent his early childhood living in the bottom flat of a tenement at 3 Inverkip Street, right by the Clyde, where the Central Mosque is now. Their home was near the John Begg whisky distillery. He remembers the barrels, the smell, the big dray horses, the neon sign that flashed into his bedroom all night – 'Take a peg of John Begg'.

Charlie's father was a busker. He would play the accordion round the pubs and then come home drunk and throw a bag of money on the floor. Charlie sometimes worked with his dad in Paddy's Market, selling old clothes out of a suitcase. 'We had hand-me-down clothes all the time,' he recalls. 'That's why I would never get rid of that coat I'm wearing in the photo. I got it bought for me, for either a birthday or Christmas, and it was the first brand-new thing I ever owned.'

When Charlie was around five or six, he saw his sister Catherine killed. Loads of local kids were out playing, as usual, by the buses parked across the road. But Catherine ran out between two buses and was hit by a lorry. 'When I looked at the ground I was in shock,' he says, 'because all you could see was her clothes. Everything was flat. I'll never forget it till the day I die.

'She was wearing this outfit that my mum knitted, a skirt with a big white stripe round it, and that's all you could see. I went to my mum and dad and they came running out – "Oh God!" Mum was in hysterics. It was terrible.'

What sort of effect has it had on him, losing his sister like that? 'What can I say? I mean, can you imagine coming out of your house and seeing the spot exactly where she died every day of your life until you moved? It does mentally affect you. You think, "If I could have stopped her ..."

Most of us had the sense not to run out. But she was only little. Three, four maybe. I've blanked it. The year, the date, everything. I didn't want it in my head.'

It must have been a relief to get away to Castlemilk. The family moved in 1959 as part of the massive slum-clearance programme, settling into a new home at 17 Downcraig Drive. Between 1961 and 1971, the population of the Gorbals and neighbouring Hutchestown fell from 45,000 to 19,000 as Victorian tenements were razed and teeming streets emptied, a pattern repeated in several other central districts. The Glasgow Corporation aimed to demolish 4,500 dwellings each year, replacing them with multi-stories, and homes in the new towns and on the vast new peripheral estates – Pollok, Castlemilk, Easterhouse and Drumchapel.

The families moving into their new homes, with their bathrooms and central heating, found them to be mansions in comparison to where they had come from. But it did not take long for problems to emerge, largely because of a lack of amenities and the distance of the estates from work. Too many people were jobless and bored. Newspaper articles from 1963 refer to Castlemilk as a 'concrete jungle' and a 'cemetery with lights' and report gang violence as a serious issue. The parents of three little boys, noted the Evening Citizen, were 'saving like mad to buy a house of their own, miles away from Castlemilk, because they don't want their children to grow up here'.

You can see something of this, perhaps, in Marzaroli's photograph, taken that same year. The multi-story being constructed in the background is possibly one of the Mitchelhill blocks, which were eventually demolished in 2005 – as part of an ongoing demolition of Glasgow's high flats, every blow-down a fresh admission of failure. There is, too, something in the tone of the photograph that seems to speak of struggle and anxiety.

We should be careful, though, not to clart the picture with

too thick a layer of our own angst. The Scottish National Portrait Gallery's guide to the photograph talks about a dislocated community inhabiting an unfriendly environment, a presumption that Peter Jackson finds insulting. 'Unfriendly enviornment?' he says. 'That's absolute rubbish. I was quite annoyed when I saw that. Flaming cheek.'

Peter is the second of the Castlemilk Lads, the boy leaning his chin on Charlie's shoulder. He's 62 now, married since 1971, with two children and a grandchild. He worked on the production line of a chemical company until his retirement in 2006, and spends three days a week caring for people with learning difficulties. He always seems to scowl in photos, he says, but wasn't the wee hard nut he looks in Marzaroli's picture.

He lives in Neilston, East Renfrewshire. At the time of the photo he stayed at 16 Raithburn Road, a first-floor flat. He moved to Castlemilk in 1959. He had been living with his paternal grandparents in Howard Street, diagonally across the Clyde from Charlie, but there was an electrical fire in the tenement and the family was moved to the new housing.

His grandparents looked after him because his mother had died of tuberculosis. His father was employed by the cleansing department and would come home with tons of stories and what were known as 'lucks' – broken toys that he had found in bins – and fix them up for the children.

'I still remember my mother,' says Peter. 'I've got vivid memories because she was ill for a long time. I remember going to visit her in hospital, my dad taking us. He would always kid on we were sneaking in, and say that we'd got to be quiet; he was making it a kind of game. My brother Richard was four years older, so he knew more than me. I just thought it was a big adventure. But the funny thing is I remember great laughter in the house when my mum and dad were there. I always remember it being a happy house.'

Peter's mother's illness, TB, is a point of connection with

Marzaroli. The photographer moved to Glasgow from Italy in the mid-1930s at the age of two, and worked in the family businesses – a café, grocer's and fish restaurant. When he was eighteen he developed tuberculosis and was bedridden for a year, gradually recovering his health in a sanatorium in Kingussie. This, according to his widow Anne, was a moment of 'catharsis'. He saw other patients dying and believed he could be next.

He began to read the great Russian authors – Tolstoy, Dostoevsky, Gogol, Gorsky – and through them developed an interest in becoming a social chronicler in his own way. This would involve a camera. It afforded him a chance to preserve moments that would soon be gone. For a young man who had felt the hand of death on his shoulder, the idea that life was fragile, fleeting and ought to be captured for posterity was powerful and pressing. So he began to take photographs.

Marzaroli earned his living as a documentary film-maker, working for Films of Scotland and the Highlands and Islands Development Board. Stills photography was a personal passion, and it was only late in his life that he began to be celebrated for his talents. His reputation as arguably Scotland's greatest post-war photographer has grown since his death.

He carried his camera with him at all times. It is said that he had 'magpie' eyes, always alert to the possibility of a photograph. He was patient, willing to linger until the light or some other aspect of the composition was right. This he called 'waiting for the magic'.

There are 55,000 negatives in his archive, of which only around 1,000 have been printed and published. Remark-ably, The Castlemilk Lads exists as just a single frame. On the contact sheet there are no other photographs of those boys. The same goes for Golden-Haired Lass, another of his most celebrated shots – a wee blonde girl in wellies trotting past the dark mouth of a Gorbals close.

Marzaroli took many, many pictures of the Gorbals: its closes and courts; its winos and workers and dirty-kneed weans in the streets. He photographed it at the precise moment when it was beginning to disappear, as the bull-dozers did their work. He shows lone tenements as islands in a sea of rubble. He shows the gigantic new tower blocks as a sort of concrete armada, an unstoppable invading force. 'I think what fascinated him about the Gorbals was the fact that it was being destroyed,' says his daughter, Marie Claire. 'He loved the community, he loved that whole idea of belonging. Because he was going back and forward to Italy, for a long time I don't think he felt he belonged anywhere. But Glasgow was where he belonged.'

Marie Claire was born in 1963, the eldest of Marzaroli's three daughters. His wife Anne often accompanied him when he was out taking pictures, but not when he took Castlemilk Lads as she was pregnant with Marie Claire. Marzaroli's many photographs of children may reflect the fact that he himself was starting a family at around this time.

What did he see when he photographed those boys that day? For what magic was he waiting? Perhaps it's some-thing to do with Charlie's clasped hands. The picture is a prayer of sorts. It feels aggressive but also plaintive. You might think you are looking at a gang. But it's not. Though these boys were classmates at Glenwood, they weren't really friends. Two years after the picture was taken they would leave school and lose contact with each other.

Robert Carnochan, he's the third boy; the one, a little out of focus, behind Peter. Robert still lives in Castlemilk. He is 61, has been married for 40 years, has two sons and three grandchildren. He worked as an engineer until a few years ago, when he was made redundant. Now he does maintenance work. He had a health scare in recent years, suffering from pancreatitis and was lucky to survive, but is much better now. He seems like a quiet and gentle man.

You can sort of understand, meeting him, why he's at the back of the photograph. 'Aye, I like the picture,' Robert says. 'Wish I was at the front, but.'

His dad was a plumber. His mum worked at the Co-op. They lived on Castlemilk Drive; Robert, his brother and sister. The family had come from Carnoustie Street in Tradeston, where they were pulling all the old houses down, and he had attended the Scotland Street school, designed by Charles Rennie Mackintosh, which is now a museum.

He moved to Castlemilk at around the age of five, in the mid-1950s, the early days of the estate. He remembers it as part countryside, part construction site, a frontier territory through which kids roamed in packs. He and his pals would steal apples and turnips from gardens, play at fighting, or venture into Burnside and explore the derelict cinema.

'I remember a lot of open spaces,' says Robert. 'I remember I got lost in the bluebell woods. I would have been eight or something like that. It was scary for a while. There was still a lot of building going on. That's how you got lost. You were in the middle of nowhere and there was no way to figure out your way home.'

It occurs to me, talking to Robert, that one day, not too many years in the future, there will be no-one left who remembers tenement life – the outside toilets and street games and tin baths in front of the fire – and the move to what must have seemed like another world. That exodus is still the dominant folk memory in Glasgow. But for how much longer? These Castlemilk lads, that generation, when they go, a whole era will fade like an old photo exposed to the sun.

* * *

It is the sixteenth of June 2012, and we are on that same hill where, so many years ago, Marzaroli photographed some pale and freckly boys. The lads are back in Castlemilk, posing in the rain for a recreation of the shot. Watching them are two of Marzaroli's daughters, Marie Claire and Nicola, and his widow Anne. 'Right hand over your left,' Anne tells Charlie. 'Don't smile. I'll hold your glasses.'

'You need to look more grumpy,' Marie Claire says to Peter.

'It's very difficult with false teeth, you know,' Peter replies.

The three talk about old times. About teachers and gangs and how Castlemilk has changed and whatever happened to so-and-so. They are glad to see each other. Though never close, they do have this strange bond in common. Plans are made to keep in touch.

Marie Claire explains to them that for many years she has had Castlemilk Lads on her living room wall; her children have grown up with it. One of her daughters, Rachael, wrote a school essay in which she admitted to being envious of the boys as they had met her grandfather and she had not. For Marie Claire, the photograph is about courage and pride and sticking together through adversity. 'It's a really important picture for us as a family,' she says. 'It gives me strength every day.'

Next year will be the 50th anniversary of Castlemilk Lads and the 25th anniversary of Marzaroli's death. There are plans for a new collection of photographs, an international touring exhibition and, a little further down the line, a permanent exhibition of his work in Glasgow. That, though, is the future. For now, it feels like enough to enjoy this remarkable reunion.

Marzaroli used to talk about waiting for the magic. Finally, on a green hill in Castlemilk, after almost half a century, it has arrived.

Jesus George

GEORGE Thomson the street preacher? I first caught sight of him at the Links Market in Kirkcaldy. He wore a long white beard in the Old Testament style and was carrying a sandwich board which denied the theory of evolution. He cut a lonely, sombre figure as he walked through the fairground, and his large placard – 'What profit to gain the world and lose your soul?' – bumped against the coloured lights strung beneath the awning of the hook-a-duck stall.

Although he stood out from the cheery crowd, he seemed to pass among them unnoticed. He attracted neither sympathy nor scorn. He was simply ignored. It was twilight, and the air smelled of burnt sugar as the preacher went silently on his way.

Almost five months later, on a bright September morning, I am standing outside George Thomson's home and looking up at the words 'Jesus Saves' written in block capitals on his green front door. Jesus Saves House, Burntisland – that was the address he had given me at the fair. The house was well known locally, he said. 'Just ask anyone where the Jesus Man lives and they'll point the way.' Some years ago there had been bother with the council; he had broken planning law by erecting a large wooden sign on the roof which read, 'Go and sin no more'. He was about to go to prison for non-payment of the fine when an anonymous benefactor stepped in and paid. The sign has since rotted away and he doesn't have the time to build another. He is too busy on the streets, 'finding people who have fallen into sin and dragging them back'.

He lives hand-to-mouth by doing a little gardening

work. A long time ago he was a farm labourer. At times during his life he has lived by faith alone. For a period in his thirties, he made his home in a graveyard and lived on foraged berries. 'I once ate deadly nightshade and it made me a little blind for a bit.'

Most of August and early September, he spends in Edinburgh, preaching to the Festival crowds. During winter he tours the university campuses – 'I love to meet students. The secondary schools are too dangerous. I've had dog dirt and stones thrown at me.' For the rest of the year, he takes the gospel to Dunfermline and Kirkcaldy.

'Preaching on the streets is different from preaching in a pulpit,' he says. 'It's got to be a short sharp message: "You're going to die one day. You're going to meet your maker. Are you ready?" They can hear that in just a few seconds as they pass by.'

At the Links Market, I had stopped him by a hot dog stall. He seemed taken aback and wary that someone wanted to talk. But it turned out that he had read an article I had written about the King James Bible, and in fact had posted copies of it to 34 friends around the world. He is precise about numbers. He explained that he was 73, that he had been 'saved' at 29, that he has seven grown children, and that he had spent the last forty years preaching the word of God in Scotland's towns and cities, most often being disregarded utterly, but sometimes finding a willing ear.

I have, for many years, been fascinated by street preachers, long-faced men in long black coats, calling down the fire and brimstone on pedestrian precincts as unheeding shoppers go to and fro, more interested in Selfridges than Sodom, Gap than Gomorrah. I've often wondered what it must be like to live that life. So would Mr Thomson be willing to have me visit him at home and accompany him on one of his trips into the city to preach? He would, on the understanding that before I ask any questions, we read together Chapter 15 of the Gospel of St Luke, the passage about the Prodigal Son. He also asked that I call him by his first name. To both conditions, George and Luke, I agreed.

We sit in the lounge and go through the text. The room has the quality of a cell: there is an alcove full of Bibles; the Ten Commandments hang above the unlit fire. The sun shines strongly through the window and on to George's face. His eyes are intensely blue; his sunken cheeks are cloaked by whiskers. It is the face of a desert hermit, a dissident in the salt-mines. After finishing with St Luke, he prays for the success of our day.

His preaching is not always a success. 'I've been attacked,' he explains. 'I was once headbutted by a man and my nose was bleeding badly. On another occasion, a drunk guy grabbed my guitar and smashed it on the pavement because I told him there will be no drunkards in Heaven. On the other hand, one day in Edinburgh I met a man who had been a Christian, but had been following the Devil's way, and wanted to know if God would take him back. When I told him the story of the Prodigal Son, he started to cry. So we kneeled down together on Princes Street and prayed.'

We take the train from Burntisland to Waverley, arriving around noon. Before leaving the station, George walks into the Victorian ticket hall with its ornate cupola. He always begins his day with a circuit of this hall, in each corner of which is a camera, so that whoever is watching on CCTV will get the benefit of the sign on his back – 'Jesus says love your enemies. Matthew, 5:44.'

Up on Princes Street, near the Scott Monument, he sets up his gear. He has a heavy wooden box, which he pulls on a trolley, painted with biblical texts and filled with religious tracts in around 200 languages from Arabic to Zulu. It would not do to accuse George of the sin of pride, but he certainly takes great pleasure in being able to provide travellers from pretty much anywhere in the world with a pamphlet informing them, in their own tongue, that they are in danger of going to hell.

'Are you Nigerian?' he asks. 'Do you speak Yoruba? Igbo?' Then he trots back to his box, fair delighted, and returns waving the appropriate sulphurous document.

He has chosen this spot because it is so busy and because the pavement is wide enough that he could not be accused of causing an obstruction. He has been lifted by the police a few times, but always considers this a great opportunity to preach to them. He is not giving a sermon today, simply handing out tracts and stopping people to talk; he would struggle to be heard over the traffic and the pipers.

For hours he stands and tries to engage people. Many take a tract and keep moving. Many ignore him completely. He is used to it. More than once, a party of sniggering tourists take his photo, but he either doesn't notice or doesn't care. Pinstriped businessmen are the group least likely to listen. Young men in hooded tops are the least respectful. One swaggers past shouting, 'Satan's coming!'

However, it is surprising just how many people do stop to talk. One young man, recently arrived from Dubai, prays with George in the street; his Muslim family, he says, do not know he is a Christian. The preacher is keen to convert Muslims, and hands a bundle of tracts to a party of smiling young Turkish women wearing hijab and carrying Jenners bags.

It is not uncommon for the public to treat the preacher as an unofficial tourist-guide. A middle-aged Australian couple walk over and say they are looking for the statue of Greyfriars Bobby. George gives them directions then seizes his opportunity – 'You're going to visit Greyfriars Bobby but where is your final destination?'

'Well,' says the man, 'We're staying in a B&B.'

'No,' says George. 'Your *final* destination.'

'Oh,' says the woman, understanding. 'We've got that sorted. We're Seventh-Day Adventists.'

Believers, it seems, love to chat. Francis Wong, a retired aircraft engineer, originally from Malaysia but now living in South Queensferry, is wearing an I Heart Jesus badge on his anorak. He says hello, then he and George have a long, animated conversation that consists largely of Bible citations. It is like listening to a pair of chess grandmasters talking their way through the strategies and moves of an important game.

'1 Corinthians, 1:18,' is Wong's opening gambit.

George counters with John, 3:3.

'Proverb!' yells Wong. 'Chapter 6! 16!' He punches the air.

Stand on Princes Street for long enough, and it's natural to develop an evangelist's eye. One needn't look far to see the lost. A young woman with opiate eyes, begging for money through front teeth rotted to brown shards, lifts her sweatshirt to show that she is pregnant. George walks over to a Scot in his early twenties, or perhaps younger, with a piercing through the bridge of his nose; the young man is high and ogling the preacher's signs. 'I like the way I'm living,' he laughs. 'I like to get fucked up. I like to get stoned all the time.'

George looks at him. 'Is that a good way to live? Do you want to go back to prison?'

'Wouldn't mind,' comes the reply. 'There's more drugs in there.'

After talking for a while, the preacher says goodbye and expresses hope that one day he will see the light.

'I don't think,' says the man, half defiant, half sad, 'I'll be seeing the light anytime soon.'

At four o'clock, George packs up his box and turns for home. It is a strange way to live your life, testifying to the power of God on a street that has no faith in the coming of the trams never mind in Judgement Day. Yet he does not seem discouraged and has no plans to stop, despite having exceeded his three score years and ten.

'No, no,' he says, sounding tired. 'There's no retiral in the Lord's work.'

A Day at the Peats

EARLY one morning in May, the Hebridean sky huge and blue, Norman Macleod and Peter Urpeth, two old pals from Lewis, are walking out on to the moor, tools slung over their shoulders, ready for another day at the peats.

We are a mile or so inland from the village of Back, in the north-east of the island. Norman, a wry, friendly 52-year-old in blue boilersuit and deerstalker, points out the highlights of the 360-degree view with proprietorial pride – the Cuillin, the Shiants, the pale peak of Stac Pollaidh. He also notes, nearer to hand, the deep brown scars in the landscape where, over the centuries, peat has been dug out.

To an outsider with no eye for it, the vast moors of Lewis can look like a bleak homogenous expanse, but to native families of longstanding they read as both personal and community histories, narratives carved with metal and muscle into the land. 'That peat bank was opened maybe 25 years ago,' says Norman, gesturing. 'My father opened it.'

Norman's father, Kenneth, died last year. He taught Norman how to cut peat. They worked together for many years. The two of them, in 1979, first opened the banks that Norman and Peter are cutting today. Kenneth Macleod was from a generation which relied on peat for fuel. They had to cut. They had no choice. In 1923, the summer was so wet that people couldn't get their peat for the winter, and they froze in their homes. Few could afford to buy coal. In those days, everyone cut peat. At one time there would have been almost seventy familes from Back alone out working on the moors. Now it's just four.

Slowly, though, it seems that folk are returning to the peats. The reason, once again, is partly economic – steeply rising prices are making keeping the house warm unaffordable for many in the Western Isles, an area with low levels of household income; in Lewis, there is no mains gas supply and much central heating is oil-fired. 'In 2001, oil was 19p a litre,' says Norman. 'The last time I bought some it was 70p a litre.'

The Western Isles have the highest rate of fuel poverty in Scotland; it is estimated that around 60 per cent of all households are affected, with many islanders, especially the elderly, being forced to make decisions between eating and heating. Against such an economic background, it is little wonder that being able to dig your winter fuel from the ground for free should become attractive. One cutter sums it up – 'If you're time-rich and money-poor this is a really good thing to do.'

So, while it would be overstatement to suggest that the moors of Lewis are as busy with peat-cutters as they were at one time, it is now quite common, as you drive across the island, to see the bend and rise of distant digging figures. It is becoming, once again, part of the sound and rhythm of the summer, a beat underpinning the fluid melody of the larks.

For Peter Urpeth, Norman Macleod's pal, peat-cutting is not just practical but a pleasure, too. He is 49, a writer and pianist, and though originally from Romford has lived on Lewis for 15 years, having married a local woman and raised a family. His wife grew up on a subsistence croft, and Peter was keen to pick up on her family's knowledge. Cutting the peats, for Peter, is a way to honour the tradition and, in a sense, dig his way into a community to which he is a relative newcomer. 'There's a practical reason I do this – for heat and hot water,' he says. 'But I'd do it even if I didn't need to.

'When you get your peats home and into a stack, to me

that's a better year end than Hogmanay. There's a real sense of having achieved something. I find it totally addictive, really. At the early stage of turfing, you are here on your own for a few days. You can be out for hours and hours and hours, and it's as if time doesn't exist. You feel very close to the place.'

Peter and Norman dig together. Peat-cutting, generally, is a two-person job. Peter cuts, Norman lifts. He uses a traditional cutting tool – the Gaelic word for it is tairsgeir, pronounced tarashker, which is about three feet long with a wooden shaft and angled steel blade. It is the approximate size and shape of an ice hockey stick. Peter inherited his tairsgeir from his father-in-law. It is thought that it was made many years ago by the late blacksmith Steallag Macleod, who died in 1972.

All Lewis blacksmiths, once upon a time, made small identifying marks that would allow a tairsgeir from, say, Ness to be distinguished from one forged in Stornoway. Steallag's was three dots on the top of the blade, a mark that his son Calum – also known as Steallag – still hammers into his tairsgeirs. Calum is, at the age of 77, the last blacksmith on Lewis making the traditional tools. 'At one time, I'd make about 100 in a year, but that dwindled a few years ago down to nearly nothing,' he says. 'Then, all of a sudden, the price of oil started going up and people started wanting them again.' He makes a few dozen in a year. 'If a tairsgeir is looked after it'll last a lifetime.'

Macleod has a smiddy in Stornoway – an extraordinary space from a distant age, brown as the moors, smelling of rust and ash and smoke. While the dawn streets are quiet, he likes to light the forge. Despite the intense heat from the flames, you can still see the breath clouding in front of his face as he bends over his anvil and beats a red-hot blade into shape. 'It warms me up in the morning,' he says, examining his finished work. 'That's it ready for work.'

The peat, as it is cut by the tairsgear, comes away in

slabs – known in Gaelic as fads – which are about a foot long, half a foot wide and three inches thick. They are wet and smooth and dark brown; the mind reaches irresistibly for comparisons with chocolate fudge cake. Inside, though, some fads are fibrous and orangey in colour; these fibres are known as calcas, and in the old days people would smoke them in lieu of tobacco. 'The poor man's fags,' is how one cutter puts it.

Peat is made from partially decomposed vegetation, mostly sphagnum moss, held in a waterlogged basin of land. Each millimetre in depth is reckoned to represent a year; so Norman Macleod's feet, as he bends to lift peat, are 1,000 years deeper than his hips.

The Western Isles have more than 145,000 hectares of blanket bog, of which approximately three quarters is in Lewis. It is an important biodiversity site. At one time, peatlands were common across much of Britain, but drainage for agriculture and industry, plus a move from peat to coal, gas and oil as preferred fuels, has meant that Lewis now, together with the Flow Country of Caithness and Sutherland, are the largest remaining landscapes of this type. There is evidence that peat has been used in the Outer Hebrides to make fire for millennia.

The timing and duration of the peat season is weather-dependent, but tends to begin in April with turfing – the removal of the first few mossy, heathery inches. Cutting proper begins in May. The cut fads, after a few weeks lying on the bank, are built up into piles known as rudhan, which resemble houses of cards. There they are left to dry and then brought home for stacking. This final gathering of the peats, in which family and neighbours muck in together, is often followed by a good meal and a few drams. The whole process from cutting to stacking can take three months.

As the peat has to last through an entire autumn and winter, the stacks outside Lewis homes tend to be large and are the approximate shape of an upturned boat. They stand out in the flat landscape, dark reflections of distant snow-capped peaks, such as Suliven, glimpsed across the Minch on the mainland. Peat stacks – the Gaelic is cruach – are part of the Hebridean aesthetic. Built to withstand an often tempestuous climate, they are also beautiful in their own way. 'A local guy 20 years ago actually tried to get a peat stack into the Tate,' one cutter recalls, 'and the gallery refused on the grounds that it wasn't art as it had a practical application.'

If one was seeking on Lewis for a man who could, truly, be said to be an artist of the peat stack, the search might well end with Donald Mackenzie from the village of Eoradale, in the community of Ness. The view from his croft shows, on one side, the house where, 77 years ago, he was born, and on the other side, a diminished but still impressive peat stack built according to a distinctive herringbone structure that recalls both the design of some Harris tweeds and the pattern left on island beaches at low tide.

Donald has been cutting peat since he was fourteen. His mother, he remembers, carried the fads on her back in a creel. He is reluctant to accept praise for the skill of his stacking, insisting that he builds in that way simply because it stops the stack from falling down.

He was, for much of his life, at sea – sailing cargo boats to Canada and New Zealand and working as a whaler in South Georgia. He also spent a number of years as a guga hunter – one of the men of Ness who, each year, sail from Lewis to the remote, uninhabited island of Sula Sgeir, there scaling guano-slick cliffs in pursuit of gannet chicks, a local delicacy. 'It's a wonder,' he laughs, 'I'm alive at all.'

His wife Katie thinks it's the sailor in him that makes him insist peat-cutting should be done just-so. Does he agree, then, that there is an art to stacking peat? 'There sure is,' he says. 'When I started, the old folk were very particular. If you didn't cut them properly, you got a good telling off.' He sighs. 'They're not so particular nowadays.'

On a moor not far from Eoradale, Calum Macdonald and his family are hard at work. Calum is 43 and works offshore, but always makes sure he is home around this time to cut peats for both his own family and his father-in-law. Joining him today are his wife Chrissie, their children, eight-year-old Ryan and six-year-old Kiera, and brother-in-law Coinneach. Earlier, before leaving for the moor, the kids were playing video games by the heat of the peat fire. Calum has been cutting peat since he was not much older than his son.

'I like to keep the traditional values alive,' he says. 'For me it's not really about the money. There's nothing better on a cold winter's night than to have a blazing peat fire and be sitting there with a dram or a glass of wine.'

Out on the moor, it is perfect cutting weather; sunny but with a bit of breeze to keep you cool. The land shimmers in a haze as the hot air above the land meets the cold air above the water. Over four hours, Calum and his family cut a length of peat bank 120 feet long by four feet deep. The proper rituals are observed: the first cut layer is thrown on to the top of the bank; the second laid along the edge in stacked diagonals, which give the bank a dragonish look; the third thrown out beyond the bottom of the bank. Peat banks are essentially heritable property, managed by the village grazing committees, and every crofter knows where his or her bank – or poll – is located; to cut someone else's peat without permission would be unthinkable.

Many of the banks have local names. Poll a'mhinisteir, for instance, is the bank of the minister, an area of the peats that at one time would have been cut for the manse as a form of tithe. 'Och,' says Chrissie as Calum wipes the peaty blade of his tairsgeir on the heather, 'that's a good day's work.'

The most significant benefit of peat-cutting, perhaps, beyond its immediate practical use, is that it keeps the islanders, who tend to live in coastal villages, in touch with the vast, wild interior of Lewis and therefore with their own pasts.

Dotted here and there on the moors are shielings, or airidhs, small stone or wood-and-metal dwellings that would have been built as temporary residences in the days when cattle were brought inland for summer grazing. These days, they tend to be used as weekend getaways for those with an appreciation for the moors, and as shelters during the cutting season. To walk among the cluster of shielings at Cuishader, in the north-west of Lewis, is a rather eerie feeling. Some are ramshackle, but obviously still in use, including one surreal presence – a converted 1940s bus, streaked with rust, which has somehow ended its days here, far from any road.

A little nearer the coast is an abandoned shieling, its turf roof collapsed inwards, fireplace choked with weeds; a Gaelic Bible, swollen with damp, falls open at the Book of Job, releasing a few woodlice that scuttle like shamed sinners for the dark corners of the room.

For Anne Campbell, a 50-year-old artist and crofter native to the village of Bragar, the peatland and shielings upon it have huge cultural importance and psychological resonance. For her, this place means as much to the people of Lewis as the Outback does to the Aboriginal peoples of Australia. It is a place of stories; family and village legends, and tales of the supernatural handed down – like a well-kept tairsgeir – through the generations.

Anne, following the example of her late father, always walks barefoot on the moor when going to the peats or visiting her shieling. She considers it an idyll in the spring, the quiet broken only by the wind in the heather and the whistling of the golden plover, which her mother used to say was singing, 'Samhradh cridheach, the e a' tighinn' – a hearty summer, it is coming.

'It's such a great feeling of freedom to be out, away from everything, getting your water from the loch and making your fire, and nothing around you but birds,' she says. 'The huge horizon lets you see for miles and miles and miles. It's a very contemplative landscape.

'I like being among our own peats and thinking about the different people – parents and aunties and uncles and grandparents – who I've cut with there, and the conversations I've had. As you're digging down through the peat, also you're going down through time.'

She pauses for a moment. 'Everything is still there. Everything is preserved in the peat.'

A Night at the Dogs

SHAWFIELD Stadium, like the ruins of ancient Rome, has a beauty that comes from decay. When the moon rises through the Glasgow gloaming and sits high and creamy above the dog track, the greyhounds aren't the only ones that feel like howling. There's a real melancholy magnificence to Shawfield. It would take a Percy Shelley or Chic Murray to hymn it properly.

The stadium opened in 1932, but the glory days, when it was quite common for tens of thousands to cram in, are over. I'd say salad days, but salads never featured prominently here, and the food outlets still run very much to pie and chips. It's Tuesday when I visit. 'You should've come Saturday, son,' says everybody. That's when they get the stag parties, works nights out, and casual punters keen to sink a few pints and maybe leave with a few quid more than when they came in.

But I wanted to be here through the week so I could meet the diehards and dug-daft men whose lives revolve around kennels and betting slips. There are perhaps 100 people here, scattered in pockets and clumps around the chilly main stand. About half of the stadium is closed off, the corrugated iron roof thick with rust, guttering hanging at angles; yellow runch weed thrusts itself from cracks on the stone terraces where crowds once stood and stamped and ground out roll-ups. It's as if someone designed Shawfield specifically to illustrate the old cliché about 'going to the dogs'. Though the stadium is still heaving each Scottish Derby day, most people tell me that greyhound racing is struggling to survive in Britain. This is the last place of

176

its type in Scotland, and there are only a few unregulated 'flapping' tracks left.

Shawfield is a remnant of the working class culture around which Glasgow constructed its self-image and projects itself to the world. The image, based on hardness and humour, was forged in places like this and the late Paddy's Market, in stale pubs and steel foundries, tower blocks and tenements, but that particular Glasgow is fading fast.

There are still those, though, for whom it is vivid. When one man, a 70-year-old called Harry, who used to be the manager of Central Station, sweeps a hand across the empty weed-choked terraces, it's clear that he can still see the men who used to come to Shawfield. 'When Benny Lynch fought here, the crowd was lined all the way to the Gorbals,' he says. 'And Clyde played here for many years too. Harry Haddock, he was one of their famous players.'

Harry, the punter not the Haddock, is a small man with a white moustache and baseball cap. He comes to Shawfield three times a week, which is every night it's open. Like most people here, he's suspicious of the press. 'Here's a newspaper man!' he exclaimed as I approached. 'What are you here to write about – animal cruelty?'

Assured that, no, that isn't the angle, he warmed up and started telling stories. Harry used to own a greyhound, and at night it slept on piles of paper from the tea factory where his daughter worked. The teabag paper was really soft and comfy for the dog, and its perforations meant that pee went right through. It seemed the very dab, but there was a snag. One night the greyhound licked the residue of tea from its bed and subsequently failed a dope test when it was found to have caffeine in its system, incurring a £500 fine.

Harry doesn't seem bitter, though. 'Oh aye,' he nods with a dignified air, 'there's a lot to be said for a night at the dogs. If you compare the cost of coming to the races to going to the football, this is much cheaper for entrance money, and you've a damn good chance of getting your money back by making little investments in the totalisator.'

The totalisator, or tote, is one of two methods of betting at Shawfield. It's a pool system which allows various types of wager. For example, you can go up to a tote booth and, for a stake as low as 25 pence, attempt to predict which dogs will place first, second and third; the amount paid out depends on the total amount wagered on any one race.

Alternatively, you can bet with the track bookmakers. They offer win-only wagers, and between each of the eight races are kept busy writing and adjusting the odds next to dogs' names on their boards. One of these bookies, Billy King, owns Shawfield and is very much master of his domain. He's a tall man with snow-white hair, bald on top, imperious in a fastened navy overcoat and neat tie. He takes money from the punters with quick, economical gestures and drops it into a big black leather bag of the sort GPs used to take on house calls. Shortly before each race, with moments left to bet, he shouts: '"Too late! Too late!" will be the cry.'

An alarm bell signals the start of the race, and there's a great rush out to the stand to watch the dogs run. In this quieter moment within the betting enclosure, one of the kennel hands approaches King on my behalf to request an audience, but he just sits back on his chair, legs crossed, and grimly shakes his head. It feels like being given the thumbs-down by Caesar in the Colosseum.

The bookie always wins, they say. But one man who won't accept that is Thomas Campbell, a professional gambler locally famous as Tommy Farmfoods or Tommy the Timer. He's 70 and comes to Shawfield three nights a week, an arrangement from which he has not deviated in half a century.

Tommy has a reputation for being the best judge of greyhounds in the place, even if he does say so himself. A small man in a herringbone greatcoat with a ruddy complexion and longish hair slicked back beneath a woolly hat, he stands by the finish line with a stopwatch, noting on a scrap of paper how long it takes certain dogs to reach particular points on the 480-metre track – 'I get third bend figures and that helps a lot'. He later feeds these results into a computer programme which detects patterns, and uses the information to make bets on the dogs' next races.

Growing up in Possilpark, he began gambling at nine years old when his father taught him how to put on lines with illegal street bookies. Now, in a Farmfoods carrier bag, he lugs around his reams of statistics, though most of it seems to be in his head too. He has a remarkable memory for dogs and numbers, and is pleased when I compliment him upon this. 'Well, I was top of my class at school,' he says. 'I've also played football against Alex Ferguson. I played for North Partick Athletic. Ferguson played for Govan Methodists. We beat them 2-1 that night and I scored a 20-yarder. He's a multi-millionaire the day. But I'm no' short of a bob or two, by the way.'

There are so many pedigree characters at Shawfield that one could almost forget about the dogs. But the races are worth watching, if only from an aesthetic point of view. The greyhounds are led out to the track by trainers looking scientist-like in white coats. As soon as the traps open, they shoot out, travelling at around 40mph after the rather disappointing electric hare, which resembles a pair of orange bloomers. The dogs kick sand up to about 10 feet in the air as they zoom past, their beauty blurred. They are clearly elite athletes and are treated as such by their trainers. William Reid, 48, who trains dogs in Wishaw with his identical twin brother, tells me that their greyhounds exercise on treadmills and in a swimming pool.

Most of the trainers and owners say there's no money in greyhounds now; you've got to love the dogs to bother staying in the game. But towards the end of the night, I meet someone who has enjoyed real success. Alex Brodie, a middle-aged man with engine oil on his hands, owns Crown Rover. Just over a year ago, he paid £4,000 for the dog; in July, Crown Rover won the Sunderland Grand Prix, bagging the £20,000 prize. 'I remember Martin Luther King had a dream,' says Brodie, who runs a bodyshop in Rutherglen. 'Well, my dream came true, the exact same as his.'

By quarter to ten, another race night is over at Shawfield. The bookies leave sharpish, and the dogs – eight of them winners, including the superbly named Lord Snooty – will soon be driven back to their kennels. It doesn't take long for the punters to head out into the dark, and I'm left wondering just how many nights like this greyhound racing has left. It seems sad and more than a little ironic that a sport based around one of the fastest animals on earth should be dying such a slow death.

The Cisco Kid Lives in Cumbernauld

I am living the fantasy of generations of Scottish women: Sydney Devine is singing just to me. 'I got a feeling called the bloo-hoo-ooz, oh Lord, since my baby said goodbye,' he croons down the phone from his home in Ayr. This intimate performance of Hank Williams's Lovesick Blues is to illustrate a point the 69-year-old performer wants to make about why country and western speaks profoundly to the Scottish psyche.

'It's the pathos,' he explains. 'The Scots have suffered oppression throughout their lives, so there's empathy there as country songs are often sad. Most are about lost love and loneliness, and I think that's why the music is so popular here.'

A few days later, at Glasgow's Pavilion Theatre, it becomes evident just how popular when Devine, in a toothpaste-white suit, performs a set of country classics for hundreds of fans, mostly female, many of whom are wearing pink glittery Stetsons. A lot of these women have been coming to this annual residency for thirty years and more.

During a cover of Jim Reeves's Welcome To My World, fans queue to hand Devine roses and receive a kiss. By the time he gets to Crying Time, a party of women in the royal box are throwing their underwear at him with admirable accuracy and, given its flimsiness, astonishing velocity.

Afterwards in the foyer, as Devine signs autographs, I speak to these fans. 'He has got my knickers in his left-hand pocket,' says Caroline Martin, a Helen Mirren lookalike from Paisley. 'They're lacy wi' wee green bows. Go and ask him.'

181

'He has still got ma red suspender belt from years ago,' says her pal Ann Henry, who is wearing specs and a tiara.

These Sydophiles burn with monotheistic passion, but the Scots as a people seem to have fallen for the genre rather than any individual performer, no matter how dazzling his breeks. According to an extensive survey carried out at music shops, concert halls and clubs, country and western is more popular in Scotland than in any other part of the UK.

If you're not into that music then its popularity may not be apparent. Scottish country goes twanging on, week after week, in social clubs and community centres, miners' welfares and masonic halls, without attracting much attention. The most recent issue of CMDS, the house magazine of the scene, lists 83 clubs, from Lerwick to Linwood to Langholm, Annan, Bo'ness and Coupar Angus.

The most famous country and western club in Scotland is the Grand Ole Opry in Glasgow. Located on Govan Road, the Opry has been going since 1974. It flourished in those early days because the drink was cheap, the welcome warm and nobody minded too much about the holes in the roof that, on rainy nights, necessitated the use of umbrellas on the dancefloor.

It's a stormy Friday when I visit, the neon sign distorted in the churning puddles. Inside, the punters are intent on wetting their whistles. A man in a Stetson and spurs asks for a double Tia Maria.

Behind the bar, there's a bumper sticker in red, white and blue that declares, 'If it ain't country, it ain't music'. Next to the whisky, another sticker says 'God made the Scots just a wee bit better'. A third, stuck above a box of Scampi Fries, proclaims, 'Old cowboys never die... they just smell that way.'

To reach the dancefloor, you walk downstairs past the DJ booth of Rowdy Yates, 56-year-old Ewen Graham, a small, round, balding man in a snazzy jumper of the sort that Noel Edmonds favoured during his House Party pomp. Rowdy Yates has been spinning discs here for 20 years, playing the music he fell in love with as a boy. 'I would have been about ten years old,' he recalls. 'Jim Reeves came on the radio singing He'll Have To Go and then Marty Robbins with El Paso, and that was it for me. I was a strange child. Everyone else was into The Beatles, and I'm listening to this stuff.'

There's a band onstage, Stealaway, two middle-aged guys in white shirts and black trousers. 'If you've got any special requests, don't bother askin' for them. We're no' daein' them,' says the singer. 'Only kidding. Here's a number by Ricky Nelson.'

By ten past eight, the first line dancers are doing their thing. Line dancing has caused a schism on the scene. The boom brought lots of new people to the clubs, but the majority weren't interested in country and western per se, and would request pop music with the appropriate beat. The craze has died down now, but there is still some ill-feeling. Hughie Price, a 68-year-old former paratrooper who dresses as a Wild West marshal and goes by the alias Niterider, has no time for these incomers. 'If you dropped a Polo mint on the floor, before it stopped bouncing there'd be three line dancers up giving it that,' he says, jigging sarcastically. 'They're not my favourite people.'

To make clear the emphasis of any given club, the listings section of CMDS magazine provides a key to the entertainment on offer: a number of asterisks indicates how much line dancing can be expected; an icon of a bandy-legged cowboy reaching for his revolvers means gunfighters are welcome.

The shootout is part of the Opry ritual. Every night after the raffle there is a fast-draw contest, in which entrants face each other on the dancefloor; their guns fire blanks and a small box between them detects who shoots first. Competitors often dress in full gunslinger gear. Tonight, these include Moira St Pierre, 63, who shoots as Linedancer, and Raymond Mackinnon, 59, an Irn-Bru-sipping vision in black known as Cisco. 'Just Cisco. Not the Cisco Kid,' a passing cowboy explains. 'The Cisco Kid lives in Cumbernauld.'

Only one gunfighter in the Opry goes without a nickname. Sandy Cummings, 72, wears a black Stetson and holds his bolo tie in place with a masonic clasp. It's a miracle he's here at all, having just returned following three blood transfusions. He seems to have had every illness going. A typical Sandy sentence begins, 'How I got my first hernia was...'

He has been a regular at the Opry for almost ten years. His wife died on the 31st December 2000, and the following Hogmanay, rather than let him mope around the house, a friend suggested he come here. He loved it, bought himself a revolver and never looked back.

Shooting comes naturally to him. He grew up in a travelling fair, learned to handle a weapon when he was seven, and had an act where he would strike a match by firing at it from some distance away. A stroke in recent years almost ended his fast-draw prospects, as his right side was paralysed, but he regained the use of his shooting hand and now is rarely without either a Colt 45 or bingo dauber on Friday evenings. 'I sit down on a chair for the gunfight, though,' he says. 'I can't stand. I've a bad corn.'

It's striking how many people at the Grand Ole Opry, like Sandy Cummings, have been widowed or have gone through a divorce. The things they have endured in their lives mirror the classic theme of country and western: heartbreak. Perhaps that's why the music is so popular in this country; the songs reflect the darkness of Scottish life. But the scene also offers the consoling pleasures of a drink, a dance and a damn good laugh.

Not that anyone at the Opry would put it that way. Ask what's good about the place and they'll tell you, 'There's never any need to send for the polis.' Essentially, it's a bit of harmless fun at the weekend. However, others on the Scottish scene take it much more seriously. Iain Grant, for instance. He is 58 and lives with his wife Catherine in a semi in Corstorphine, Edinburgh, with a bird-bath in the front garden and a conservatory out back. So far, so suburban. But Grant has a passion that sets him apart. 'You hear of people finding God, eh?' he says. 'Well, I found Wyatt Earp.'

Grant lives his life as a tribute to Earp, the iconic 19th-century lawman who took part in the gunfight at the OK Corral, arguably the most famous shootout of the Wild West era. Sitting in his living room, he cuts an anachronistic figure in his black Victorian clothes, silver star and Pa Broon moustache. Yet this is how he looks most of the time. The only exception is when he goes out to earn his living as a professional piper, at which point he wears the kilt. Otherwise, be it for a trip to Asda or his daughter's graduation ceremony, Grant dresses as Earp. He signs his e-mails 'The Old Marshal', his mobile plays The Magnificent Seven theme and when someone presses the doorbell, the recorded voice of Ian McShane yells out 'Welcome to fuckin' Deadwood!', which sets Molly the Westie barking.

'It's really not funny, Iain,' says Catherine when he demonstrates the doorbell. 'My mother comes in and says, "What did he say?" "Don't ask, mother, don't ask".'

Catherine, a retired teacher, has short silver hair and bright red nails. The Grants have been married for 33 years. She indulges his fascination with the Old West, accepts that he's an unorthodox person and has accompanied him on trips to Tombstone, Arizona, where he has been made an honorary citizen. However, she draws the line at dressing at all times in the Victorian clothes he buys for her and playing the part of Earp's lover, Mattie Blaylock. She is essentially a regular lady of middle years who enjoys reading magazines and watching Loose Women – and has found herself hitched to an obsessive. 'My friends think I put up with a lot,' she jokes. 'Apparently you can get an annulment if your husband turns out not to be the man you thought he was when you married. Well, I didn't know I was marrying bloody Wyatt Earp, did I?'

Grant's fascination with Earp began during his own childhood, in Leith, when his father bought him a toy version of the gun used by the marshal. However, it wasn't until 15 or so years ago that he decided to dedicate the rest of his life to the man. He struggles to understand exactly what it was that clicked inside, and won't allow himself to say that he is the reincarnation of Earp, though he has clearly given the matter some thought. Once, at a country and western night, a man approached Grant, introduced himself as 'a wee bit of a medium' and promptly 'threw a wobbly', lying shaking on the floor. Grant would like to try hypnotic regression, but his wife doesn't approve.

All of this makes him sound flakier than he appears. He's actually a very friendly and funny guy who is loving living this way. There's maybe a hint of melancholy to him, though. Does he never feel that Wyatt Earp has somehow squeezed Iain Grant out, that his own life has been lost? He nods. 'It's gone.'

And is that not a sad thing in some ways? 'Yeah,' he says. 'It does sometimes frighten me a wee bit.'

Spend enough time on the Scottish country scene and a distinction becomes clear. The men – it's mostly men – are not actually dressing up as cowboys; they're dressing up as themselves as children dressing up as cowboys. It all goes back to a period when Saturday mornings meant watching Roy Rogers at the pictures and then recreating the action on the green, green drying greens of home.

Nowhere is this clearer than in Tranquility, a Wild West town built lovingly by Alistair Baranowski, a former postmaster, in the garden of his home near Huntly, Aberdeenshire. Beaming with pride beneath his ten-gallon hat, the 56-year-old provides a guided tour of the town hall, saloon, jail, bank, general store, undertaker's and cemetery, all constructed from wood by Baranowski and his friends in the reenactment group Northern Rough Riders. On Sundays they get together to stage historical gunfights or scenes from Sergio Leone westerns. One might call these meets A Fistful of Doric.

'A dinna ken fit it wis,' says William Kidd, a 62-year-old known as Kansas Billy, when asked what draws him to the Wild West. 'But it always stuck in my mind fae when I wis a school kid. I remember wur teacher was asking everybody in class fit they wanted tae dae when they left school. I said I wanted to be a cowboy, and he just kinna laughed.'

Tranquility feels authentic. Baranowski has taken care to fit out the interior of his buildings with period-looking furnishings. So it's strange to glance out into the landscape and notice that the town is set, not in some dry frontier gulch, but amid fertile farmland. The sound of gunfire in the air comes from pheasant-shooting on a neighbouring estate.

Five Northern Rough Riders are here today, all retired or semi-retired, except Steve Ramsay, 45, alias Buck, who drives a bus for Stagecoach.

Alan McEwen, 60, hails from Macduff and calls himself Duke. 'Two years ago, I bought my wife a Winchester rifle for her Christmas,' he says. 'That's what she wanted. I've been collecting guns since I was, whit, 18, 19 years auld. I used to throw a couple of quid in a jeely jar and wait until I'd enough saved up.'

Lewis Shewan, 55, known as Dakota, is six foor four and built like Desperate Dan. He admits to having a 'small shrine' to John Wayne at home in Banff, and wears his holster, like the actor, on his right buttock rather than on his hip. 'I'm John Wayne daft,' he grins.

When considering why the Northern Rough Riders and

other Scots are so wild about the Wild West, it's possible to go deep. In the 19th century, thousands of Scots emmigrated to America, among them Highland cattle drovers who found work as what we now know as cowboys. It could be, then, that the weekend westerners from Glasgow, Corstorphine, Tranquility and elsewhere are merely responding to some sort of genetic calling which coils like gunsmoke through their DNA.

Or it could be a lot simpler than that. 'Ah think we're ah jist a bunch a big kids living a childhood dream,' smiles Kansas Billy, shortly before taking that famous wagon trail, the A96, back to Aberdeen. 'That's whit it is. That's whit it is.'

Val at the Crown and Anchor

ABOVE Aberdeen harbour, the sky is pink, chill and shrill with the cries of gulls. It is early evening and the lights are blazing on vast ships, named for Norse gods, which have voyaged here from Bergen, Lerwick and Copenhagen.

Hard by the harbour, on Regent Quay, is the Crown & Anchor, its frontage red and gold, a pub which has been washing salt from the throats of seafarers since the 19th century. Behind the pumps is Val Morrison, a barmaid there for 20 years. What the Statue of Liberty is to New York, Val is to Aberdeen – an awesome matriarch, the first and best woman the men see when they arrive back on dry land; in place of a tablet and torch she has a rolled-up copy of the Press and Journal which she uses to belt any drouthy sailor who gives her too much lip. 'She's like a mother to us,' says Daniel McKenzie, 26. 'Val kens every boat in the sea.'

Aged 61, standing five foot not much, with short bleached blonde hair and sparkling greeny-blue eyes, Val's name is known from Rockall to German Bight, Skudeneshavn to Singapore. There is many a mariner, tough as teak, who has stood green-faced on a pitching deck in the Forties and been comforted by the thought of Val doing Cilla Black at the karaoke.

To watch her work is extraordinary. The atmosphere in the pub when she arrives to start her shift fairly starts to crackle and spark. It is like a famous actor walking on to the stage for their nightly performance. She greets the men with profane warmth and a magpie cackle, accepting hugs and wisecracks as due tribute. She has a tongue of sharpened steel and a heart of molten gold. 'Hello, my dearie,' she says. 'Where have you been a' day, ye wee shite?' She is becoming well known, now, as the star of BBC Scotland's hit documentary series The Harbour, and was delighted the other day to be asked for an autograph in Asda. But as she says, 'Darlin', I was famous lang afore that.'

She takes drinks orders, of course – 'Whit are yous wantin'?' – but this question is a mere matter of form. She knows without being told what everyone needs. She has a tremendous memory for names, faces, boats and bevvy, though even she was taken aback one time when an entire Norwegian crew came through the door and ordered nineteen Fluffy Ducks – a cocktail of Guinness, Tia Maria, blackcurrant and Coke.

The oil industry has an international workforce, which means the Crown & Anchor is arguably Scotland's most cosmopolitan pub. You are more likely to hear 'Skål!' than 'Slàinte!' when a glass is raised. Norwegians, I'm told, can be daft laddies on the drink; Poles and Latvians always want the strongest lager; vodka and Coke, as served here, often arrives in separate glasses of spirit and mixer, according to Scandic custom. James, a Catalan sailor, meets with Val's approval when he downs the dregs of his pal's pint before letting the barmaid take it away. 'You,' she beams at his thrift, 'are getting more like an Aberdonian every day.'

This is, largely, a man's pub. The captain of the darts team, Angela, is a woman. But other than Angela, the female of the species is represented this evening by Joan, who sits at the bar reading erotica on her phone while her husband, Ian, leaving soon for Korea, knocks back shorts and reminisces with Val about the grand times they've had. 'Fa was it,' she asks, lost in a fond memory, 'I chased along the street with the brush one night?'

Over at one of the tables, a retired engineer, Bjørn

Eikejet, is drinking whisky and ice with his friend, Svenn Varaberg. The pair meet here once a week before strolling along to the Norwegian Seamen's Service to read newspapers and watch telly in their native language. 'I have to tell you a story about Val...' says Bjørn. Apparently, he had spent time working out of Aberdeen during the 1980s and became sweet on a local girl, Janette. But then work took him away. He was gone for 13 years. On his first night back ashore he, naturally, popped into the Crown & Anchor. There he told Val about the girl he had loved and lost. Val, of course, wasted no time in fetching down the phone book and calling her up. Her match-making skills must be formidable, as Bjørn and Janette have been together for years now and he has settled down in Aberdeen.

Ari, a Finnish engine fitter working on a Danish ship, sips lager and explains that he is recently returned from a job in Newfoundland towing icebergs away from oil rigs. Tomorrow he is off to Shetland. This is his first time in the Crown & Anchor in three months. Val gives him a welcoming embrace. Another of her boys home safe.

'Ari,' she asks. 'Another drink?'

'Of course,' he shrugs. 'I am from Finland.'

He goes over to the jukebox. 'Ari,' says Val. 'If you don't put on Willie Nelson, you're dead.'

'No, please,' he begs. 'I want Whitesnake.'

The Crown & Anchor is a snug pub with dark wood panelling and nautical touches. A model of HMS Victory, which Val found in a charity shop, sits at full sail above a fridge. The brass bell for last orders is rung by a rope in the shape of an anchor. At one time, Aberdeen's quayside was full of such 'crew bars' busy with seafarers, but now there's just here and the Fittie along the road. A widespread zero tolerance policy on alcohol within commercial shipping and the oil industry has holed pubs like this below the waterline.

Val is in love with ships and the men who work in them.

191

Watching the light and shadow drift across the frosted glass windows, she knows when a boat is entering or leaving the harbour, and takes great delight in being able to name which one. She can tell different vessels by the noise of their engines, she claims, or the vibrations on the floor of the pub. 'It'll either be the Normand Neptune, the Highland Valour, the Mariner Sea or the Vos,' she predicts, sending Ian out the door to check. 'The Highland Valour?' she says when he returns. 'Yes!'

Away from the pub, at home in Torrie, she goes online to track the progress of ships she knows, sending emails to regulars to wish them safety in storms, and letting Jill the landlady know when such-a-such a boat is on its way back into harbour so she can stock up on the favourite drink of the returning crew.

Somewhat ironically, Val herself is both a teetotaler and committed land-lubber. She once took a trip to the Faroes, where she had been invited as a dignitary by islanders grateful for her hospitality, but the long rough voyage put her off for good. She sometimes boards ship to share a cuppa with the skipper but never now leaves the harbour. Neither does she go on holiday. The world, she figures, comes to her, so why bother? Anyway, she would miss the Crown & Anchor.

'This pub,' she says, 'is my life. It's like a safe haven. There's always laughs and jokes. It boosts your spirit. I was very ill last year with an operation that went wrong. But coming in here and speaking with the guys was my road to recovery.'

The men who drink here call her 'Ma'. She has had a difficult relationship with her own son and thinks that her care for the punters is, perhaps, a way of making up for that. One young lad tells me that, following an injury he sustained while recovering a dying man who had fallen from an oil rig into the sea, it was to Val, not his wife, that he unburdened his feelings. She is also a dab hand at sensitive relationship advice. 'You've no chance, darlin,'' she tells one man who has his eye on the captain of the darts team. 'She's seen mair sex appeal in a chip. And she disnae like chips.'

Val has been known to loan money to men for drink. Also, she has taken huge sums away from flush riggers, to keep them from spending all their pay at the lapdancing, and given it back to them the following day when they returned, hungover and contrite, to the pub.

She has, too, a tremendous knack of throwing men out without them realising they're being thrown out. 'Come on, dearie,' she says to one hulking drinker who had been growing rowdy, 'you and me are goin' awa.' Popping an egg piece in his gob to deter argument, she takes his hand and gentles him out the door. He goes meekly and at once, grateful for the sandwich, like a bairn led to bed.

It is approaching closing time. Last orders. Bobby Darin, on the jukebox, sings Beyond The Sea. Darts thwock, pool balls click. The drinkers, by this time, are a mere rump – a few Scots, three Danes, a lone Spaniard. Val will get away home soon for a few hours' sleep and then be back the following morning to open up and start the weekend. You Are My World. That's her song at the Saturday night karaoke. This pub is Val's world. We just drink in it.

Fox Hunting

IT is a beautiful late autumn day in Selkirkshire. From hilly farmland near the village of Lilliesleaf one can look across several miles of green countryside towards the rolling Cheviots that mark the border with England. A shaft of sunlight slants down through the clouds, falling on a distant field and picking out a figure on horseback, a man in a scarlet coat galloping after a pack of hounds and followed by a dozen or so riders. The urgent, staccato sound of a horn carries quite clearly through the mild morning air and confirms that this is indeed a fox hunt.

This classic rural scene, familiar from a thousand paintings on the walls of country pubs, might be taking place a decade or even a century ago. Yet this is November, 2011, almost ten years after a law was passed that, most people believe, banned the blood-sport forever. In fact, fox hunters – in a wily move reminiscent of their cunning, jinking quarry – have survived the politicians' attempts to exterminate their way of life and are thriving in 21st-century Scotland.

'Hunting is not,' as one female rider observes, 'something people round here would ever give up lightly.'

Indeed. Of Scotland's ten mounted hunts, five are based in the Borders and one in Dumfriesshire. This is, in part, a quirk of topography – the landscape of southern Scotland offering plenty of open, relatively flat countryside, ideal for hunting on horseback. But there is also, one might hazard, a psychological dimension to the enduring pursuit of the fox in these parts. Folk here are thrawn.

Just look at the continuing popularity of the Common

Ridings, those great annual equestrian celebrations of community that take place in many Borders towns; they are an
expression of the same local taste for costumed ritual and
deep immersion in landscape. The important thing is that
they endure.

Cancellation of a Common Riding would be unthinkable. And so it is with fox hunting. It too has 'aye been'
– well, for a couple of centuries, anyway – and has carried
on because hunters have found a way to do so within the
law, but also because resistance to change is a quality
Borderers imbibe with mothers' milk.

The Protection of Wild Mammals (Scotland) Act was
passed – in the teeth of furious opposition led by the Scottish Countryside Alliance – on 13 February, 2002. The
legislation outlawed the hunting of wild mammals with
dogs, but made some exceptions. It is legal to use dogs
to flush a fox from cover in order for it to then be shot,
so long as this is done as a form of pest-control. The act
further states that no offence is committed if the dog kills
the fox during the course of this activity, in other words
if it was not the intention of the huntsman that the dogs
should do so.

These loopholes have allowed fox hunting to continue
in Scotland. Hunts now present themselves as pest-control
operations offering a service to farmers. The packs of
hounds, followed by riders, chase the fox towards waiting gunmen who attempt to shoot it. If the fox is killed
by the hounds before it runs towards the guns then that
is regarded as an accident and therefore within the law.
Hounds are also used to kill foxes that have been wounded
by the gunmen or are otherwise seriously injured or
diseased. Once the fox is dead, either by bite or shotgun
pellets, the hounds still sometimes chew on it.

Trevor Adams, huntsman with the Duke of Buccleuch's
Hunt for the last 23 years, suggests that of all the foxes
killed by his hunt, one third are dispatched by hounds.

However, as a result of the introduction of guns, many more are now killed than before the change in law; in the case of the Buccleuch, it is thought that up to three times as many foxes now die in a season. This means that roughly the same number of foxes are being killed by hounds as before the ban, and there is no reason to believe that the Buccleuch is unrepresentative. Indeed, the protocol on how to hunt foxes within the new law was developed by the Buccleuch and endorsed by the Master of Fox Hounds Association, the governing body for fox hunting in the UK. The new approach was then tested in court when, in 2004, Trevor Adams became the first person to be prosecuted and the first to be acquitted under the new law. The huntsman is 'majorly proud' of the role he has played. As he puts it. 'I'd love my gravestone to say, "Here lies Adams. He was the saviour of fox hunting in Scotland."'

The Duke of Buccleuch's hunt is the largest in Scotland, covering a huge area from west of Hawick to east of Kelso, from the foothills of the Cheviots to the bottom of the Lammermuirs. It was founded in 1827 and hunts three days a week within the season, from the end of August until mid-March. On November the ninth, at a little after 10.30 am, over 40 members of the hunt are gathered at Newhouse Farm, near Lilliesleaf, preparing to move off. First, though, there is the matter of the Stirrup Cup, the traditional pre-hunt drink.

Gloved hands reach down from horseback to accept plastic cups of port or whisky served from silver trays. Stomach-lining is provided by trays of sausages and home-made fruit cake. Some find it helpful to have a small stiffener as an aid to leaping fences. In the section of the Buccleuch website dedicated to dress code, hunters are advised not to forget their hip flasks. Sloe gin is, apparently, the favoured tipple.

Most of today's riders are dressed in the subdued tweeds known as 'ratcatcher'. The Buccleuch hunt made a decision to stop wearing red jackets following the introduction of the new law in 2002 as a visible sign of change. Only the three men running the hunt – the huntsman Trevor Adams, the field-master and the whipper-in – continue to wear the traditional dress, mostly because it makes them easier to see. The idea that these red jackets are called 'hunting pink' is scoffed at as a wrongheaded townie notion.

'Townie' – meaning one who lives in the urban sprawl – is a disdainful term in common use among the hunters who consider that the ban was an injustice imposed on them by a political intelligentsia that has no empathy with rural Scotland. 'It was done by people who don't know anything about the countryside,' says Anne Brydon, who at 78 is in her 69th season riding with the Buccleuch. 'They are ignorant. They are townies.'

Tony Blair, in his memoir, claimed the hunting ban of 2004 – which changed the law in England and Wales – was one of his main regrets of his time as Prime Minister, writing: 'I didn't feel how, for fox hunters, this was part of their way of life'. Had he wanted to do so, he could have done worse than spend the day with the Buccleuch. There is no doubt this is a ritual that devotees feel in their bones. Foxhound aficionados talk admiringly about the intricately plotted bloodlines of their pack, and there is something similar among the riders themselves; they often come from long-established hunting families and go on to sire further generations of enthusiasts. 'We are hunters,' explains one member of the Buccleuch. 'We've got a hunting gene.'

Take, for instance, today's host, Marjorie Hepburne-Scott, whose farm this is. Her late husband Francis died last year just a few days shy of his 90th birthday. Hepburne-Scott's father had hunted with the Buccleuch, and her husband was at one time chairman of the hunt, so by providing hospitality and access to the land, his widow feels she is carrying on a tradition her husband adored. 'He is buried up among those trees,' she says, pointing up the hill. 'Francis had been hunting since he was a small boy of six. He was blooded.'

Blooding – the quasi-baptismal ritual of smearing blood from the dead fox on the face of a newcomer to the hunt, often a child, has been long since abandoned, though sometimes still the fox's brush is cured and presented as a trophy to an initiate. Given these rather grisly practices, it is surprising to hear hunters express admiration and even affection for foxes. Yet such comments are widespread.

'The fox is probably my favourite animal,' says Trevor Adams. 'It's one of those things that you so struggle to explain. My father would rather shoot a human than a fox. The fox is king and the world without him would be a much poorer place.'

Adams is a stocky Englishman of 53, quietly authoritative, with silver hair and pale blue eyes, the son of a dry-stone waller; his red coat has five brass buttons each bearing the Buccleuch crest. What is it about the fox that he particularly likes? 'Well, of course, he provides me with all the fun in my life. So I admire him for that.'

But if Adams wasn't a professional huntsman? How would he feel about the fox then? 'I would still love him. A marvellous mammal. My worst road trip is when I see a fox run over because it is such a waste. Yet I am employed in the destruction of them. All of this is going to sound contradictory. They deserve a good end. We shoot foxes because we have to. The parliamentarians made us do that. That's not me doing it out of choice. I'm doing it to stay within the law.'

Surely, though, shooting is a quicker and less cruel end than being killed by dogs? 'Well, I would think that if the fox had the vote, he would prefer the older way when he was pitched against his wits to get away from the hounds rather than having some lead pumped through his heart.'

Shooting foxes was regarded, pre-ban, as rather improper. The practice had a name that made it sound like a crime

– vulpicide. Even now, among hunting people, the feeling of distaste lingers. John Cook, the senior 'terrier man' with the Buccleuch, is one of two men responsible for shooting foxes during today's hunt. He is tall and ruddy-cheeked, wearing camouflage clothing and a deerstalker cap. He makes no secret of the fact that the task is not to his liking, and explains that healthy foxes are now being shot, whereas before the hounds would pick off the weakest and the strongest might well escape. Crouching over the corpse of a fox he has killed, its muzzle bloody and tongue lolling, he speaks regretfully: 'They really don't have a chance.' Later, his wife Frances says: 'Oh, he hates it. It's so unfair.'

The Buccleuch Hunt has a membership of around 150, the majority of whom are mounted; the remainder follow the hunt on foot. Riders pay subscriptions ranging from £300 to £1,000 per season, depending on how many days they intend to hunt. One might pay £5,000 for a horse, £150 each week for stabling, plus additional costs for equipment, clothes, transport, and for the farrier. It isn't cheap, and certainly still attracts the expected share of blue-bloods. The hunt essentially belongs to the Duke of Buccleuch, the UK's biggest landowner, and it is no surprise to see the Duchess of Roxburgh go trotting by on a white horse, or to notice one of the foot followers tip his cap to her. Most of the riders to whom I am introduced describe themselves as farmers. There are, apparently, increasing numbers of white-collar professionals living in Edinburgh who travel down to the Borders to hunt at weekends, but even in those cases the majority have come from hunting families. It is a way of life into which one is born.

Emma McCallum, 39, was brought up in one such family and is now raising her own. She has children aged seven and nine and has encouraged them to hunt with the Buccleuch, believing it teaches independence and confidence. She worries about them falling and getting injured, but is against wrapping children in cotton wool.

Fox hunting, for McCallum, is 'escapism from real life. There's an adrenalin rush. There are a few times I've had a fence in front of me and thought, "Should I? Shouldn't I?" But when your blood's up and the hounds are running in front of you, you want to keep up and watch them. Some people need a bit of fear in their life, and it does give you that. Many times you find yourself shaking and think, "God, did I really jump that?" You get home in the evening on a high because you've frightened yourself a little bit. When you are hunting every week, it is like an addiction.'

Unquestionably, fox hunting is risky. The 61-year-old chairman of the Buccleuch, Allan Murray, is currently recovering from a bad fall in which he broke eight bones, including a shoulder and four ribs, and punctured a lung. The late ninth Duke of Buccleuch, who died in 2007, broke his back in a hunting accident in the early 1970s and was in a wheelchair for the rest of his life; this Trevor Adams describes as 'the ultimate sacrifice'.

Fox hunting is a minority interest. It is estimated that there are somewhere between 1,000 and 1,500 mounted followers in Scotland. That's very few considering the Scottish parliament spent almost three years discussing the issue. Given that the vast majority of the Scottish population have no connection with fox hunting and will probably never see it in real life, it is difficult, perhaps, for most of us to understand the appeal in attempting to kill an animal for sport.

Make no mistake, though fox hunting is presented as a form of pest control, few if any of the riders with the Buccleuch – or, surely, with the other hunts – pay their annual subscriptions because they want to help farmers protect their hens. Trevor Adams is quite open about it. 'We are very definitely in the entertainment business,' he says.

For some, the so-called 'thrusters', that entertainment comes from riding hard and jumping fences. For others, the real appeal is the hounds, especially the sound they make when they scent a fox. This is known as 'speaking' or 'giving tongue' and is a fetish among hunters. 'When they are in full cry it's an amazing sound, especially if it's echoing in a wood,' says Eric Paxton, the 54-year-old former Kelso and Scotland rugby player, who works as an agricultural engineer and hunt with the Buccleuch. 'I played in the final of the Melrose Sevens twelve times, and it is the same sort of noise and feeling.'

Johnny Richardson, the 19-year-old whipper-in, has hounds speaking as his mobile ringtone. 'When they are absolutely screaming, you turn into an animal,' he says. 'I can't describe it. It just puts you into a different world.'

One of Richardson's jobs is to feed the hounds their daily ration of horse flesh, and though there are 70 animals in the pack, mainly bitches, he knows each by name. During a hunt, he carries a white whip which he uses as a way of showing the hounds the direction in which he wants them to move. They are never actually struck, he explains, looking horrified at the thought. The job title 'whipper-in' is the origin of 'whip' used in its political sense – in both cases, it's about keeping a group in line.

Richardson is from Kirkby Lonsdale in Cumbria. It is his ambition to one day become a huntsman and carry the horn, just like Trevor Adams and like his own father. The first time he went out hunting was while inside his pregnant mother. It is something he has done all his life. He worked as whipper-in for his father from the age of nine. This job is, for him, deeply important and profound. He has grown up with the ban, and moved to Scotland in part because hunting north of the border is closer to what it was like in the old days.

What was it about hunting before the ban that was better, in his view? 'Well,' he replies, 'you were obviously allowed to conclude a hunt by letting the hounds kill a fox.'

And what was better about that? 'The hounds hunted a

lot better than they do nowadays because when they kill a fox that's all their Christmases and birthdays at once. They absolutely love it. It's the natural way for them. Because they knew they were going to get one, it made them hunt that much harder, the voice would be a lot stronger, and it would be so much more exciting. You went a lot further in those days as well. You found a fox and it'd run a hell of a lot further. Back then the hounds would have gone twenty miles easily.'

So there was a greater intensity perhaps? 'Yeah, that's just the word. I wish I could go back to that. But I still think there's quite a good future in it. Hopefully the new government in England will do something.'

In England and Wales, foxes can be hunted as a form of pest-control but no more than two hounds can be used. Thus, the thrill of galloping after a pack has been removed. The Buccleuch, by contrast, works with around 25 hounds at a time, or to use hunting's curious arithmetic, twelve and a half couple. Fox hunters in Scotland are no longer lobbying for a change in the law. They are grumblingly content with the present situation and consider it unlikely that a Holyrood vote would go their way. Scottish hunters say they would not cross the line and start allowing the hounds to catch the fox, as they are worried that if they were caught doing so, the Scottish Parliament might decide to outlaw their sport entirely.

At present, fox hunting in Scotland is not policed. Lothian and Borders Police would respond to any complaints of law-breaking, but there are no officers out there making sure that foxes are shot rather than killed by hounds. Neither do there seem to be many hunt saboteurs – known as 'antis' – monitoring what is happening. For all the political and media attention given to fox hunting in the run-up to the ban, almost a decade on, as the huntsman flashes scarlet through the fields and woods, he does so largely unobserved.

During the day I spend with the Buccleuch Hunt, only one fox is killed. A second is shot but escapes wounded into woods at the side of the A7, pursued by the pack screaming across the road in full cry. It seeks refuge in a badger sett, where, because of the legislation that protects badgers, the hunt must leave it alone even though it may die from its injuries.

One, possibly two deaths, then, but fox hunting itself is in seemingly rude health. Whatever you think of it, whether morally repugnant or a splendid tradition, it would seem that this is the sport they couldn't kill.

'The antis won the battle,' says Allan Murray, chairman of the Buccleuch, with evident satisfaction, 'but they haven't won the war.'

The Lodging House Mission

'SEE if it wisnae for this place?' says Trisha. 'I'd probably be dead the noo.'

Trisha is 36 with long blonde hair and pale blue eyes. She is about double the weight she was two years ago, when she was a ghost in the grip of a drug addiction. Now, she takes methadone, the heroin substitute, eats regular meals, and stays away from the narcotic temptations of the streets – all of which is made possible by her attendance, most days, at the Lodging House Mission.

The Lodging House Mission is at 35 East Campbell Street in the Calton area of Glasgow. It is a 19th century Italianate church building which would once have been grand but is now rather faded. You'll find it near the Barrowland Ballroom. Shortly before 8am, when the Mission opens, there are already a few men sitting on the steps outside, woolly hats pulled low, wanting in out the cold for breakfast. This is one of the three big charity centres – the old-fashioned term would be 'soup kitchen' – offering shelter and nourishment to the city's homeless and vulnerable. 'At the height of the great depression we served 34,000 lunches a year, and last year we served 32,000,' says the manager Neil Watton. 'So that tells its own story.'

Stories are the one thing people here have in abundance. Everyone has a tale to tell. The man who escaped from a PoW camp in Italy. The guy who stabbed his father with a potato peeler, and, stealing a dead man's identity, fled abroad. Soon, hearing all this, you are immersed in drama and sadness. Alex, a 47-year-old in a baseball cap, recalls that when he and his elder brother were both kids, just six and seven, an old wall fell on them while they were out playing. His brother threw himself on top of Alex, saving his life and losing his own. The family flitted from Maryhill to Easterhouse, trying to outrun the bad memories, but you feel that Alex has never quite been able to get away. He does not keep well, and has been homeless, and though he now has a tenancy in Broomhill, he still comes to the Mission four days a week because the alternative – 'sitting in the house, demented' – does not appeal. He comes for the company.

There is a strong sense that this is a community, even a kind of family, made up of people who, very often, feel they have been rejected by wider society and their own kin. The main hall is large and bright with striplights. A tapestry at the far end says, 'Lord, let Glasgow flourish by the preaching of thy word'. A menu penned on a whiteboard offers mince and tatties for 75p, sponge and custard for 35p. Soup, tea and coffee are free. Folk sit on plastic chairs at wooden tables. Some keep to themselves and keep their eyes on their plates. Others play cards or chat. It is noisy, busy and upbeat, a social club for the socially excluded.

Though food is the draw, this is much more than a soup kitchen. Classes are offered in a wide range of subjects including art and literacy. Attempts are made to get people into college and work. Fourteen people from the Mission, including Trisha, sang at the Royal Opera House in Covent Garden as part of the Olympics festival. The idea, with all of this, is to build structure back into lives which, for a long time, have had none. Not everyone can be saved, of course. The Mission memorial book is full of short tributes to short lives; the words 'suddenly' and 'untimely' occur again and again. This old man drank himself to death; this young man shot up heroin contaminated with anthrax.

Few who use this place call it the Mission. It is known as Trotter's, after John Trotter, who was chaplain between 1958 and 1977. The street has a long memory. The main hall smells strongly of cooking and vaguely of disinfectant. Some of the younger men have the blank, heavy-lidded eyes that indicate they have scored heroin or valium.

Most appear peaceful enough, but you can't always tell by appearance. One small, gaunt man in his sixties comes through the door in a suit, tie and neat tan overcoat. This is him back after a three-month sentence for assaulting a member of staff. He's always on the wind-up, calling the younger guys junkies, picking fights like picking scabs. 'He's awright when he's sober,' says Neil Watton, 'but see if he has a couple of drinks? Bedlam.'

Not everyone conforms to intoxicated type. Take Kit. He doesn't seem to care for the word homeless, preferring to call himself a pilgrim. A Christian and an aesthete, he can often be found upstairs playing Chopin's piano works to the empty pews, playing from an old green-bound book of scores he bought second-hand for a pound. Kit is 46, originally from the north of Thailand. He has degrees in electrical engineering and computer science, but struggled to find work. He was raised as a Buddhist but had a conversion experience while reading Les Misérables high in a tower block in Manchester while suffering from disappointment in love. He found himself weeping on his knees. Since then he has walked everywhere – the Pennine Way, the West Highland Way, across Glasgow every day, glorying God as he walks. He is living in a hostel and teaching himself Hebrew, Sanskrit and Ancient Greek. The Mission is far from his home. 'But this is also home,' he says.

The Mission is the busiest place of its sort in the city, and most likely the busiest in Scotland. They get about 150 people coming through the door every day, up from 100 just a couple of years ago. There are thought to be around 7,000 homeless people in Glasgow, around a fifth of the total Scottish number. Government statistics show that the numbers of homeless are falling, and yet the Lodging House Mission and other similar places are all experiencing sharp rises in demand as the recession bites. The needy are getting needier and there are more of them all the time.

Homelessness manifests itself differently now in Glasgow from how it was just a few years ago. The big council-run hostels have all closed, and, though there are private hostels, the city authorities prefer to move people into housing authority flats. But rough-sleeping, out on the streets, still happens and is still dangerous. One man recalls being asked for a cigarette and, on refusing, being slashed through the tendons of his hand; on another occasion, the same man, while dozing drunk in the train station at Carntyne, was bitten on the fingers by a rat and the poison spread up to his armpit.

So many stories. Randolph alone could write a book. He is 76, an owlish teetotaller wearing a woollen sweater-vest spotted with blue paint. He speaks good English with a strong East European accent, but was in fact born in Rangoon. When the Japanese attacked Burma, his family moved first to Arizona, and then to Czechoslovakia, Bulgaria and Yugoslavia, where he grew up among Russian expats, anti-communists who had fled Stalin and who passed around samizdat copies of Tolstoy, Gogol, Lermontov and Pushkin.

In 1953, Randolph went on the road. He travelled across Europe – 'a gentleman of independent means' – doing odd jobs, sometimes begging, spending his nights in churches and hostels, his days in libraries, reading law, economics and philosophy. He did this for decades. It was a wanderlust, but also a lust for silence and exile. He wanted to be alone. Eventually, in the Nineties, he moved to Britain. Getting old, he needed a steady place to eat and sleep. 'I could either go to monastery or to madhouse or to prison,' he said.

The monastery was out as he didn't fancy all the praying. The madhouse was out because he would have no freedom at all. So he settled on prison. He would have to commit a crime. But which crime? Something serious enough to merit a longish sentence, but not so serious that he would spend the rest of his life in there.

'So,' he says, delighted, 'I make a bank robbery.'

He held up American Express on Princes Street but made no attempt to escape, pled guilty, and spent two years in Shotts prison, at the end of which time he felt much fitter and in better mental health than before.

On release, Randolph settled in Glasgow, in a homeless hostel in Dennistoun, but now lives in retirement housing in Bearsden. He comes to East Campbell Street most days, finds it comforting and feels like the people here are his family, even though he doesn't talk to them much, preferring to sit by one of the large arched windows and paint bright exterior views of the Mission. The lines of perspective are remarkably straight given his trembling hands.

Trotter's, it seems to me, is a remarkable place, a great untapped resource of anecdote and character and rough humour. On my way out, I nip into the gents, and there's an old fella in there, bunneted at the urinal, singing Rothesay Bay.

'It must be sumbdy's pay-day,' comes a wry voice from a closed cubicle.

'Everyday's a pay-day for me, son,' says the old man. 'All ah need's the sunshine.'

'Aye,' says the voice, 'but there's precious fuckin' little of that n'aw.'

The Royal Caledonian Ball

'WELCOME,' says Lord Biddulph with a waggle of his estimable eyebrows, 'to the best ball in Scotland! Um, in London!'

Lord Biddulph, known to his chums as Nick, is 54, loose-lipped, loose-hipped, altogether loose, a jolly, rose-cheeked Toby jug of a man, full to the brim of bonhomie, with a foaming head of fun. Down from the Borders for the evening and intent on a good time, he is short, stout, his faith in reeling devout, and he seems perpetually to be on the move – dancing, mingling, slipping his arm around a beautiful lady or two (and introducing them as such) or slapping some good old fellow on the back. His trajectory is always joywards. It is as if someone fired a cannonball in 1959 and it hasn't come down since. His kilt, in Cunningham tartan, is by his estimate a century old, but wears its years well, as does its wearer. 'You must have the odd drink,' he advises, conspiratorially. 'But you mustn't have too much or you forget the steps, you see.'

The Royal Caledonian Ball is the oldest charity ball in the world. It is the one night of the year when Scotland's high society descend on London, in their hauteur and couture, for dinner, drinks and most of all for dancing. These are people who were instructed in the finer points of the Dashing White Sergeant as soon as they could walk, and for whom the free whisky on every table seems to function as rocket fuel, carrying them smoothly through Friday night and into the orbit of Saturday morning. Later, following the start of the grouse season, will come a string of balls in Scotland – among them Oban, Skye, Angus,

Perth, Lochaber and the Northern Meeting. But that is for another day.

Tonight is the 165th Royal Caledonian Ball. It was inaugurated in the Victorian era by the Duke and Duchess of Atholl as a pick-me-up for their homesick Scottish friends in London, a whiff of the Great Glen in the midst of the Great Wen. It has been held most years since, except during the Boer and World wars and following the death of Edward VII. No matter the decade, no matter the century, everyone always has a wonderful time, the only possible exception being the ball of 1997; it took place on the evening of Tony Blair's landslide which, I'm told, cast rather a pall over proceedings. Since 1930 the ball has been held at Grosvenor House on Park Lane, the hotel with the biggest, grandest ballroom in London, certainly capable of accommodating the 700 or so guests here tonight. Tickets cost between £135 and £225 and benefit several Scottish charities. The guest list is a spectacle in itself. It is a pleasure to lean over the balcony, look down at the blue blood on the dancefloor, and wonder which lovely lady is Miss Victoria Pentecost, which Mrs Imogen Lyndon-Skeggs, and which Fanny, Lady MacGregor of MacGregor.

On the door, in a natty tartan bow-tie, is Terry Kemp, 66, the retired chauffeur of Viscount Dupplin. His job is to check the tickets and that each guest is attired correctly. There is a strict and rather complex dress code. Gentlemen are expected to wear Highland evening dress, evening tails with white tie, or mess kit. Dinner jackets are verboten. Ladies should wear floor-length evening dress; tiaras and tartan sashes are optional but encouraged. There are, of course, little individual flourishes here and there. One handsome young man, Peter Taylor, a student of art history at St Andrews with more than a touch of Sebastian Flyte about his appearance, is sporting an extraordinary detachable fur collar over his tail suit. Is it fake fur? He shakes his head. 'Raccoon.'

I arrived early, in time for the drinks reception at which viscountesses with flowing tresses dipped long-taloned fingers into glass bowls of nibbles and popped them, sparingly, between glossy lips. I was keen to talk to the staff, in particular to Miho Barbarich, 63, who brings to his role as floor manager the steely command of a regimental sergeant major with the unflappable poise of a Zen master. I asked one of his colleagues to point him out to me, and this was what they said: 'He is bald. And he is Miho.'

It was sufficient. He is indeed bald and he is indeed Miho. He is also a legend in the hospitality trade. He moved to London from his native Dubrovnik 45 years ago, finding work first at the Savoy, cleaning glasses, before rising, like a perfect soufflé, to his current eminence at Grosvenor House. 'Everything has to be perfect. In this business, everything you do has to be precise and planned in advance, and the timing is paramount,' he tells me, flourishing a complicated document that looks like a football manager's tactical diagram. 'But when the dancing starts, it is something mag-nee-fee-cent.'

Upstairs, in a room off the balcony, the pipes and drums of the London Scottish Regiment are preparing to perform, some of them sipping bottled lagers or whisky and ginger ale, others getting into uniform. Four leopardskins, part of the get-up of the drummers, hang on a clothes rail like onesies. These were once real leopards, shot back in the days when such things were still acceptable, and each has been given a nickname by the band. One skin of especially high quality is known as Rizla.

Rob Green, a 29-year-old Londoner, is standing in T-shirt and underwear, ironing his plaid. He used to be a Highland dancer but found there was more beer to be had in a pipe band. Although he himself is English, his grandmother was from Glasgow and his great-grandfather came from Lewis. 'That's a beautiful story,' jokes a passing drummer. 'It almost makes up for how shit you play the pipes.'

Drum Major David Foulis, known as Nobby, is a 66-year-old Glaswegian, specifically a Partick man, and has been in the army since joining the Argyll and Sutherland Highlanders at 17. His barrel-broad chest is bright with campaign medals – Northern Ireland, South Arabia, Malay Peninsula, Borneo – and each hand has a fading tattooed swallow, souvenirs of Singapore. 'I was in the Crater with Mad Mitch,' he says, referring to his 1967 posting in Aden, fighting nationalist insurgents under the command of Lieutenant Colonel Colin Mitchell. 'Anything for the troops, that guy. Charisma coming out his arsehole.'

Nobby gives the strong impression of being considerably tougher than the toughest pair of old boots one might hope to find, mentioning in passing that just four weeks ago he suffered a 'wee haemorrhage' of the brain. 'I can't believe you're here tonight,' I tell him. 'Neither can my wife,' he grins.

At 10.00 pm, wielding his mace, Nobby leads out the band, playing Scotland The Brave, to mark the start of the ball. The London Scottish Regiment are followed by the set reels, a prelude to the dancing proper, in which the most accomplished dancers strut their stuff. Ralph Anderson, an earnest 27-year-old resplendent in a lace jabot, urges his party down the stairs to the dancefloor with the stern passion of an officer ushering paratroopers out the door of a plane: 'Right! Go! Go!' Ralph – pronounced 'Rafe' – hails from Selkirkshire and works for a stockbroker. One must 'take a strict line' when instructing dancers, he says. 'It requires military precision.' He himself was taught by his father to dance at the age of two – 'There's pictographic evidence' – and considers reeling to be an artform. 'If the alternative is going to a disco and getting drunk and shaking your body around, well ...' Ralph pulls a face of profound revulsion. The Bee Gees must give him the heebie-jeebies.

Children of some of the guests have been allowed to stay up late and watch the set reels from the balcony, while they

212

themselves are watched over by nannies, around a dozen Mary McPoppinses in ballgowns. 'Can you see mama?' one asks her charge, a little girl wearing a tartan sash and a pronounced pout. 'Hmmph!' says this child, unimpressed. 'There's more clapping at my school assembly!'

That must be some wild school assembly, because the Royal Caledonian Ball is a foot-stomping bacchanal from start to finish. There is a break at half-past midnight for a restorative breakfast of kedgeree and porridge spooned from silver servers by white-jacketed waiters, but then it's once more unto the breach until after three in the morning. A woman is on hand to repair ripped gowns and split troosers. Glengarries lie on tables next to Prada clutches.

Seen from the balcony, the ball is a skirling, whirling kaleidoscope of tartan and tiaras. Every opening accordion chord from the Simon Howie Broadcasting Band is met by a groan of mixed agony and ecstasy as yet another reel begins. The most impressive mover of all is Euan Ivory, a rather burly, genial young chap from Glenisla with mirth to match his girth, and grace to match his mirth, who floats like a butterfly, lowps like a flea, birls his partners like so many roulette wheels, and generally treats the dancefloor as though it were his fiefdom and he its feudal master.

The last person I see before leaving, just after everyone has sung God Save The Queen, is the Lord Biddulph. He, clearly, does not intend to return to Kelso empty-handed. 'Hey!' he calls over to one of the waiters, who is beginning to clear up. 'I'm taking the whisky!'

Doo Men

'AH'M a doo man,' says Bonzo. 'They call us the doo men.'

Bonzo is Gerald Bonini, a 46-year-old from Gartham-lock, in the east end of Glasgow. He's standing shivering in a Hoops tracksuit, speaking gently to the white pigeon cradled in his hands. 'Hello, lady,' he murmurs. 'Hello, girly.' Bonzo also owns a dog called Naka, after the Celtic midfielder Shunsuke Nakamura, but birds are his first and best love.

Behind him is his 20 foot tall wooden doocot, or pigeon loft, secured with five padlocks to keep out thieves and with broken glass in the bottom to shred the paws of rats. Within a few hundred yards, on a large grassy area of waste ground strewn with crumpled cans, there are maybe ten similar doocots, owned and built by different men. Each is monolithic, yet dwarfed by the two huge, circular concrete water towers for which Garthamlock is known. This network of doocots and towers gives the scheme the feel of a ritual space – a kind of council-house Callanish.

When Bonzo calls himself a doo man, he means that he is one of an estimated 1,000 men in Scotland, the vast major-ity of them in Glasgow, who spend their days engaged in an activity known as doo fleein'. Here's how it works. A doo man arranges his pigeons in pairs – a doo and a hen – and they spend Monday to Thursday enjoying intimate com-panionship. He separates them on the weekend and sends his still horny pigeon out into the sky. A nearby doo man, seeing this, will send up a hen. The idea is that the birds mate and each will then attempt to bring the other back to its doocot. As soon as the birds alight on the landing

214

board, the watchful doo man pulls a wire that operates a trap shaped like a pram hood, and thus takes ownership of his opponent's pigeon. The captured bird is then given to a doo man in another area of the city, who gives a bird in return, and the whole circle goes on revolving as it has in Scotland since at least the Victorian age.

If you want to fly doos, it's helpful to have a plentiful supply of two commodities – spare time and spare ground. It is an ideal pastime if you happen to be unemployed and living in one of the big post-war housing schemes from which whole streets have been cleared. As the saying goes, 'A doo man is a buroo man'. It doesn't cost much. The feed is cheap, the water's free and doocots can be put together from scrounged and found wood and metal. Doo fleein' also gets you out of the house. On hot days you'll find the doo men sitting out on benches, sharing a carry-out, their faces red with heat and drink, the sky black with birds.

But doo fleein' has its dark side. Cheating is not tolerated. 'Oh, there's a lot of fightin',' says Bonzo. 'Jeezo, man, there's mair stabbins and slashins through birds than anythin' ah know. Ah've been on the rampage one time masel.'

On that occasion, according to Bonzo, a rival doo man was standing in his own doocot and holding on to his hen, which was visible, thus tempting Bonzo's priapic pigeon – a prized white male – without any danger of losing his own. 'Ah scudded him right in the face. Ah took the doo back aff him and said, 'Don't you ever do that tae ma fuckin' birds again or ah'll rip the fuckin' heid right aff ye.' Don't get me rang, ah lost the rag, but he shouldn't be stealin' aff people. He should let the birds fly free.'

What's interesting about the strength and violence of this reaction is that it has nothing to do with money. The birds themselves aren't worth much – around £6.50 for a doo and £15 for a hen – but the men grow very attached to them; they may have had a particular pigeon for a number of years, and it hurts to lose it.

'Aw, it's a drainin' feelin',' says Bonzo. 'It's like being bereaved. Ah lost a big silver doo and I went into mournin' for two weeks. Ah'd had the doo ten year. It was like ah'd had my wife for ten year and lost her. So ye hit the booze. 'Ah'm no wantin' tae fly any mair!' But ah sobered up efter two weeks and went back to ma birds. Ye've got tae take the good wi' the bad. It's the passion, it's the buzz, the adrenalin rush. It's the best sport in the world.'

* * *

Garthamlock, Barlanark, Dalmarnock, Parkhead and Possil, Blackhill, Cranhill, Barrowhill – there are doocots in them all. These represent a guerrilla architecture in the city, and their rise and fall mirrors the successes and failures of Glasgow's housing policy. Where flats are cleared, doocots spring up; when land is earmarked for development, the doocots come down. Doo men abhor a vacuum; any waste ground is fair game.

If you want to meet doo men, go near some doocots. It won't be long before someone asks what you're up to. They might wander over from a nearby house or pull up in a car. They may welcome your interest or tell you where to go. They'll definitely be suspicious. Stealing is rife. It's common for doocots to get 'rattled' and the birds sold in either a distant district or in Edinburgh, where there is also a sizeable scene.

Security is therefore a preoccupation. Doocots are sometimes fenced off or protected by fierce dogs. It has been known for baby monitors to be installed. A while back, in Glasgow's Tollcross, a man called Shuggie, who worked in a foundry, welded steel sheeting right round his doocot. Yet one night thieves climbed the fence and used an oxyacetylene torch to burn through the back and steal his birds. It's said that man never flew doos again. Shuggie's heart was broken.

216

Lilybank, a small district of the east end within sight of Celtic Park, boasts the highest concentration of doocots in the city – no fewer than 25. Among these sits a steel shipping container, covered in graffiti, with a makeshift chimney smoking away on top. This is the headquarters of Matt McConnell, a stocky 51-year-old with a white goatee and peaked cap. He can be found here most days, drinking lager, attending to his birds and warming his arthritic hands by the rusty iron stove.

The shipping container is within sight of McConnell's doocot and contains everything a doo man might need – bevvy, binoculars and birds. The doos are locked away in their pens behind two steel doors and a wire gate, effectively inside a safe. McConnell isn't taking any chances. A few years ago his doocot was burned to the ground, with all his birds inside, by thieves frustrated that they couldn't break in to it. The shipping container is his response. 'This is the Rolls-Royce,' says 20-year-old Jason Kerr, a fledgling doo man who has stopped by to top up his supply of birds. 'No' everybody's got a place like this.'

Though it's Saturday, it's too wet for the doos to fly, and so McConnell has time to talk. He explains that the skill of the doo man comes in selecting just the right bird to go up against whatever your opponent puts in the air. It's like chess, he says; a question of strategy. Also, you have to be willing to sacrifice pawns – pigeons that aren't so skilled – in order to learn the strengths and weaknesses of the champion bird that you really want. This can go on for a long time.

The birds that evade capture for years, capturing other pigeons all the while, become hated and coveted in their particular communities, loved only by their owners. 'Ah've got a doo, his nickname's Eliot Ness,' says one doo man. 'He's untouchable – 12-year-auld and never been caught.'

Doo men tend to boast about their own birds and denigrate the stock of their opponents. Good pals through the week, they become deadly rivals at weekends. 'When you've got a pigeon in your hand, ready to put it oot,' says McConnell, 'you don't have any friends.'

A few years ago, according to McConnell, doo fleein' was dying, no youngsters coming into it. But the recession and rise in joblessness has brought new blood to the scene. 'This is keeping a lot of younger people off the streets. It keeps them away from vandalism because they've got something to do. The council should designate an area where you can keep pigeon lofts, and recognise this as a sport.'

Stephen Cairney, 30, is unemployed and shares McConnell's doocot. When he was younger, he was involved with gangs. 'See if ah didnae hae the doos,' he says, taking a break from smashing up wooden palettes for the fire, 'I'd probably be in the jail.'

McConnell, a former paratrooper and panel-beater, is unable to work because of ill health. He can testify to the psychological benefits of the sport. 'It's quite calming,' he says. 'I had a quadruple heart bypass when I was 41 and, oh, I was depressed for a long while after. At points I couldnae go oot the hoose. I lay in my bed all day. But this has been a kind of therapy for me, you know.'

*   *   *

Sunday night in Parkhead, the moon a thin pale disc like a communion wafer. On Springfield Road, there's a double billboard advertising McDonald's and Sky. Cut into the wood between these two bright expressions of the modern world is a narrow doorway, leading into a Glasgow of the past. Dim yellow light and harsh laughter spill out to the street. Pass through and you find yourself in a low and dirty room, lit by bare bulbs powered by a generator, fragranced by Silk Cut incense. This is the doo shop.

At one end is a counter, behind which are pigeon pens;

the paint is flaking and they are lined with pages from the Daily Record. Every Sunday night, birds are bought and sold, and there is a raffle in which others can be won. The place feels ramshackle and temporary, but has been here for more than 50 years. It was built by George Dunn, a 74-year-old who has some claim to being the city's longest-serving and most respected doo man. He retired about a year ago and doesn't keep pigeons now, but he still visits from time to time. Asked what it has meant to him to be a doo man, he can't stop the tears. 'It was an important thing, aye,' he chokes. 'I caught my fair share.'

There are about 30 doo men in the small room, and a few young boys kicking a football. The Old Firm match finished a few hours ago with a defeat for Celtic, but the atmosphere is gallus and giddy. Many people are drinking beer or Buckfast, or both. Birds are swapped and insults traded. Wit and aggression are cross-bred here. One man says he used to keep pigeons on his window-sill in Barlinnie.

Someone gives an impromptu lecture on the type of pigeon used for the sport. These are horseman thief pouters, known for their puffed-up chests, a breed that was used centuries ago by the poor to catch other pigeons for the pot. Hens are harder to capture than males, which are easily lured by sexual wiles. Doos seem to favour light-coloured hens, so the men dye their female birds with peroxide. 'It's like when ye're goin' tae the dancin',' explains a young doo man wearing a baseball cap. 'If there's a blonde, ye're gonnae find her mair attractive.'

Robert McLeish is 54 with short silver hair, a pattern shaved into the sides. He has mixed feelings about the doos. 'I caught pigeon lung off the fuckers,' he says. 'One in a million catch it, and I did. My chest's solid brick-hard.' He knocks a fist against it. 'I shouldnae even be here. I was told tae get rid of ma doos. But they're awfy hard to get rid of.'

Pigeon lung, or avian alveoliti, is a respiratory illness caught from inhaling the dust that comes off the feathers.

McLeish was told two years ago that he had just two years left to live. Yet, as someone who has wrung the necks of many diseased pigeons, he is philosophical. 'I've killed enough of them,' he says, 'and now they've killed me.'

The doo shop is more a social club than a business. It's a Sunday night ritual. 'People think we do this for money, but that's wrong,' says Edward Rutherford, 32, who runs the place with his brother Kevin. 'We do it to keep the sport alive.'

It's striking that this hidden spot is only a short walk from the huge fenced-off area where the arenas and athletes' village are being constructed ahead of the 2014 Commonwealth Games. Think of all the money and attention being directed at that, and yet this indigenous sport goes unrecognised. Perhaps it's because of the people who do it. Just as pigeons are widely regarded as dirty and unhealthy, the proverbial rats with wings, the doo men come from a social milieu that is not the side of Glasgow the city authorities wish to project. It is the Glasgow of negatives – the jobless, the toothless, the city of scars.

Yet this is also a proud community. The doo men take pride, for example, in the condition of their birds. They keep them fed, watered and cleaned, administer medicines when needed and speak to the doos in a low and tender patois intended to resemble the birds' own calls. 'The bottom line,' says Rutherford, 'is if you look after the pigeon, the pigeon will look after you.'

There is also a great deal of pride in the long tradition and a strong sense that this is about family. Several of the doo men have been coming to this shop since they were kids, brought here by dads who came as young men themselves. George Dunn is a godfather to these people. Kevin Rutherford, from Blackhill, says that when he and his brother were children, their dad used to keep pigeons in the coal bunker. Now he brings his own son, also Kevin, to tend the doos.

Young Kevin is only five, cute in a Celtic top and with chocolate round his mouth, but he's already crazy about the birds. He speaks to them, feeds them, cleans their pens. He's also very confident when handling them. If doo fleein' has a future, then Kevin and others like him are it. What's his favourite bird? 'A wee blue storry hen,' says the boy.

What is it he likes about the doos? 'Cos they're good.'

And so will he, when he is grown up, build a doocot of his own? At this, as his father sweeps up the raffle tickets, Kevin just nods.

Oystermen

FIRST light, and Stranraer is not yet awake. Down by the harbour, seagulls perch on the gaudy roofs of shuttered fairground rides, while clouds – some gilded, some smoky pink – scull across the pale sky. It is time to go fishing for oysters.

The Vital Spark is a Clyde-built boat, almost 40 years old. Seven days a week during the oyster season, which starts in September and runs until April, she works the waters of Loch Ryan, a long and narrow sea loch on the Galloway coast. This is the only place in Scotland where wild native oysters – Ostrea edulis, to use the Sunday name of this coveted beastie – are still fished commercially. The fishing rights were granted to the Wallace family by the crown in 1701 and are still held by that local estate to this day, meaning that the Vital Spark is the only boat out there bringing up oysters.

There are two of a crew. Rab Lamont and John Mills are Stranraer natives each just a little older than the boat in which they sail. Neither man likes oysters or, more accurately, has ever been able to bring himself to try one. 'Aye, the boss's catch is safe with us two,' says Rab. They sustain themselves instead, during the long cold days, with endless mugs of coffee, endless roll-ups, and rounds of toast and marmalade which, being tough seamen, they do not cut daintily but instead fold in half and gobble in snatched moments while the dredge is on the bottom. The wheelhouse is a mausoleum of toast crumbs and half-smoked fags lying in scallop ashtrays. An old battered metal kettle, which one imagines to be encrusted on the inside with barnacles, puts in a hard shift on the hob.

222

Rab and John love their job. They view bad weather – whether it be a temperature of minus 14 or the northerly wind that comes howling down the loch – as a pleasurable challenge rather than something to be tholed. They have known each other for 30 years and seem to get along, to go together like oysters and stout, which is just as well given they spend eight months of the year in each other's company daily. Fishing is forbidden during the breeding season, which means any month without an 'r' in it, so the summer is when the oystermen catch up on their drinking and DIY. They seem to enjoy the company of guests, although they have certain reservations about bringing women on board; like many fishermen, they consider this to be bad luck, and still rue the day when they hosted 'a 25-year-old barmaid from Toronto' and found themselves unable to catch a thing. 'Aye,' says John, 'she was a fuckin' demon, right enough.'

John is a big man; dark haired, solid and possessed of an extraordinarily gruff laugh. This begins somewhere around his wellies, comes growling up behind his muddy oilskins, and emerges eventually from his throat as a sound so sonorous it could warn shipping from the coast. Someone once told him he was 'the George Clooney o' the fishin'' – a compliment to which he clings like a drowning man to a mast. He has been a fisherman since leaving school and has sailed right round the British Isles. Although he is only 43, he gives the impression of being a grizzled, weathered veteran, the last generation, as he sees it, to learn the trade right. He prides himself on being able to splice rope, mend nets and tie all the nautical knots. He likes to keep the boat clean, giving it a good scrub each Friday, as is the tradition. He has been on the Vital Spark for four years.

Rab, the skipper, is 47, wiry and tough, with close-cropped silver hair. He sometimes takes a break from puffing on a fag to puff on an asthma inhaler. He used to work as a steward on the ferries sailing to and from

Northern Ireland, but has been an oysterman since his late thirties. His greatest burden, he feels, is having his ears bent by John's off-colour jokes and wind-ups. 'He once told me that Ailsa Craig was the Isle of Man. Think of spending twelve oors a day wi' that and you won't wonder that I'm grey.'

We sail first up the eastern side of the loch, overlooked by the hills. Here, because the water flows better and there is less silt, the oysters have a classical oystery shape and are therefore favoured in the restaurants and bars of London, where they will sell for between two and three pounds each. The Loch Ryan Oyster Fishery Company supplies the Ritz, Savoy, Harrods and Selfridges. In Scotland, they sell oysters to Andrew Fairlie, Martin Wishart and to Rogano. They also ship to Italy, France, Holland and Canada, foreign palates apparently favouring slightly smaller oysters.

John shucks open a few for me to try with lemon juice. They have a deliciously briney, brackish, lip-smackish zing. These wild oysters, as opposed to the non-native rock oysters which are now cultivated in the UK all year round, are the sort that Charles Dickens would have been able to buy from street stalls at three for a penny, that Julius Caesar would have eaten while invading Britain, that Casanova shared with his lovers in their morning bath.

Although they know the waters by such local and personal names as the Scar, the Smiley and Pelican Toes, the oystermen also use a navigational computer to help them in their work. Known oyster beds are marked on the screen with red crosses. But these are beds where oysters are still growing and so they must to be avoided. An oyster takes about ten years to reach the right size and weight – 75 grams and above. Undersize oysters are returned to the bottom and the coordinates noted. 'We'll be back here in three, four years' time,' says Rab, tipping a basket-full back into the loch. It is like laying down wine or maturing whisky in a bond. The point, too, is to make the oyster beds sustainable and not to fish them out. 'See, you're no' just fishin' for the now, you're fishin' for the future,' says John. 'You've got to think ahead. Cos this is the last yin in Scotland.'

According to Scottish Natural Heritage, native oysters have been in steep decline for over 100 years as a result of over-fishing and pollution. They have long been part of the Scottish diet, as shells gathered from Mesolithic middens show. Scotland's biggest and best known fisheries were, from the 13th century, in the Firth of Forth, with large fleets of oystermen working on both the Fife and Lothian coasts. By the start of the 19th century, fisheries there were landing 30 million oysters a year; Charles Darwin, while a medical student in Edinburgh, sometimes sailed with oystermen from Newhaven. By 1957, Ostrea edulis was thought to be extinct in those waters, although recent discoveries suggest it is making a small recovery.

Thanks to careful management, Loch Ryan has survived much better. It is expected that around forty tons, half a million oysters, will be fished this year. There are thought to be sixty million down there, twenty feet below the waves. Victorian-era record books, in the possession of the Wallace family, give a flavour of the money that could be made from oysters and the risks that men would take to take to bring them ashore. 'Blowing a gale of wind from the north,' reads the entry for October 7, 1889. 'Boat swamped and three of our men nearly drowned. Not fit to dredge.'

The dredge of the Vital Spark is a large square chain pouch on a galvanised wire. Rab and John take it in turns to fish, the other steering the boat. After seven minutes scouring the bottom, as the Spark advances at around one and a half knots, the dredge is brought up, beribboned in brown seaweed, and its contents released, rattling, on to a metal table at the back of the boat. The two men sort the oysters by size, quick as Vegas croupiers, and remove all unwanted creatures – cockles, mussels, shrimps, crabs, Buckie whelks. Orange starfish, killed by leaving them to dry on the edge of the boat, are considered to be enemies as they eat oysters; these starfish are also, apparently, prized by certain pigeon fanciers, who leave them around their lofts, believing that they will fatally poison any cat foolhardy enough to eat one.

The dredge brings up rubbish too. At one time it was known to find crockery embossed with swastikas, artefacts from surrendered U-boats which were held in the loch before scuttling. Nothing so darkly glamorous today, though. 'There's a can of beer with an oyster stuck to it,' says Rab, holding up an old can. 'Does that no' sum up Scotland?'

In the course of a day, Rab and John will fill four large baskets full of sellable oysters – around 2,500 of them. In the absence of other boats, they compete with one another, each man keen to catch as much as possible. It is always an exciting moment when the catch comes out the water; a slight air of one of those claw games from the fair. So they don't get bored. Every day is different. The wind. The tide. The catch. The craic. This is the perfect job for them, they say; 'away oot the road', the world their oyster, the oysters their world.

'Right,' says Rab, handing his pal a slice of toast and marmalade. 'Fold yer gums roond that, and I'll go and lift the dredge.'

Extreme Cleaners

'HOW are you with smells?' asks Marie.

She has the back of her van open and is reaching inside for a face mask. We are standing on the street of a large Scottish city, in a canyon of tenements, about to visit the flat where, two or three days ago, a man bled to death.

Marie Fagan, a sharp-eyed, blunt-spoken woman of forty, runs Clean Scene Trauma with her partner Billy. The company offers a professional cleaning service in the aftermath of violent crime, suicide, accidental death and any scenario in which blood, bodily fluids and harmful items need to be removed. They go into the bland rooms of budget hotels and clean carpets crimson with the evidence of drug deals which became knife fights. They lift dirty needles from filthy squats and from the floors of fast-food toilets. They clean up after those obsessive hoarders whose homes are mouldering mausoleums in which lie interred the husks of their own neglected lives.

Most people would find this sort of work impossibly vile, but Marie has two of the most important qualities for an extreme cleaner – a strong stomach and a strong interest in life on the margins. 'The worse it is,' she says, 'the better.'

We climb the stairs of the close. There are big splinters on the landing floor from where the police battered the door. Marie and her colleague Lesley Wright, 45, change into white protective suits; masks and goggles and double-gloves. It's better not to do this on the street. Too many folk would be wondering. Discretion is what this job's all about.

The key in the lock. You hold your breath as you go in, unsure what you're about to find. A tiny flat. Junk mail at one end of the hall floor, stained footprints at the other. The bathroom is an atrocity; the sink full of blood. You want to look and you want to not look. You want to know and you want not to know. What the hell happened here?

'We don't ask,' says Marie. 'To me, it's not right to ask. When you're on the job you can't help but wonder. But you never really know, and the questions kind of float about your head forever.'

On entering a home, Marie likes to find a photograph of the deceased. Likes to know their face. Not out of nosiness. Out of what? Compassion, maybe. And as a kind of comfort. Somehow, knowing something about the person – a name, an age, their appearance – lessens the sense of dreadful absence by giving a glimpse of the life that has ended. It is also a way of dignifying the labour. Say the property is a rented flat. The work is being paid for by the letting agency. But Marie, in her head, is really working for the deceased and their loved ones. She's cleaning so that when the family come by to uplift belongings, they don't see anything that would upset them. Her job, in a way, is telling white lies.

Here, though, is the truth. Blood, when it's been lying a while, is dark as a ripe plum and has the consistency of jelly. You never quite get used to the feel of it rising up your gloved wrists. The smell rises, too, as you start to clean. Forget jelly. This, as Marie puts it, is like the back of a butcher's shop. The stink clogs and clots at the back of the throat.

Not everyone could do this job. But don't make the mistake that the people who can do it are cold and hard. 'You do feel sad,' says Marie. 'I'm not really religious, but I always kind of say a wee prayer. It's just a bit of respect for the person.'

It's strange to be in the flat. There's a touch of the Mary Celeste about it. Fags unsmoked. Clock unwound.

A birthday card lying in the kitchen, addressed but never sent.

'For a man, that's a nice clean wee cooker,' says Lesley, nodding approvingly from within her white hood.

'Aye,' says Marie, 'he's kept the flat tidy. He seems to have been a nice clean-living man. It's a shame.'

Marie photographs his wallet, on a table in the bedroom, to prove that she has not touched it. She cuts away an area of stained carpet and checks the floorboards. She strips the bed, bundling the duvet and sheets into bright orange clinical waste bags for incineration.

She and Lesley between them heft the mattress down the close stairs and out to the van. In the street, life goes implacably on: people and traffic; the shrill joy of kids at their playground games. This is the thing about extreme cleaning. You very quickly become aware of aspects of society – the quiet tragedies; the dim sadnesses – which never make the papers. 'We had three suicides last week,' says Marie. 'One was a guy who'd drunk salt and his kidneys blew up. One was heroin. The third was a girl who'd slit her wrists.'

The extreme cleaners know things. They know that heroin users, when they've found a nice dark spot in which to shoot up, say a burned-out derelict underground bar, will sometimes live there for a long time, laying down on the cold floor a new flattened cardboard box each time the present layer grows too dirty and damp, and creating for themselves a sort of nest. Cleaning such places, Marie and her team will peel back each layer, careful as archaeologists, finding needles and scorched foil in each. Recently they found the passport of a young woman and handed it in to the police; another piece of flotsam from another shipwrecked life. When lifting needles they wear pierce-proof gloves and boots with metal soles. They are vaccinated against hepatitis B and C.

Extreme cleaners know what poverty means; the desperate

things it makes you do. 'We had a job at Kinning Park,' says Marie. 'Bad winter. Two or three years ago now. The guy had been breaking into factories. Stealing lead. But the roof was covered in snow so he didn't see the skylight and fell right through on to the concrete floor. Seemingly he was quite a youngish guy. I bet he had a couple of weans and was skint and trying to get money for Christmas presents.'

There can be a kind of very dark comedy to extreme cleaning. Laugh or you'd cry. Marie recalls a man in his twenties in Glasgow who had mental health problems. This particular Saturday, he had got himself a carryout, sat down to watch one of the Saw films, slashed his arms, bled into cups and thrown blood all over the walls. He was known to have hepatitis C, so his carers called the cleaners. When they turned up, the man was quite the genial host, blithe among his bloodstains, offering wine and cider.

'This was always my dream,' says Marie. Her family have been in the industrial cleaning business for more than twenty years, but she long had a fancy for this particular niche. She used to watch the CSI shows and, rather than try to work out whodunnit, she would think, 'I wonder who cleans that?'

Most of us would probably assume that the responsibility for cleaning up the aftermath of violence or drug use would lie with the police. But this is not the case. The police do often make arrangements, but they are not obliged to do so. Assistance is available from Victim Support Scotland for families affected by violent crime who cannot afford to pay for specialist cleaning.

Marie did the course at the National Academy of Crime Scene Cleaners in Bristol, learning about pathogens and pest control and needle sweeps. 'People laugh at me,' she says. 'A lot of my pals like to go online and look at shoes and bags, then they come to my house and I'm on the internet looking for mattress bags and the best stuff to clean blood. I can't explain it, but I'm passionate about it.'

She takes a particular pleasure in dealing with hoarders, of whom she speaks with affectionate pity, sometimes having to spend weeks negotiating and gaining their trust so as to be allowed into their properties. She knows their quirks: their abhorrence of cleanliness; their love for labyrinths of piled papers; the way that many hide caches of booze and own far too many cats. One old hoarder from Argyll was terminally ill and sent home from hospital to die. Marie was asked to gut his flat so that it would be safe for his carer. She remembers pulling down a vast cobweb, yellow with nicotine, which covered the whole kitchen ceiling, like a silken ochre mantle.

'Time had stood still for that wee man,' she says. 'He didn't sleep in a bed. He slept on the same bit of the floor of the living room, on an old-fashioned rug in front of the fire, for years and years since he was a boy.'

It is teatime when Marie and Lesley finish cleaning the blood from the flat. Dusk has turned to dark and fallen leaves have choked the gutters. Soon, they will drive back to Moodiesburn with the stained mattress in the back, satisfied that the dead man's family need not see what they have seen. The kindly gift they bestow, with sanitising spray and disposable wipes, is ignorance.

'There's a lot more goes on out there,' says Marie, 'than people would believe.'

The World Stone Skimming Championships

RON Long, a man proud to introduce himself as an old tosser, shakes an angry fist at the dank Hebridean sky. 'A pox upon it!' he shouts in a strong Welsh accent. The 67-year-old retired fireman is unhappy about the rain and wind. They will not help his bid to become the World Stone Skimming Champion.

We are standing on the edge of Scotland's west coast, a few miles south of Oban, waiting for the small ferry boat to take us across to Easdale Island, which has hosted the championships since 1997. Ron has been named 'Old Tosser' for the last two years after skimming a stone further than any other competitor aged sixty and above. Today he hopes to retain that title and go one better, winning the entire event. But the weather has got him spooked.

Since taking up stone skimming three years ago, he has become something of an expert on fluid dynamics and does not like the way the wind will create waves on the surface of the flooded quarry where he is due to compete.

'Ideally, the water should be mirror-flat,' he says, rain dripping from his moustache. 'It'll be a matter of technique, skill and a large dose of luck today. But the truth is that the stone will never go any further than you can throw it anyway. You get nothing for nothing in this world, and bugger all for sixpence.'

The ferry arrives. Just a wee boat, open to the elements, but the very thing for carrying a few people on the five-minute crossing from the Isle of Seil, which is itself linked to the mainland by the famous Bridge Over The Atlantic.

232

Easdale is tiny and car-free. The first things you notice as you get off at the harbour are the upturned wheelbarrows, each with a number or Gaelic name painted on the side; these are how the locals humph their shopping back home. A rough signpost made from slate nailed to driftwood gives the distance to various places of significance: Paris, 715 miles; Basra 2,471 miles; Pub, 41 metres.

Easdale has a population of seventy: fifty adults and twenty kids, eleven dogs and five cats, mostly living in the terraces of whitewashed cottages which were once home to quarriers. Easdale is one of the Slate Islands, a small archipelago which, from the 17th century until early in the 20th, provided much of the slate used in the construction of homes throughout Scotland and beyond. Easdale slate is known to have been used in Wellington, Dublin, Belfast, parts of Canada and perhaps in New York. By 1794, Easdale alone was producing five million slates each year. An old Pathé newsreel screening in the local museum explains that the island roofed Glasgow and Edinburgh – 'only on such tiles will Scottish cats make whoopee'.

A huge storm in 1881 flooded the quarries throughout the Slate Islands, hastening the decline of the industry. The last commercial slate was dug out of Easdale in 1911. Many of the quarrymen and their families moved to Glasgow to find work in shipbuilding. The population, which in 1881 stood at 452, dropped as low as four, but since the 1960s has been creeping back up. Many of those who live here now are descendants of the original quarriers, lured back by family history and the attractions of raising kids in a slow, safe, neighbourly place. And it is those same flooded quarries, once almost the death of the island, which are now helping to finance its second life. The World Stone Skimming Championships, played out on the glassy arena of the quarries, will this year raise around £7,500 for community development.

'But really it's just great craic,' says Donald Melville,

known as Mellon, the chief organiser of the championships. 'If it was purely commercial, it would be quite a
bore.'

Mellon winds red and white tape around the perimeter
of the quarry, weighing it down with rocks, to keep spectators and contestants back from the steep edges. The quarry
is roughly rectangular, 66 feet long, and divided up today
with a string of orange buoys marking the distance of each
throw. Distance is the mark of success, not the number of
skips, though each stone must bounce at least three times.
The water is deep, dark and green, a placid cousin of the
nearby roaring Atlantic. Mellon points out neighbouring islands: Mull, Luing, Scarba, the Garvellachs. Hazy
through the mist of rain are the crumbling gable-ends of
Belnahua, long abandoned by islanders, a fate that might
have befallen Easdale had it not been so conveniently close
to the mainland.

The start of the competition is still a couple of hours
away, but already Ron Long and other hardcore skimmers
are down at the quarry, foraging for stones and practising
their throws. Stones are provided by the championship
organisers, but some competitors prefer to select their
own. All stones must, however, be true Easdale slate and
conform to a regulation three inches in diameter. They are
checked before throwing by Mike Cafferty, landlord of
the island's pub The Puffer, who is armed with a piece of
wood with a hole in it. 'If the stones don't fit through here,
tough,' says Mike. 'You'd be surprised by how seriously
some people take all this. There was a guy in the bar last
night who said he was using one arm to lift his beer and
saving the other for the skimming.'

Manuela Kniebsch, the 2010 women's champion, who
has travelled from Aachen in Germany, throws a few. One
doesn't skip at all, instead plunging into the water with a
loud plop. Manuela grimaces. 'Oof,' says Ron Long, sup-
portively. 'Dead man's fart we call those.'

Ron lives near the River Severn and practises skimming three or four times a week. During the summer he won the All-England Championship at Ambleside and has designs on the Welsh title. There's something very whimsical and carefree about stone-skimming, but Ron is ultra-competitive. 'I have a dedicated fitness regime. You have to use all kinds of muscle groups to get it done right.' He has been working with a chiropractor and is 'on more pills than a German brewery' for the pain in his throwing arm. 'I am completely desensitised,' he declares. He is developing a line of artificial skimming stones made from concrete in the hopes that his beloved sport can spread to areas unblessed by Easdale's natural bounty. One day, he hopes, stone skimming will feature in the Olympics.

His main competition for the title is Dougie Isaacs, a 36-year-old unemployed driver from Blairgowrie who looks a bit like Liam Gallagher, warms up with a pint, and spends much of the day disconsolate beneath a large golf umbrella. Yet the man can throw. He has been world champion three times and is looking to keep the title. Yet he shrugs when asked to explain how he does it – 'I've just got the bionic arm sort of thing, eh?'

The championships get under way at noon. There are a few hundred people gathered on the rocks. The air smells of sea salt and hip-flask whisky. A band plays hillbilly tunes. A frisky Westie called Skye keeps getting in the way of the skimmers and is eventually lifted by her master, the ferryman, and plonked in a rowing boat from which new vantage point she watches the action with an air of great magnanimity. Everyone cheers when the Royal Dutch Stone Skimming Association arrive, eight jolly Netherlanders singing and marching behind their flag.

There are 320 competitors, of which a couple of hundred are men. One group of young women, calling themselves the Skimmy Dippers, psych each other up: 'Come on, Cat! Be one with the stone!' Mellon, keeping score and keeping dry in a small wooden hut, is a partisan compere. 'Ye big ginger tosssuuurrr!' he bellows when one red-haired local lad, 14-year-old Simon Fraser, achieves a massive throw of 55 metres. Mellon, need I add, intends this as a great compliment.

Everyone skims three stones while standing on a slate podium by the water's edge. Judges lined around the quarry estimate the distance and convey it to Mellon using megaphones. Good throws are met by oohs and aahs and applause. There was a hoolie the night before in the community hall and several competitors have hangovers. One pale woman skims her stones and then staggers off asking for hair of the dog. I don't think she means Skye. Possibly Talisker.

In the course of the day, only three skimmers manage to hit the back wall of the quarry – Ron Long, Dougie Isaacs and Paul Crabtree, a tall and lugubrious retired police officer from Gloucestershire. This shared feat means they must compete in a three-way head-to-head for the title. 'This is going to be classic!' says one excitable local. 'It's time for the toss-off!'

Bending, swivelling, grunting and chucking in the torrential rain, the three men give it their all. Dougie Isaacs wins the day, champion for a fourth time, undisputedly the world's greatest tosser. He raises a clenched fist and heads off up the rocks to the pub. Will he defend his title next year? He's not sure. He might, instead, enter the mobile phone throwing championships in Finland.

It's the end of a long day. Time to get the ferry back to the mainland. Let's give the last word, though, to Larry Phinney, a bald and burly 53-year-old truck driver from Manitoba, Canada, who has come all this way to witness the stone-skimming. 'It was really great,' he says, 'to see that many people get together and have fun throwing a rock.'

Jacobites

THESE days, in Scotland, you are more likely to encounter midgie bites than Jacobites. The movement, which fought for the restoration of the Stuart monarchy, was largely exterminated in the violent purges following the Battle of Culloden, Bonnie Prince Charlie's bloody last stand.

Yet in the 21st century there are still men, and a few women, as familiar with the heft of a broadsword and the weft of a plaid as they are with broadband and PlayStation, and who consider Queen Elizabeth a cuckoo in the nest. These Jacobites – Jacobytes, if you will – may use online forums to discuss their beliefs and they may sometimes carry BlackBerries in their sporrans, but their hearts and heads belong to the 18th century.

On an overcast Saturday lunchtime in early August, a dozen or so of these Jacobites are gathering at Balgonie Castle, near Markinch in Fife. Balgonie has been visited by several Scottish icons over the years including Mary Queen of Scots and Rob Roy MacGregor. Today, the castle chapel will see six men initiated into A Circle of Gentlemen, one of Scotland's leading Jacobite groups.

The Circle started as a secret drinking society in 18th century Edinburgh, a way to toast the cause without fear of government reprisals. Revived in the 1990s, the group remained under the radar until last month when one of its members, Alasdair MacNeill, spoke out angrily against tourists picnicking at Culloden.

'A family of four and their two dogs were sprawled across a grave mound having a picnic,' he told the BBC.

'The father was leaning against the headstone eating a Scotch egg and smoking a cigarette.'

MacNeill, 41, lives in Inverness, works in IT, and is a member of the Circle's eight-man Council. Like everyone else here today, he's wearing period dress. Modern-day Jacobites spend a lot of time and money on the clothes they wear to events like these. There isn't a Jacobite shop you can walk into and buy the look off the peg; you have to do your research and get things made. 'We're not a reenactment group, so we're not big hairy people with half a deer on our backs.' MacNeill explains. 'We dress more like the polite end of society. The savage look appeals to tourists who expect to see Bravehearts all over the place, but that's not what we're about.'

Matthew Donnachie, the leader of the Circle, has based his outfit on a portrait of Bonnie Prince Charlie, with whom he identifies. In addition to his tartan trews and embroidered waistcoat, he is wearing a deep blue jacket, its gold-plated buttons cast from original period fasteners, the silver lace trim 200 years old and sourced from America. He also carries an authentic Jacobite sword.

Donnachie, 39, runs a cosmetic dentistry business in Inverness under the name Doctor Denture. He grew up in Dunfermline as a great admirer of the work of Duran Duran, in particular their flamboyant keyboard player Nick Rhodes, which is where he gets his dandyish dash.

Being a modern-day Jacobite is about more than dressing up, although that aspect is meaningful given the post-Culloden ban on Highland garb. But not everyone on the scene agrees on exactly what being a Jacobite is about. For some, including the group who call themselves Na Fir Dileas, of whom more later, it is specifically to do with a desire to chuck out the royal family and restore the Stuart line to the throne of an independent Scotland.

James the VII and II, a Catholic monarch, lost the thrones of Scotland, England and Ireland in the revolution of 1688, and was replaced by his Protestant daughter Mary and her husband William of Orange. Between that year and 1745 there were a number of armed risings which attempted to put the Stuarts back in power. These culminated at Culloden on 16 April 1746, when the forces of Charles Edward Stuart, Bonnie Prince Charlie, were slaughtered by the British army.

The Circle of Gentlemen did once support the restoration of the Stuarts, but have now dropped that policy. 'We've been to so many functions where someone will stand up and say, 'Here's to the King, sir!' Well, that's a hollow toast and embarrassing,' says Donnachie. 'It doesn't mean anything. The King is in a mausoleum in the Vatican. The direct Stuart line is gone. The remote line is now the crown prince of Bavaria, and if you think he would be any better, or any more connected to Scotland than the Windsors, then you'd be very much mistaken.'

Donnachie is outspoken and rather brash, and, when talking about the values of the Circle, speaks about the need, in a multicultural society, to retain and promote indigenous Scottish identity and culture. 'The ways of the western world are under attack just now,' he says, 'and so I think you are better with a Christian monarch rather than mumping and moaning about which Christian monarch.'

He's talking about Islamic extremists, and becomes defensive when I press him on this, even posting a notice on the Circle's website expressing concern that I am interpreting the group incorrectly. The Circle, he insists, is neither religious nor political and certainly not racist; he finds anti-Englishness, in particular, embarrassing. 'There's a lot of cranks out there who want to rebuild Hadrian's wall,' he says. 'We can't afford to have ourselves attached to people like that.'

Though none of the Jacobites I meet are keen to talk about it, some will admit that their movement can attract isolated extremists, or 'tartan Nazis' as one member of the

Circle describes them. Both the Circle and Na Fir Dileas are strongly against bigotry and careful about whom they let become members.

In fact, Donnachie could be described as the Tony Blair of Jacobitism – committed to making the movement credible to the mainstream. For him, being a Jacobite means being a guardian of Scottish history, hence the stooshie over the Culloden picnickers. The battlefield is a sacred site for the Circle, which each year hosts a Lament for Culloden, and for Donnachie in particular as he proposed to his wife Donna there, one year, in the snow.

The romance and heroic failure of the Jacobite movement – these things appeal to Donnachie. Earlier this year he visited the Stuart mausoleum in Vatican City, bringing with him heather and thistles from the Highlands and laying them on the altar. 'Donna was standing around going, "When am I getting to go to Prada? When am I getting to go to Gucci? You and that bloody Prince! It's the bane of my life!"'

At a little after 1.00 pm, the Circle of Gentlemen walk into the central grassy courtyard of Balgonie Castle, where they are met by the Laird, who has lived here with his wife, son and a succession of rescued deerhounds since 1985.

Balgonie, as he is properly known, is 79 and was born Raymond Morris in Walsall, England, but considers himself Scottish. He is one of the men who today will be initiated into the Circle. He is wearing Highland dress in his own registered tartan and has a white beard. An accomplished craftsman and painter, he has spent over twenty years restoring the castle to how it would have looked in the 14th century, though much of it is still ruined; summering swallows build mud nests in the rafters and fly through the corridors. The Jacobite flag, scarlet with a white square in the centre, flutters on the battlements.

The Laird's love affair with Scotland began when he was five and a holidaying aunt sent a postcard of Edinburgh with a pipe band on it. It all went from there. In 1948, he joined the Gordon Highlanders for his national service, and five years later 'emigrated' to Scotland to work in forestry. He is a great champion of the kilt and has not worn trousers for at least 35 years. For him, being a Jacobite is simply about patriotism and cultural conservation. 'Anything to do with Scottish tradition, I like to see helped along.'

He leads the way into the impressive barrel-vaulted room he uses as a wood-carving studio. 'There's a little something you don't see very often,' he says, gesturing to a large box lying against the far wall. 'That's my cremation coffin.' Balgonie made and decorated this himself. Along the sides he has painted ancient Celtic designs. On the lid it says, 'The much honoured Raymond Stanley Morris of Balgonie and Eddergoll, 1930-2009. Requiescat In Pace.' On each January 1st, he paints over the old death date and adds a new year.

Balgonie is explaining this when Matthew Donnachie wanders over. He has a question. 'Are you ready to join the Circle, your grace?'

The six men who are to become fellows of the Circle of Gentlemen are blindfolded and led, one by one, through a heavy oak door surrounded by white flowers and into the chapel. I am not permitted to see the initiation ceremony, which lasts around ten minutes, but Donnachie later explains that it involves swearing an old Highland oath on a ceremonial dirk. Also involved is a carved silver Medusa's head, modelled on the boss of Bonnie Prince Charlie's shield, one of a number of artefacts used by the original 18th century Circle.

After the ceremonies have been completed, the Jacobites enter the great hall for a candlelit lunch of lentil soup and sausage rolls, whisky, wine and Drambuie, a beverage said to have been invented by Bonnie Prince Charlie. In the centre of the top table there's a crystal bowl of water.

Drinks are poured into pewter or silver goblets and passed over the bowl silently before being handed out. This is a Jacobite tradition, a way of toasting the exiled 'king o'er the water' without having to utter those seditious words.

It is clear from talking to members of the Circle that everyone has their own highly personal reasons for calling themselves a Jacobite. Peter Chambers, a 60-year-old antique furniture restorer from the countryside near Carluke, believes that he is the reincarnation of Angus MacLeod, a member of Bonnie Prince Charlie's army. During a past life regression he saw himself being pursued and killed by Hanoverian troops in the aftermath of Culloden. 'So what we do here is close to my heart,' he says. 'It's not a hobby. It's a spiritual journey and emotional experience.'

For Matthew Donnachie it was a trip to Skye when he was 18 that turned his head. He was seeing a girl from there, and her grandmother, who had the Gaelic, told how her own family in the aftermath of Culloden had suffered at the hands of redcoats looking for the Prince. The family had twin little girls and one of these was hung from a tree by a whip. Donnachie, near tears, was struck by how the old woman told the story as if it had happened just the day before. Nearly 250 years on, it was clearly still traumatic. He found himself getting angry and his obsession began right there.

Perhaps the most interesting of the Circle, however, is Michael Corby. A founder member of The Babys, a British group that enjoyed success during the 1970s in America and elsewhere, Corby has that Jagger/Richards deeply-grooved gauntness but at 58 is still striking and has bright blue eyes to go with his silver tongue. 'Despite the appearance of Dorian Gray,' he says, 'I'm a cadaver awaiting its final ceremony.'

At Balgonie, Corby was wearing a Victorian take on the Jacobite look; dirk, sword and a pistol on his belt, his long hair tucked beneath a plumed bonnet. But a few days later, at his home, he is every inch the retired rock star in black jeans and fancy cowboy boots, swagged in silk scarves and necklaces. He sits in front of a huge stone fireplace, legs crossed like a fancy mantis, smoking small cigars and flicking them into a Delft ashtray which, apparently, Britt Eckland stole from a restaurant in Fulham when they were having dinner there. Corby's conversation is full of references to what Jimmy Page, Rod Stewart and Alex Salmond once said to him about one thing and another.

He would rather I didn't write where he has his home, for fear that fans from Argentina might camp out on the doorstep, but suffice to say that he lives in part of a wildly impressive Baronial hall somewhere in Lanarkshire which he likes to call 'Disgracelands'. There are holes in the front of the building through which residents would once have been able to shoot at Covenanters, but these days the greatest threat is from trespassing neds who knock over the 14th-century sundial and drain the fishpond, killing the poor Koi carp. Corby yearns for the days of boiling oil.

Like Balgonie, Corby was born in England ('a misfortune I cannot deny') but does not consider himself English. His father was from Aberdeenshire, his mother from Ireland. They moved south for business. The family had money, having invented the trouser press, but also had blue blood in their veins. Corby grew up in the grounds of Windsor Castle and attended Wellington public school; he speaks with the sort of accent usually described as 'plummy', though the odd Scotticism – 'hame', 'pish' and 'shite' – creeps in following the opening of a whisky liqueur.

His extended family, living in the Home Counties, had an ex-pat obsession with where they had come from, and so Corby was 'indoctrinated' in the ways of Scotland, raised on marmalade and shortbread, and taught never to forget his roots 'up the road'. Ironically, when he finally moved to Scotland a few years ago he was made to feel incredibly English; people, hearing his accent, would tell him, in choice language, to go back to where he came from. This annoyed him because, as far as he was concerned, he was home, in fact hame.

Talking to Corby, it becomes clear that there are many factors which may explain why he should be drawn to the Stuart cause. He had a very difficult relationship with his parents after their marriage split, felt unwanted, and at seventeen ended up begging on the streets of London. Also, he was eventually kicked out of The Babys, the band he had founded, and that led, in turn, to the end of his marriage and eventual estrangement from his son who lives in America. So the idea of being usurped and exiled is very familiar to him.

Corby has no wish to restore the Stuart monarchy, but identifies very strongly with the historical Jacobites, empathising with the suffering of those killed during reprisals following Culloden. He also claims as an ancestor Lord Lewis Gordon, a commander during the 1745 uprising. 'I have a Jacobite soul and a Jacobite heart and I have Jacobite blood in my veins,' he declares, 'and I shall be quite happy to present that when I make my case on Judgement Day.'

Much the same could be said of the other significant Jacobite group in Scotland. Na Fir Dileas, Gaelic for 'the loyal men', are political radicals. Their vision is this: in an independent Scotland a referendum would be held on whether the country should become a republic, should continue as a monarchy under the Windsors, or whether the royal House of Stuart should be restored. If Scotland voted for the third option, as Na Fir Dileas hope, then anyone calling themselves the rightful heir would have their claim assessed by a panel of genealogists and lawyers. Once chosen, the new Stuart monarch would sit at the head of an elected second chamber and have the power of veto over bills. The people, however, would have the power to depose and replace the king or queen.

Although its members have their own private beliefs, Na Fir Dileas do not have an official public line on who is the rightful heir to the Stuart throne. In the past they supported the claim of Michel Lafosse, a Belgian-born man living in Edinburgh who styled himself Prince Michael of Albany, and who returned to Belgium in 2006 amid Home Office claims that he had used a forged birth certificate to apply for a British passport.

It was a painful and discrediting episode for Na Fir Dileas, but they remain passionate about the Stuart cause and committed to the idea of themselves as a Jacobite clan. Numbering around forty across Scotland, they meet about twice a month, and communicate every day on the forum of their website. There are also regular expeditions, in period dress, to the sites of Jacobite flashpoints.

Late in the morning on a Saturday in August, I meet members of Na Fir Dileas in Glenfinnan. They are camped near the famous viaduct over which, as I approach their caravans and tent, chuffs a steam train called The Jacobite. In a few days time it will be the anniversary of Charles Edward Stuart's arrival in Glenfinnan, when he raised his standard and began the 1745 uprising; Na Fir Dileas are here to mark that occasion. While waiting for others to arrive, Margaret Scott-Stewart, a big, friendly woman of 55 in a tartan tunic and blue bonnet, smokes Royals and sings Charlie Is My Darling.

She and her husband Alistair have travelled from Innellan, near Dunoon. What's it like to be here? 'It feels like going back to my roots, seeing what it was like for my ancestors to have their Prince come home,' she says. 'The point is to honour the dead. To show that they've not fought in vain. That we will keep it going and we will remember them.' She sobs at this. 'It's quite emotional. This is my life and it means a lot to me.'

This is the crucial point about contemporary Jacobites – they still hurt at the thought of losing their King and kin.

Somehow, even though they were born centuries after the fact, the wounds inflicted at Culloden and elsewhere gape in their own psyches.

At half-past noon, thirteen members of Na Fir Dileas march up to the hilltop site looking down on Loch Shiel, where Bonnie Prince Charlie is believed to have raised his standard. They form a circle around the stone on which he stood and on which his footprints are carved. It's a dramatic landscape, seared by sun one moment, scoured by showers the next.

Alistair Scott-Stewart reads out the Prince's manifesto, the Jacobite flag is flown, and a toast drunk. 'We are here to show loyalty to the House of Stuart and to let the Hano-verian usurpers know we are not beaten yet,' says Terry Innes from Alloa. 'To the King!'

Next, the traditional duo Whiterose perform an a cap-pella version of News From Moidart, a song which tells of the Prince's arrival on the Scottish mainland. Whatever your political views, it's undeniably stirring, even a little eerie, to hear it sung on this particular spot with rain and the smell of brandy in the air, and the sound of the pipes from the Highland games below. There's a sense of the centuries collapsing in on one another, time being blurred.

'To us, 1745 doesn't feel that long ago; in evolutionary terms it's nothing,' says Marti Morrison, captain of Na Fir Dileas, lingering on the Prince's rock after the ceremony. He is a 47-year-old lorry driver from Dunbar, an intense man with a strong physical presence, wearing a black velvet jacket and kilt. A long-standing member of the SNP, his attraction to Jacobitism began when he was 26 and his mother died. Looking through old photographs, he discovered a picture of himself as a toddler wearing a kilt and bonnet with the white cockade, the Jacobite emblem. He realised that this was who he was.

Morrison bends to pick, as a souvenir, some of the purple heather growing around the rock. 'A lot of people like to take the mick out of our attire,' he says, 'but we take a lot of strength from the values of the men of that period. It was a time when a man's conscience and honour were important, and I've always tried to be an honourable person. That's what tells me in my heart that I would have been a Jacobite, and that's why I am a Jacobite, and I'll always try to keep this going for as long as I live.'

The Jacobite cause is sometimes known among its adherents as 'the auld sang'. Strange to think that in the fields of Fife, the Highland glens and cyberspace's nooks and dens there are still those who sing it.

Memorial Benches

THAT summer's day was the start of it. Walking in Green-bank Gardens, a National Trust property just to the south of Glasgow, a small silver plaque on a bench caught my eye:

'Muriel Broadbent, Muriel Low, Oh what a wonderful girl to know. 1914-1983.'

Such an elegant little memorial, love garbed as wit, and it was easy to imagine Mr Broadbent, 'a proper old gent' never without his trilby, according to the head gardener, visiting this beautiful spot and thinking of his late wife, whose maiden name had been Low, and whom one could almost see, thanks to the plaque, in her own youthful bloom.

Once I'd noticed the Greenbank bench, I started looking out for these tributes. They are everywhere in Scotland. On the lower slopes of The Cobbler, that well-loved mountain near the head of Loch Long, there is a bench dedicated to Tam McAulay, a passionate climber and relentless patter-merchant who died five years ago at the age of 60, swept over a waterfall on Rhum. His body was recovered by friends and his ashes later scattered at Dumbarton Rock.

That's the thing about these benches – each one is a story, a life. In Edinburgh alone there are more than 1,500. Taking a stroll through Princes Street Gardens and reading the plaques is to brush briefly against the texture of many lives, and to get a strong sense of distances travelled, both temporal and physical. There are people who were born up a close during Victoria's reign and died in America during that of the Beatles.

More moving than the stark dates of birth and death are the brief messages on the plaques, which make one understand that these were real people who took real pleasure in the place where they are now commemorated. 'In memory of Tim Wright whose Scottish dance music was heard so often in the gardens,' it says on one bench overlooking the Ross Bandstand where, during the 1940s, Wright – a pianist – and his band would perform. Another, for Charles Doward Farquhar, who died in 1960, aged 70, notes that he was, 'A lover of music and this grand scene.' I'd like to think he heard Tim Wright play.

Léan Scully, 'who made a festival of this city', is remembered on a bench in the gardens near the Royal Over-Seas League, the private members club where she stayed during her annual visits from Dublin during the festival, and from where she always watched the fireworks above the castle with a glass of champagne or crème de menthe to hand. On her death in 2007, aged 71, she left the Edinburgh International Festival a legacy of £3.66 million, a parting gift for the pleasure she had taken in so many classical concerts.

'She was a larger-than-life lady,' says Nicky Pritchett-Brown who was in charge of fundraising at the time. 'She was fabulous and fun-loving and felt so at home here. I like to think she's up there somewhere, looking down, and enjoying what's going on at the festival now.'

Scully's is a happy story, in its way, but there are sadnesses in the gardens, deep emotional shadows as if cast by a low winter sun. Dr Julian Roebuck was just 25 when he died in a car accident over 20 years ago. His bench is near the Ross Fountain, that elaborate gilded ornament depicting in female form the arts and sciences, two disciplines beloved of Roebuck, a scientist with BP who also played the French horn. His dad Martyn, now 74, talks about his son's achievements with evident pride. They were friends as well as father and son, and were getting to know each other again after Julian's years away at university.

He died on the evening of 24 January, 1990, driving back home to Edinburgh following a game of squash in Grangemouth. A sharp frost caused black ice on the M9. He skidded and collided with the crash barrier, the car turned over and was hit by another skidding vehicle. The black ice only lasted for three quarters of an hour, Martyn explains, and his son also had the misfortune to hit the end of the crash barrier, which was made of concrete; a little to the right and he might have survived. Martyn's mind seems to snag on these facts, as if it were a matter of minutes and inches which killed his boy. 'I don't think I've ever got over it,' he says.

There are love stories here, too. James and Margaret Bryce, commemorated on a bench right in the shadow of the castle, were born and raised in Edinburgh then emigrated to Toronto where, eventually, they reached the end of their lives – she in 1979 from breast cancer; he in 2010, just two days shy of his 92nd birthday.

Jimmy, as he was known, was one of eleven children. At seventeen, he ran away and joined the RAF, spending the war as a navigator on Lancaster bombers. On leave, he met Margaret at the Palais de Dance in Tollcross, walked her home to 81 Gorgie Road, and they sat on the step outside the tenement getting to know each other. They married in 1944. Their daughter Patricia, who is now 66, makes a point of sitting on that step every time she is visits from Canada. This summer she will sit, for the first time, on her parents' bench. 'It means the world to me,' she says. 'It's in a spot that they both loved. They are together in their home.'

Edinburgh's Royal Botanic Garden is a special, soulful place in the city; visit early in the day and the only sounds are birdsong, leaves underfoot and the wind in the trees. In centuries past, the garden grew plants for use in medicine;

now it acts as a sort of balm on city-scoured minds. People fall hard for the Botanics and it is little wonder that, after their death, so many are remembered here.

Maggie Stevenson, 'who,' according to her plaque, 'enjoyed the seasons', died of cancer in 1997 aged 65. Born in Glasgow, she moved to Ghana with her husband and two young children in 1957. On the boat over, she met a man, Bill Stevenson, who was moving to the same town, Kumasi, to work as a literature lecturer. He became a friend of the family.

In 1959, Maggie's husband and her six-year-old son died in a road accident. She returned to Scotland to raise her daughter, and some years later, she and Bill, by this time also living in Edinburgh, became a couple. In 1977, they married. They lived in a top floor flat off the Royal Mile, and Maggie – a keen gardener with no garden – became a Botanics regular. She especially liked to visit in winter to see the alpines. After her death, Bill, who had comforted her in her grief, found some comfort in his own by visiting the bench which bears her name.

George and Rena Petrie, commemorated on a bench beneath the spreading limbs of a Hungarian oak, lived for many years in a large sandstone house on the north-western corner of the Botanics; they had spent their childhoods living in the same street in Trinity. 'Rest and be thankful,' it says next to George Petrie's name and dates (1911-1997). This has a triple meaning – he is at rest, of course, and the passer-by is invited to rest; but it also refers to his passion for motor-racing. He honeymooned in Le Mans and was a keen spectator at the Rest And Be Thankful hill climb. He owned the first E-type Jag in Scotland. He was a master blender of whisky, famous for his nose. He kept secret recipes in his safe, the most prized being his recipe for Glayva. Rena (1912-2001) was an immensely strong woman, who married George in 1938, and cared for him when he developed Alzheimer's. Theirs was not, according to the children, 'a boring domestic saga'; though they were private, undemonstrative people, their depth of feeling for each other was obvious.

One of the most intriguing plaques in the Botanics commemorates James Robertson, a quantity surveyor, originally from Ayrshire, who died in 1997 aged 50 after suffering a brain haemorrhage: 'Breathing in I am space/ Breathing out I am free'. It is a Buddhist text, the choice of his friend Pat Piper. They had been close since the late 1970s, spending time together in the pub and at the pictures; for a while he rented a room in her Bruntsfield flat. It was the most important friendship of Pat's life, and she cries a little when talking about him. They enjoyed walking in the Botanics, and would pause by Inverleith House with its vista of serried steeples and gables. 'We used to sit looking over Edinburgh and put the world to rights,' she says.

I am sitting there while I writing this. Twilight is coming on and it's cold, but there is a tremendously warming feeling of communion – with Pat and Jim, and all the citizens who have taken pleasure in this place. All things must pass. This we know. But in the meantime, what could be better than to pass some of one's own precious time on a comfortable bench, gazing out at a city full of stories, and loss, and love?

The Renfrew Ferry

HALF-PAST six on Thursday morning and the Renfrew Rose is making its first trip of the day across the Clyde, in doing so sailing a little closer to oblivion. High heejins at Strathclyde Partnership for Transport have decided that the ferry service between Glasgow and Renfrew costs too much, so March 31st, 2010 will be the last day in a 500-year history of river crossings. A boat is usually followed by a wake; in this case it feels like there's one being held on board.

'It's very sad,' says Tommy Gray, 49, crossing from Renfrew to his welding job at BAE Systems in Scotstoun. 'You get an affection for the ferry. You get to know the guys who work on it.'

Gray has his bike with him, and is wearing a cycling helmet, the light on the front bright in the morning darkness. He has taken the ferry to work for 34 years, travelling to his job in the shipyard as his dad and grandad did before him. When the service ends, he faces an extra five-mile commute each way through the Clyde Tunnel.

Will he really cycle that far each day? 'Whit else d'ye suggest ah dae?' he snorts. 'Pack ma swimmin' trunks?'

At this hour, most passengers are making their way to BAE, which everyone still calls Yarrow's. Men in woolly hats carry their pieces in plastic shopping bags. There's a little swear-strewn chat. Tabloids are unfurled and spread out on knees. News of Celtic's latest defeat is digested, followed by a curse or chuckle depending on the reader's particular persuasion.

Some of the younger men are clearly hungover, the very

definition of peely-wally, and clutch their Irn-Bru like life preservers. The grooved benches of the Renfrew Rose are excellent for keeping bottles from rolling off and smashing on the steel floor.

There are, at most, nine men on board, though the boat can hold fifty. At one time, this ferry and the others which used to cross the Clyde would have been packed with workers going to the yards which lined both banks. However, the decline of shipbuilding, together with the construction of the Clyde Tunnel and Erskine Bridge, has meant that passenger numbers have been decreasing for years. The welders, platers and sparks going to their work before dawn are a doubly precarious breed – the last shipyard workers on the Clyde making one of the last ferry crossings.

It takes less than two minutes to traverse the 200-metre stretch of water. The Renfrew Rose turns neatly halfway across, elegant as one of the swans that throng the shores, so that its gangway faces the approaching slipway. The engines are noisy, the air cold and filled with the smell of diesel. By seven, dawn is breaking over the shipyard and the radar of HMS Diamond, a Type-45 destroyer, is silhouetted, like a minaret, against the sunrise.

In the wheelhouse, where a single paper rose is jammed into the window frame, Joe McLaughlin is turning the steel wheel and thinking back over his twelve years of service. He's a stocky man in his forties with short grey hair and a tartan tie. He loves his job as ferry supervisor. You might think crossing the Clyde 48,000 times a year would grow monotonous, but McLaughlin is never bored. 'I think I've seen everything,' he says. 'I'm no' being morbid, but see the biggest satisfaction I get? It's when somebody's committed suicide, or fell in the river, and we find the body.

'The one that sticks in my mind is the Polish skipper that went missing, it must have been in 1999, and six weeks later I was standing on the deck talking to a passenger.

As the boat pulled away, this big massive tree floating in the water started to turn and his body came up out of the water, caught in a branch. It was like something out of a horror movie. I always remember trying to catch him with the boathook and hearing this dull thud, like wood, when the point was hitting his body. I sent a card of condolence to his widow in Poland on behalf of the Renfrew ferry. It was nice to think that woman had closure now.'

As the ferry is one of the few vessels on the Clyde, the police often ask the crew to look out for missing persons either floating in the water or trying to cross. They've fished out a lot of bodies and body parts over the years, which is never pleasant, and have developed dark humour to cope with such grim tasks. John Malinowski, a large ferryman with 34 years service, recalls asking a police officer whether a particular corpse was a Rangers fan. 'What makes you think that?' the officer asked. 'Well,' said Malinowski, 'he's a bit blue.'

Four or five times a year, someone falls into the water from one of the banks, either by drunken accident or with sober purpose, but so far the ferrymen have saved everyone, even if that means risk to their own lives. Sometimes they foil suicide bids before they get going. There was, for instance, the old woman filling her pockets with pebbles who informed a concerned Malinowski, 'It's awright son, I'm jist goin' tae droon masel.'

The crew know their passengers very well. First name terms are common, and the ferrymen have created a pantheon of regulars. There's Bill the Baker, Bert the Butcher, Squeaky Voice, Granny Ferry, and a man with long hair and a beard known as Jesus. On Clydeside, there's none of this walking on water nonsense. Jesus takes the ferry.

There's also a guy, known simply as Gordon, a former paratrooper. He likes a drink and enjoys it especially by the heat of a bonfire on a patch of waste ground at the end of a footpath on the Yoker side. This drinking spot is known, colloquially, as the Clyde River Bar. 'So Gordon,' says McLaughlin, 'if he missed the last ferry, he'd a black poly bag, and he'd take his clothes off, put them in it, and swim across.'

Spend any time on the ferry and it becomes clear how important it is to the community. Between eight and nine you see the kids who live in Renfrew and go to school in Glasgow, or vice versa. You also meet the people who have taken the ferry since they were kids themselves. They remember back to when it was a chain ferry, known as the Skye ferry on account of the number of islanders who worked on it. Those were the days when the boat ran all night and you might well find yourself invited to join the crew for a dram.

Dan Crawley, 77, heading to the shops in Paisley with his wife Jean, says he's been taking this boat, 'for as long as the Clyde's been navigable'. Liz Grant, 51, travelling to work in Clydebank, started a petition to save the ferry and gathered more than 2,500 signatures in three days. 'We grew up in the east end of Glasgow and my dad worked in Renfrew,' she says. 'He used to tell me he took the ferry to work, but I used to think a fairy came and took him.'

Gerry Parker, 45, standing on deck en route to Glasgow, sweeps an awestruck hand past the riverscape. 'See for your average commoner? This is as close to the river as the majority of us are going to get.' He has written a protest song about the scrapping of the ferry and posted it on YouTube. 'There's not many songs about the Renfrew ferry,' he says, 'apart from that teuchtery one, The Song Of The Clyde.'

Alexis Buchanan, 36, is a dental nurse who lives in Knightswood but works in Renfrew. Upset that the ferry service will soon end, she is willing to go to extraordinary lengths to avoid a lengthy commute. 'I'm going to buy a dinghy on eBay and cross the river myself. All right, I might get the jail, but they'll have to catch me first.'

The ferrymen take their place in this community seriously. They'll carry funeral parties down to the shipyard so widows can scatter the ashes of husbands on the waters where they once worked. They'll dress up as Santa and sail past the local nursery school at Christmas. They'll accept, with a smile, the sympathy of regulars, no matter how indelicately put. 'Thass fuckin' pish,' says one man, Big Chris. 'Izzat yooz oot ae a joab, noo?' The crew are indeed worried about their own livelihoods, but seem just as concerned with the impact the loss of the ferry will have on their passengers.

One man who will feel its loss deeply is Alexander Morrison, 93, standing on the Renfrew side, throwing hunks of plain loaf to the swans and gulls from a Mother's Pride bag. He was born in a cottage only a few yards from here and has spent all his days watching the ferry go to and fro. He's dressed in a peaked cap and blue coat and says he has 1,000 photographs of the boat at home, plus screeds of data. He worked in the shipyards, first at Simons-Lobnitz in 1931 and then moving to Babcock's. 'He was the best driller on the Clyde,' says his pal, Charlie Newlands, 65. His last job before he retired was working on the boiler of the Waverley.

Meeting Mr Morrison is to sense very acutely how close we are to periods that feel quite distant. His father, for instance, was born in 1865, and he himself has been an eyewitness to all the maritime history of which the Renfrew ferry is a frail, lingering part. He has attended the launch of every ship on the Clyde for the past 60 years, and you can ask him a random question such as, 'When was the Queen Mary launched?' in full expectation of an accurate reply. 'Ah mind it was a terrible wet day ...' he'll begin and go from there.

For most people, the Clyde looks nearly empty, but for Alexander Morrison it's full of ghost ships, sleek and vivid memories. Now, as he considers the end of the ferry that is one of the few remaining vessels on the river, his blue eyes come to rest on the boat and grow sad.

'They're telling me they're gonnae dae away wi' that,' he says. 'Ah wish they would wait till ah'm away and then they can dae whit they like.'

A Ploughing Match

DRIVING north inland from Pittenweem, scanning the fields left and right, there is at first no sign of the ploughmen. Suddenly, though, I round a bend and there they are – approximately seventy tractors moving with a tailor's precision and patience across the land of Lochty Farm.

The ploughshares gleam like needles in the morning sun, and the grassy fields, as they are tilled and the dark earth exposed, turn from tweed to corduroy. It is half past nine, and the annual Highlands Of Fife Ploughing Match has begun. It is a grand title for a much-loved event known to all participants with fond informality as 'the plooin''.

The Highlands Of Fife, sometimes called the Riggin O' Fife, is an area of high ground in the north-east of the region. The farmers here are proud to live and work in the 'beggar's mantle', a reference to James VI's famous description of Fife as a beggar's mantle fringed with gold – the gold being the coast. Less affluent than the fecund East Neuk, the Riggin' has a strong sense of community, as well as of shared history and economic struggle.

Many of those competing or spectating here today have roots in the area going back many generations. Their ancestors ploughed the same Fife soil and were eventually laid to rest within it. In the hospitality area – the long, dim trailer of a drainage supplies truck – Jane Lang, a small lady with a red coat and white hair, examines a display of photographs of the match held in 1939. She has recognised her father. 'And that's my Uncle Dod,' she says, pointing to another black and white, flat-capped figure.

Competitive ploughing is not well known in this country.

Things are very different in the Republic of Ireland, where the annual national match attracts in excess of 60,000 spectators. In Scotland, however, it remains very much a minority interest. That's a shame in a way as some of the best ploughmen in the world are Scots.

The current stars are Andrew Mitchell Snr and Jnr, known as Faither Andrew and Young Andrew, a father and son from Haughs of Ballinshoe farm near Kirriemuir. Between them they have won the World Ploughing Competition three times, and this May will both compete in Sweden to regain their titles. In theory, they could both win their class and come home with a brace of trophies, but they think that is an impossible dream. 'It can be a wee bitty like the Eurovision Song Contest,' says Faither Andrew, a 53-year-old with curly hair and apple cheeks. 'Some of the Eastern Bloc countries vote for themselves.'

Competitors in ploughing matches are given a certain amount of time in which to complete a particular area.In the world championship it is two hours and forty minutes to plough 100 by twenty metres. Here, in Fife, the area is smaller and there are five hours in which to cover it. To the spectator, therefore, it appears rather somnolent. It is certainly far slower than if these men were actually ploughing their own fields for practical purposes. 'If he was doing this for real, he'd be flying along at four miles an hour,' says Pete Small, the Highlands of Fife Ploughing Association's archivist, pointing out one septuagenarian ploughman whose jug ears are glowing red with cold.

The trick is to plough straight, to make your furrows uniform in width and depth, to leave the earth free of grass and feeling firm. Men frequently get down from their tractors with a tape measure to check their progress; competitive ploughing is as cerebral as physical. Others pat and handle the ploughed earth, correcting mistakes; though this isn't strictly within the rules, a blind eye is turned at regional events. Extra marks are awarded for fine points, inexplicable to the outsider, known as feerings, finishings and 'ins and oots'.

One of the judges, 79-year-old Dougie Johnston, is dapper in his shirt and tie, checked bunnet and boots with the steel toe-caps worn through the leather. He examines a well-ploughed rig, making notes in a little black book, and pronounces himself highly satisfied. 'Oh, I just love to see that,' he says. 'To me, it's like looking at a beautiful woman.'

It would be a mistake to think that farmers are dully pragmatic people with no feel for beauty. There is undeniably an aesthetic dimension to a ploughed field, and everyone here is aware of it. They readily compare ploughing with painting or sculpture or the presentation of a fancy meal. There is, for example, no pressing agricultural reason why furrows should be straight. The crop won't grow any better as a result. But no self-respecting farmer would dream of allowing crooked furrows. John Stewart Collis puts it very well in his memoir The Worm Forgives The Plough, an account of working on a farm during the Second World War: 'The straight furrow is the labourer's acknowledgement in the validity of art for art's sake.'

The ploughing contest is a grand day out. Two wee boys fashion ersatz stooks from clumps of stray grass. One old man with a long white beard and a deerstalker covered in souvenir ploughing match badges says he has come for the 'camraddy', of which there is plenty. Many of the competitors have been here since 7am, raring to go. 'See in the morning when the guys turn up?' says Pete Small. 'You're beating them back with a stick. There's a fever grips them when there's a ploughing match.'

Ally Fraser, the past president of the association, laughs his assent. 'The adrenalin is pumping in these old guys. This is like Viagra to them.'

There is also the attraction of the laid-on refreshments. At noon, a hot pie and a can of lager is placed at the end of each rig, and there always seem to be a couple of bottles of Grouse on the go.

Competitive ploughing begins in September, and there are matches on most weekends until the spring. The uniform seems to be the boiler suit and bunnet with optional paunch. Attending these occasions is a sensory experience: the growl of the engines; the warm, pleasant stink of diesel, paraffin, whisky and horse muck; the snell wind that would take the face off you.

Ploughmen compete in a range of classes, their ploughs running the historical gamut from horse-drawn to hi-tech. Dave Nelson, 69, from Crossgates near Dunfermline, is here with a fine pair of Clydesdales called Danny and Stanley, all done up with silver-studded harnesses and ribbons. 'This, to us, is like a game of golf would be for an office man,' he says. 'You get a day away from your troubles. It's magical.'

The horse-drawn ploughs draw the crowds, but it is the contemporary machinery which draws gasps. The Andrew Mitchells, Faither and Young, both work with formidable bits of kit. The senior man's reversible plough, powered by hydraulics, swings through the air in forceful and elegant arcs. It is Emmerdale meets Transformers.

Faither Andrew is 53 and didn't start ploughing competitively until he was 35. Young Andrew is 22. He has been at it since he was thirteen and over the last few years has dominated the Scottish Ploughing Championships, winning in each of the last six years. He is the Roger Federer, the Bobby Fischer, the Tiger Woods of the plough, though rather less wealthy and renowned. You are lucky to earn twenty quid for winning a match. Young Andrew first became world champion at seventeen, the youngest ploughman to ever take the title. 'My best moment was when he won in Ireland in 2006,' says his dad. 'That meant more to me than winning myself.'

Competitive ploughing is very male. The wives and

girlfriends of competitors are known as ploughing widows and they tend not to come along, which is understandable.

One exception is June Grieve, wife of Wullie Grieve. June is definitely not a ploughing widow. She accompanies her husband to many of his matches and enjoys his success greatly. 'How can I say it?' she laughs, standing with her dog Diesel at the head of Wullie's rig and watching as he steers his tractor. 'He's 74, he's been ploughing for 50 years, he always wins a prize and he just loves it.' June rakes an appreciative eye over her man's furrows. 'That looks beautiful there.'

Though the ploughmen are by nature undemonstrative and grounded, these occasions are not without emotion. One man recalls taking a cup of earth from the farm on which he won a championship and scattering it on his father's grave. For another ploughman, Ross Grieve, twin brother of Wullie, ploughing gave him the motivation to recover from serious illness. A decade ago, suffering problems with his spinal cord, he was in hospital for five months, for two of which he was completely paralysed. 'Awb'dy said I would never make it. Six times they had to resuscitate me. I was away and they brought me back.'

It was the thought of ploughing that kept him going, that got him through the five months spent learning how to walk again. He nods towards his brother. 'When I was lying ill, I telt this man to look after my tractor and get it set up for me.

'Ploughing is in my blood,' he adds. 'It's all I've ever done. And I'll keep going as long as I'm drawing breath.'

Arthur's Seat

HURRYING, hurrying through dark Edinburgh streets to keep an appointment with the dawn. The horizon, at a little after six, is a pale and chilly blue, growing pink to the east. The silhouetted steeples of the Old Town are witch's hats; the great cresting wave of Salisbury Crags frozen on the point of drowning them.

This is the hour of Scotmids and Spars, of joggers and early commuters. A jet etches a line into the stained glass sky. The clarity of light promises a hot day. The weather-cock on top of St Giles' has his beak wide open, as if to greet another fine morning.

I'm on my way to Arthur's Seat. Such warm weather so early in the year is a sort of gift, and deserves a gesture of acknowledgement. What better way to show appreciation than to climb the hill, an extinct volcano, which has for so long given grandeur to the city and pleasure to its citizens? Sir Walter Scott, in his novel The Heart Of Midlothian, noted that there is no more enchanting place to watch the rising and setting sun than these crags above Edinburgh. Today, I'll test that theory.

On St Margaret's Loch, at the foot of the hills, swans glide across the rosy water, pausing to beat their wings as if in sarcastic applause of the midnight barbecuers who have left such a mess of charred tinfoil and empty beer bottles. Holyrood Park, in which Arthur's Seat and the other hills sit, is managed by Historic Scotland; the challenge for the eight rangers is to keep the place beautiful even though it receives an estimated 1.5 million visitors each year.

Hugo Arnot, in his 1779 history of Edinburgh, wrote

that 'seldom are human beings to be met in this lonely vale, or any creature to be seen, but the sheep feeding on the mountains, or the hawks and ravens winging their flight among the rocks'. These days, the park is never empty of people. At any time of the day or night, at any time of the year, you will encounter dog-walkers and runners. During hot spells like this, the place is hoaching and becomes a perfect expression of that rare phenomenon – Scottish happiness.

It's still cold as I climb the lower slopes. Whinny Hill is living up to its name, the gorse in flower and smelling of coconut oil. Mary Queen of Scots is said to have enjoyed this scent when, in 1564, she hosted an engagement banquet here. That's the thing about the park – it has been enjoyed by the great figures from our history. A boulder at the side of the path leading to the summit is marked with recent graffiti, noting that Britney, Heather and Niall were here. It's a list to which one might add David Hume, Bonnie Prince Charlie and Robert Louis Stevenson.

Nearing the top of Arthur's Seat, which rises to 251 metres, I stare down at my feet, so as to save the pleasure of the sight from the summit. This is a popular strategy. There are plenty of whispered breathless wows as new arrivals raise their eyes to the view. It's golden and hazy up here. The shadow of the hill falls almost to the Meadows. The hills of Fife poke, crocodile-like, above the haar. What are the sounds? Seagulls and sirens, trains clanking into Waverley and the fretful growl of morning traffic. The city is spread out all around – dainty and moreish. It feels as though one could reach down and pick up Holyrood Palace or flick the buses along North Bridge.

A group of friends in their twenties and thirties, colleagues from a digital agency, arrive at around 8am. This is a ritual. They come here once a week to breathe the cool clean air. 'It's a nice way to start the day, and makes you appreciate the city,' says John Harfield. 'At work all you

see are the four walls.' Today, they have brought an ironing board with them, and attempt to iron a pair of jeans in
the face of a wind which does its best to blow the denims
off to Leith. It's a joke for the benefit of their boss. They
take photos on their phones.

Russell Carter, a tall Alaskan geophysicist, aged 25,
is leaning against the sharp brown rocks of the summit
with a look of perfect contentment on his face. 'I'm here
on business and leave in two hours,' he says. 'I came here
when I was ten and climbed it with my family. I couldn't
bear to leave the city without coming up here again.'

You meet all sorts on the top of Arthur's Seat: couples
sharing Strongbow and saliva; school-trippers from Hano-
ver punching the air to the Rocky theme; a wee boy in a
Spider-Man costume shooting imaginary webs in the direction of the Forth Bridge. It's especially fascinating to watch
the glistening runners who arrive at the top, tap the trig
point, tap their stopwatches, and barely glance at the view.
They are absorbed in an internal struggle of pounding
hearts and personal bests. The tinny motivational music
leaking from their iPod headphones is a transmission from
the remote world each inhabits.

Though Arthur's Seat and the surrounding crags are
remarkable, those of us who see them often can begin to
take them for granted. Clearly, though, there are many
people who appreciate Holyrood Park very much. Walking
around, one meets connoisseurs with specific preferences
for particular seasons and times of day when the light falls
on the Pentlands just so. This is the place they come – with
pets and pals and lovers – treading memories into every
path.

Over on the Salisbury Crags, Roisin Russell, 48, is enjoying a picnic lunch with her friends Dave and Eve Beynon,
a South African couple in their fifties, and a big friendly
dog called Jambo, named not for the football but after the
Swahili word for hello.

'This place means a lot to me,' says Roisin. 'I've been coming here since I was sixteen and moved to Edinburgh.' She points round the park. 'I've had a pee there, and a crap there, and I had sex there when I was eighteen.'

Dave and Eve laughingly tell her to shush. 'We arrived in Edinburgh on Christmas Eve nine years ago,' says Eve, 'and I thought I had come to fairy-land. We are still in awe of places like this. Everywhere you go there's another secret.'

As the day wears on and warms up, the air takes on a lolling, lotus-eating quality. At the foot of the crags, along the Radical Road, four female students are sunbathing in bikinis. All are American. One is called Bliss Baker, a name that suits the day. None of them is studying geology, or else they would know that the sloping lump of sandstone and dolerite immediately behind them, known as Hutton's Section, enabled the 18th century scientist James Hutton to radically alter our understanding of how the Earth was formed. 'It's, like, a nice little windbreak,' says Bliss.

The afternoon heat burns off the haze and ships become visible on the Forth. A brace of buzzards spiral in slo-mo on the thermals. Two white-vested acrobats, right on the cliff edge, tumble and leap, taking pleasure in the sunshine and their own capable bodies. A party of four women, in hijab and tracky bottoms, set out for the summit. Climbers, enjoying the feel of hot rock beneath their chalky fingers, move with balletic grace up the crags.

On Queen's Drive, a young blonde woman parks her Fiesta, and lies back, eyes closed, bare feet up on the dash, listening to Enya, right arm drooping out of the window, long silver nails flashing in the sun.

Back up on top of Arthur's Seat, a small crowd gathers to see the day out. Germans, Russians, French, English, Scottish and Vietnamese; a Babel of voices. Someone opens a bottle and there's a sudden smell of champagne. Everything is growing purplish and indistinct. Crows, which have spent the day in leafy purdah, sense a kinship with the lengthening shadows and come whirling round the summit. At 7.40 pm, the red sun slips down the back of Ben Lomond like a coin in the meter and lights start coming on all over the city – the Castle, the Balmoral clock-face, the lighthouse on Inchkeith.

Hurrying, hurrying down the hill, through the gloaming, trying to get back to the streets before it's too dark. Today has been glorious; from dawn to dusk, the park has buzzed with people enjoying the simple business – which sometimes seems horribly complex – of being alive. Days like this, weeks like this, don't come along too often. 'You do realise,' folk have been telling each other all day, 'that this is Scotland in March?'

In years to come, when we remember little else, some of us may be lucky enough to remember the pleasure of that surprise; that and the fading smell of the whins.

List of original publications

Murmuration – first published in Scotland On Sunday, November 25, 2012

The Fetish Club – first published in Scotland On Sunday, January 8, 2012

A Glasgow Ambulance – first published in Scotland On Sunday, December 20, 2009

The Monks Of Pluscarden – first published in Scotland On Sunday, June 17, 2012

The Forth Bridge – first published in Scotland On Sunday, November 20, 2011

The Ba' – first published in Scotland On Sunday, February 21, 2010

Barlinnie – first published in Scotland On Sunday, February 12, 2012

The Fortieth Lambing Of Bert Leitch – first published in Scotland On Sunday, April 29, 2012

Glasgow Central – amalgamated from two articles, previously published in Scotland on Sunday, March 17, 2013, and The Herald, September 7, 2013

Karaoke At The Horseshoe Bar – first published in Scotland On Sunday, December 4, 2011

The Hawick Common Riding – first published in Scotland On Sunday, November 6, 2011

The Naturists Of Loch Lomond – first published in Scotland On Sunday, May 9, 2010

Ladies' Day At Musselburgh – first published in Scotland On Sunday, June 19, 2011

The Last Voyage Of Jimmy McFarlane – first published in Scotland On Sunday, June 24, 2012

Showfolk – first published in Scotland On Sunday, May 29, 2011

The Waterloo – first published in Scotland On Sunday, March 20, 2011

The Anatomy Rooms – first published in Scotland On Sunday, October 24, 2010

Ye May Gang Faur And Fare Waur – first published in Scotland On Sunday, May 27, 2012

Up-Helly-Aa – first published in Scotland On Sunday, January 30, 2011

The Fishermen Of Dalmarnock – first published in Scotland On Sunday, September 17, 2010

Kingussie vs Newtonmore – first published in Scotland On Sunday, August 21, 2011

Thistle vs Rose – first published in Scotland On Sunday, May 23, 2010

At The Berries – first published in Scotland On Sunday, July 3, 2011

Whatever Happened To The Castlemilk Lads – first published in Scotland On Sunday, June 19, 2012

Jesus George – first published in Scotland On Sunday, September 4, 2011

A Day At The Peats – first published in Scotland On Sunday, May 27, 2012

A Night At The Dogs – first published in Scotland On Sunday, September 6, 2009

The Cisco Kid Lives In Cumbernauld – first published in Scotland On Sunday, December 6, 2009

Val At The Crown And Anchor – first published in Scotland On Sunday, November 4, 2012

Fox-hunting – first published in Scotland On Sunday, December 4, 2011

The Lodging House Mission – first published in Scotland On Sunday, July 8, 2012

The Royal Caledonian Ball – first published in Scotland On Sunday, May 12, 2013

Doo Men – first published in Scotland On Sunday, May 30, 2010

Oystermen – first published in Scotland On Sunday, September 30, 2012

Extreme Cleaners – first published in Scotland On Sunday, December 2, 2012

The World Stone Skimming Championships – first published in Scotland On Sunday, October 2, 2011

Jacobites – first published in Scotland On Sunday, August 23, 2009

Luigi Corvi – first published in Scotland On Sunday, November 21, 2010

Memorial Benches – first published in Scotland On Sunday, March 4, 2012

The Renfrew Ferry – first published in Scotland On Sunday, January 31, 2010

A Ploughing Match – first published in Scotland On Sunday, October 2, 2011

Arthur's Seat – first published in Scotland On Sunday, April 1, 2012